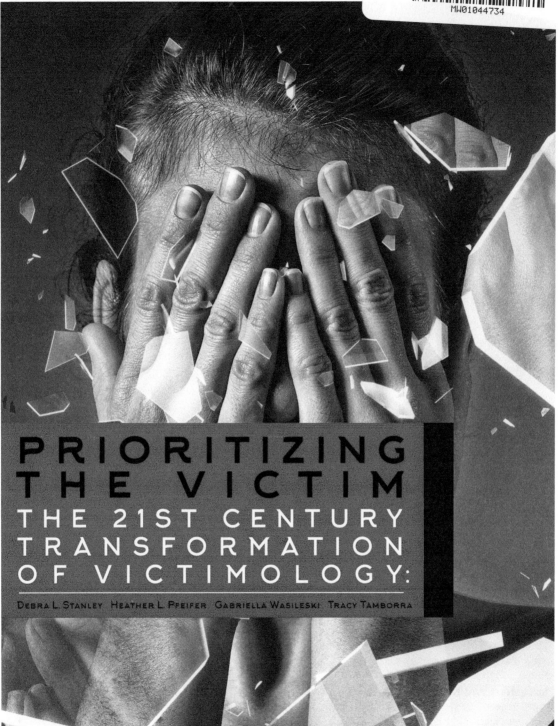

PRIORITIZING THE VICTIM

THE 21ST CENTURY TRANSFORMATION OF VICTIMOLOGY:

DEBRA L. STANLEY   HEATHER L. PFEIFER   GABRIELLA WASILESKI   TRACY TAMBORRA

Kendall Hunt
publishing company

Cover image © John Pfeifer

www.kendallhunt.com
Send all inquiries to:
4050 Westmark Drive
Dubuque, IA 52004-1840

DEDICATION

To all the courageous and passionate souls who stand in the shadows as they support crime victims through their journey of recovery.

To all the 20th Century visionaries who are fondly referred to as the "buffalos" who laid the groundwork and built the field of victim services, brick by brick …

We all thank you.

BRIEF CONTENTS

Section I – The Historical Deconstruction of Victimology

Section II – The Impact of Law and Politics on Crime Victims

Section III – The Transformation of the Field of Victimology into the 21st Century

CONTENTS

Section I – The Historical Deconstruction of Victimology

Section II – The Impact of Law and Politics on Crime Victims

Section III – The Transformation of the Field of Victimology into the 21st Century

Index

PREFACE

I am so grateful to have had the experience of knowing so many of the "old buffa-los," the pioneers of this field, and it has been an honor to work alongside so many champions. It was the passion and commitment of the "buffalos" that built this field—layer by layer; without you, thousands of injured souls would be suffering alone.

This book is written for the new generations of brave souls who have and will continue to step into the shoes of the former leaders, activists, scholars, and victim service providers. It is vital to the future of victimology and all the future crime victims that the next generation of "buffalos" be as brave and fierce as the first. Remember the history and the many passionate and determined voices that led the way, carry their message forward, and continue to do the hard work that will eventually lead to the recognition and respect that the discipline of victim services deserves.

Deb Stanley

SECTION I

THE HISTORICAL DECONSTRUCTION OF VICTIMOLOGY

Historical Overview of Victimology and 21st Century Challenges

Objectives

After reading this chapter, you will be able to:

- understand the context of the historical evolution of victimology,
- discuss the impact of social movements on the development of victimology, and
- describe the major federal responses to victims since the crime victims' rights movement.

History of Victimology

Crime victimization has been a part of society since the beginning of time. Yet, for centuries, society and the criminal justice system virtually ignored the existence of crime victims. Crime victims were first referenced in a philosophical essay by Cesare Beccaria, *On Crimes and Punishment,* published in 1764. Following Beccaria's essay, early philosophers and criminologists wrote about the "culpability of the victim" and focused on the role they played in criminal events. Specifically, when these early writings mentioned victims, the emphasis was on victim blaming; in effect, holding them responsible for their own victimization. Thus, crime victims were not portrayed as individuals worthy of empathy and compassion, but as possible partners or contributors to their offender's behavior.

The first publication that specifically details crime victimization was Edwin Sutherland's *Principles of Criminology* textbook, in which he devoted an entire chapter on victims (Sutherland, 1924). Sutherland's work shifted attention for the first time *toward* the study of crime victims. Yet, it wasn't until the 1930s and 1940s that researchers began to devote considerable focus on studying crime victims, which ultimately laid the foundation for a new field of study to emerge called Victimology.

One of the first scholars was a German criminologist, Hans von Hentig. His earliest work explored the victim and criminal interactions (1941), and he then later published a book on the relationship between the criminal offender and the victim titled *The Criminal and his Victim: Studies in*

> **Benjamin Mendelsohn**
>
> (1900–1998) lived to see the field of victimology mature through the 1990s.
>
> He regularly attended the International Symposia on Victimology, and at the 1979 Symposia he witnessed the formation of the World Society of Victimology (WSV). In 1981 he was honored at the WSV meetings with the Hans von Hentig Award. Today the WSV, in honor of the pioneer, presents the Benjamin Mendelsohn Young Scholar Award of victimology to individuals who have had made promising contributions to victimology.

the Sociobiology of Crime (1947). Von Hentig's work laid the groundwork for academic research in the study of victims of crime, which other scholars soon began to build on. The most influential of these was Benjamin Mendelsohn.

Mendelsohn, a French lawyer, published in law journals throughout his career; his first substantive publication on crime victims focused on the rapist and his victim was published in 1937. As an attorney, he encountered victims daily in the courtroom, and believed that there were recognizable personality patterns found in most victims that, he came to believe, contributed to their victimization. Much of Mendelsohn's early work focused on the victim and offender relationship, and eventually led him to create victim typologies. These typologies described the varying circumstances leading up to a criminal event, the relationship between the victim and the offender, and the actual type of crime itself. Mendelsohn first used the term "victimology" in 1947 in one of his law articles. However, it was nearly a decade later by the time he formally proposed the concept of victimology as a new "science of victims" in his publication titled *A New Branch of Bio-Psycho-Social Science, Victimology* (Mendelsohn, 1956). The social movements of the 1960s and 1970s influenced much of Mendelsohn's later scholarship which lay out a blueprint for developing the science of victimology and detailed the organizational steps necessary for victimology to emerge into a respectable field of science to better understand victims (Mendelsohn, 1976). Given his role in the advancement of victimology as a new field of study, Mendelsohn was subsequently regarded to be the "father of victimology."

Defining Victimology

Victimology is a science of the study of the causes of criminal victimization. It studies data that describes phenomena and causal relationships related to victimization. This includes events leading to the victimization, the victim's experience, its aftermath, and the actions taken by society in response to these victimizations.

A *victimologist* is someone who studies the causes of victimization. Contemporary victimologists are often defined as specialists focusing on a specific category of victimization such as interpersonal violence, child victimization, homicide, sexual assault, street violence, human trafficking, immigrant victimization, cyber-victimization, etc. Some of the more popular typologies of victimization are those that examine lifestyle and routine activities that increase the likelihood of risk.

However, it was not for another twenty years after Mendelsohn's introduction of the field of victimology that scholars began to concentrate on the *impact* of victimization. While the early concept of victimology focused on the victim's actions and behavior on their victimization experience, a new theoretical paradigm—cultivated by the social movements of the 1960s and 1970s—shifted researchers focus towards the plight of victims. One of the most significant factors to help shift the paradigm was the institutionalization of the National Crime Victim Survey (NCVS) database in 1972. The principle goals of the NCVS data was to 1) provide more detailed information on victim-related crime incidents, and 2) provide the field of victimology with its own victimization data source that would drive research, policy, and best practices. This data enabled researchers for the first time to measure the extent of domestic violence and other interpersonal violence in American society, and explore the socio-political response to the problem. The NCVS enabled researchers to examine the causes of victimization to be explored in an entirely new manner, and help raise awareness among the general public, as well as the criminal justice system, about the impact these crimes have on victims. Ultimately, this research helped to facilitate the development of federal initiatives and agencies, and funding to support more formal victim services for the treatment and protection of crime victims.

During the 1990s, researchers continued to explore interpersonal violence, however, they expanded their focus and began to explore all categories of victimization and all victim populations. Feminist criminologists, many of whom had their own personal history of victimization or close affiliations with victims, moved into the field of Victimology, and began to highlight specific populations of victimization, including domestic violence, sexual assault, same-sex violence, dating violence, child abuse, immigrant victimization, elder abuse, as well as other populations. Types of victimization that had been ignored in prior generations were now at the forefront of Victimology. Moreover, this era of research included a "solutions-based" focus that searched for ways to enhance support for victims, expand victim services, advance the theoretical foundations of the field, educate those in the victim services profession, promote greater community awareness and collaboration, and advocate for more resources and funding, legislation, and laws.

Victimology in the twenty-first century is now a respectable stand-alone discipline with its

© Boris15/Shutterstock.com

own data, research, theories, and best practices. The field has matured as new theories are validated, and new sources of crime victimization survey data continue to inform us on the details of victimization. Most importantly, the field of Victimology continues to flourish with a rapid increase of professionals shifting their research portfolios toward crime victims and producing major contributions to the literature.

But it is not just today's scholars that have helped to continue to advance the field of Victimology. A great deal of credit must be given to a small group of powerful and passionate advocates, fondly referred to as the "old buffalos," who were some of the first advocates during the social movements in the 1960s and 1970s—often volunteers who worked with crime victims prior to when any formal services were in place. These advocates focused their attention on the type and extent of harm inflicted on the victim. They also proposed legislation and contributed to the construction of numerous federal agencies established specifically to address advocacy and support, funding, and resources to victims. Many of these advocates were subsequently appointed to lead many of these agencies at the federal, state, and local level. Today, they tirelessly continue to assist and empower victims, giving them a voice and advocating for them legislatively, as well as mentoring young scholars and victim service providers to empower the next generation of professionals who will lead the charge.

Social Movements' Impact on Victimology

As noted previously, Victimology as a field of study was really birthed from the social and political sentiment in the 1960s and 1970s. The social movements of this era in American history—civil rights, Black power, women's rights, LGBT, children's rights, and victims' rights—began to shift scholars attention to crime victims in a more supportive way. Five major concerns emerged from these social movements that renewed the interest of scholars and the public alike to better understand and support crime victims:
1. the high rate of child victimization,
2. revelation of the domestic violence and sexual assault incidents,
3. anxiety over the growing crime problem,
4. limited legal and social remedies, and
5. lack of victim compensation funds.

The women's movement and the victims' rights movement, in particular, played a siginficant role in shifting attitudes and moving the field of victimology forward. Feminists, advocates, and domestic violence and rape victims were the first organizers of victims' rights, with platforms built around the need for restoration and healing of female victims; and, helped bring greater public awareness to victims

(Koss and Harvey, 1991; NOVA, 2019; Young, 1997). The feminist movement focused a great deal on bringing attention to the interpersonal violence occurring behind closed doors, and fought for equal justice that included both gender and victim equality. The leaders of this movement challenged the traditional indifference shown toward female victims, most of whom were victims of interpersonal violence in the household, and rejected the early victimology theories that were based on "victim blaming" concepts. They also gave a voice to many of the silent victims overlooked in society (e.g., dating violence, sexual assault, domestic violence victims, children who were maltreated by a parent/guardian, and the elderly) and fiercely advocated on their behalf. For example, more than a century prior to the start of the children's rights movement provisions to the law were added to provide states the right to remove abused or neglected children from the guardianship of their parents. Yet, these laws were rarely used to remove an abused or neglected child; instead, states were more likely to remove an unruly child from the home. However, things began to change after the efforts of the feminist movement and child advocates during the 1970s and 1980s to renew the public's concern about the welfare of children. Ultimately, their advocacy led states to pass stronger legislation to protect children from abuse and neglect, as well as the creation of Children's Bureaus and the addition of guardians ad litem to serve as an impartial legal advocate for the child in the courts to better protect and shelter child victims.

During this same time period, the victims' rights movement was focused on raising awareness about victims' rights, or more accurately, the lack of rights afforded to victims in the criminal justice system. Over the next two decades, advocates lobbied tirelessly to establish specific rights for crime victims to ensure the appropriate protection and support for all victims, and give victims access throughout the legal process. The efforts of these advocates led to the creation and passage of a litany of crime victim-related laws. While fewer than 100 such laws were passed in the early days of this movement, by 2019, over 30,000 crime victim-related laws have been enacted and every state has passed victims rights legislation. The efforts of the advocates of the victims' rights movement also paved the way for national and state constitutional amendments. Today, 32 states and Puerto Rico have passed victims' rights amendments to their state constitutions. Although a similar amendment was drafted for the U. S. Constitution in 1984, it has yet to be adopted.

In the early 1980s, crime victim reformers and national organizations drew further attention to the problems of interpersonal and domestic violence, highlighting common forms of female victimization in the research. This decade saw victims rights and services begin to significantly expand to better meet the specific needs of female crime victims, as well as target other victim populations, including LGBT, elderly, and undocumented immigrant victims (NOVA, 2019; Young, 1997). Many victims and advocates have banded together to establish national and local support groups, and to continue to raise awareness. For example, domestic violence and sexual assault victims and their supporters joined together to create an annual "Take Back the Night" national platform to restore a sense of safety, power, and freedom; while family members of victims of drunk driving created Mothers Against Drunk Driving (MADD) to actively lobby for legislative changes.

The 1980s also saw the passage of key federal legislation on victims rights and the expansion of victims services that set the standards for the states. Including:

- The development of President Ronald Reagan's National Task Force on Victims and Crime in 1982. Its mission was to 1) increase the rights and protection of victims, 2) investigate issues and concerns associated to crime victimization, 3) raise public awareness of the plight of victims, and 4) establish new legislation to support victims.

- The passage of the Victim and Witness Protection Act in 1982 to protect funding for victim-witness protection programs. In 1974, the Law Enforcement Assistance Administration (LEAA) fund was established providing over 50 million federal dollars to victim-witness programs housed in state attorneys' offices across the country. When the LEAA funds began to dry up in the late 1970s, the Victim and Witness Protection Act was passed to ensure continued funding for these programs.

- The passage of the Victims of Crime Act (VOCA) in 1984, which established the Crime Victim's Fund that is funded by fines collected through federal criminal cases, penalty assessments on convicted persons, and proceeds of all forfeitures in federeal criminal cases. These funds are then distributed via grants to states to help support victims of crime. Today, the fund balance is over $12 billion.

- The establishment of the Office for Victims of Crime (OVC), the largest federal agency to support crime victims, in 1988. As part of the U.S. Department of Justice, OVC's mission is to provide aid and promote justice for crime victims, and is responsible for the management of the Crime Victims Fund.

Many more laws and initiatives have followed in the three decades since—each of which has continued to advance the field of Victimology and expand the rights and services for all victims of

> "The criminal justice stystem has long functioned on the assumption that crime victims should behave like good Victorian children—seen but not heard. The Crime Victims' Rights Act sought to change this by making victims independent participants in the criminal justice system." *Kenna v. District Court* (2006) [435 F.3rd 1011, 9th Circuit]

crime. However, advocates, survivors, and scholars alike express there is still a great deal that needs to be done.

Overview of 21st Century Challenges in Victimology and Victim Services

Despite all of the progress made in the field of Victimology and in victim services over the past century, we are still not yet where we need to be. Some of the challenges we face in the 21st Century include:

1. We still have limited data sources for accurately and consistently measuring the full extent of crime victimization, studying the causes of victimization, and expanding the depth of research needed to improve our understanding and response to crime victimization.

2. Very few victim service programs have been evaluated. While data may be collected anecdotally, and agencies may maintain client data, overall, we have limited knowledge of which programs attain their intended goals and objectives. Without the necessary outcome evaluation research, the field has minimal evidence on what services are a best practice.

3. Changing victim populations are also a challenge; agencies may be designed for a specific victim population, and may not have the resources needed to change their target population.

4. Competing for external funding to stay viable is an ongoing concern for most programs. The financial dependency many agencies have on external funding makes them vulnerable. Most community-based agencies are nonprofit, dependent on federal dollars via grant programs. Public victim service providers are often the lowest priority in criminal justice budgets; victim service units in police department and corrections are always in jeopardy of being cut before public safety officers are eliminated. Moreover, public funds are competitive, and agencies do not always receive ongoing funding from year to year. Some grant years may be more prosperous than others, and in other years the funding source may dry up, forcing an agency to close its doors despite a continued demand to serve victims. Although VOCA and VAWA funds are both at the highest dollar amount since their inception, many smaller agencies don't have the resources or the expertise to apply for competitive funding. Many service providers in law enforcement and corrections work alone, and they have no other staff to assist with grant writing. Hence, the search for external funding is always a source of worry for many agencies.

5. In addition to funding, agencies struggle with reaching victims; programs located in the more remote or rural areas struggle with accessibility. Victims

often don't come forward and admit their traumatic experience for fear of revenge on the part of the offender, fear of having to testify, and/or a number of other personal reasons. Agencies also struggle with being known as a resource in the community; if they don't have a networking resource, getting the word out to victims may be difficult.

6. Also related to the more remote or rural communities is a lack of referral resources and ancillary services for victims. Most victim service providers can not provide all-inclusive services (e.g., medical, clinical, or behavioral health services), therefore they rely on referral agencies. In the more remote communities, there may be a limited source of necessary recovery services for victims. This challenge may be an issue for heavily populated communities as well, due to the limited services to support large volumes of victims.

7. Service providers working in remote or rural areas may not have a network of providers to rely on for support and sharing knowledge and expertise, and professional support. Collaboration and community partnerships are essential to the successful recovery and well-being of crime victims; however, building those relationships may be challenging in a rural community.

8. In addition to a lack of networking, isolated service providers may not have easy access to training or professional development opportunities.

9. Victim services is a transformative field that has a substantial role in the successful recovery and safety of victims. The changes in law, policy, and practices in the criminal justice system, and the nature and scope of victimization, continuously shift the demands and redefine the role of service providers, requiring ongoing training and professional development. Limited training, university education, certification, and credentialing is still an issue in many communities.

10. A final challenge for many service providers is keeping up with the complex and multifaceted long-term recovery needs of victims. The field is frequently required to change the service modalities to ensure that the most effective resources are available. Service models may no longer fit the needs of current victim populations. Providers should listen closely to the victims they serve. Some agencies attempt to be all things to all victims, and it's a monumental task to have resources centered in one place. The best source for reevaluating the mission, goals and practices are to hear from clients who are willing to identify their explicit needs and concerns. Agency assessments and process evaluations should be an ongoing course of action for all agencies to remain relevant and viable in a competitive and changing field. Qualitative surveys are essential to agencies that truly want to learn from their clients and provide the most suitable services.

To assist communities with addressing each of these challenges, the Office for Victims of Crime [OVC] is committed to "transforming Victim Services" in the 21st century through a comprehensive and systematic delivery approach; as well as, is committed to more flexible funding, filling the research gaps, and changing the way in which victims' needs are addressed and met. Ultimately, the goal for Victimology and victim services in the 21st century is to be vigilant in creating a safe place for victims to step forward and report their victimization and promoting a more unified effort to reach all underserved populations, and ensuring safety, support, and access to recovery services for all crime victims.

Overview of this book

This book provides the reader with a comprehensive overview of the evolution of Victimology and crime victim services, detailing the major events in history that led to the development of the field of victimology, and offers insight into the changing social and political ideologies that have influenced the way crime victims are treated within the legal system as well as in the community. Landmark legislation and cases are reviewed, as well as on the many political decisions that have influenced the support and development of crime victim services. Advancements in both research and victim services are highlighted, and a candid assessment of the gaps that remain in our collective response to victims of crime help to identify the path forward to to recovery.

Chapter 2 provides a statistical overview of how crime victimization is measured, the challenges such measures present, and how that information is used to guide policy and practice. Our knowledge about the consequences and seriousness of victimization is dependent on the extent of reported incidents of victimization. However, many victims are reluctant to report their experiences to law enforcement. Thus, we must find alternate sources to help capture this information. One of the most important sources of information on crime victimization comes from the National Crime Victimization Survey (NCVS). It provides a more detailed view of the precipitating factors of interpersonal crime victimization; explains the victim-offender relationship; and, reveals more accurate rates of incidents, as data originates from actual victims' reporting. However, it is not without its limitations. Thus, researchers have worked diligently to improve the quality and quantity of crime victimization data by seeking our more participants and expanding the scope of the types of victimization, re-examining the type of survey instruments used, and amending the data collection process. Each of these efforts have helped to increase the reliability and validity of the data, and as a result, we have a more complete picture of the nature and scope of victimization.

Chapter 3 provides a thorough overview of the typologies and theoretical developments in exploring and explaining the causes of victimization. Many theories did not have the original intent of specifically studying victimization, victimology evolved from studies that focused on criminal behavior, law, or practice. This chapter describes the predictors of victimization, and explores the research based on individual demographics and characteristics of offenders, and the multidimensional role of victims in the criminal event. It addresses the limitations of the theoretical research used to explain and describe victimization, and how research should be used to develop appropriate services.

Chapter 4 provides a comprehensive overview of legal and social remedies afforded to crime victims, dating back to the American Revolution and tracing them forward to the present day. A chronological summary of landmark developments in the treatment and ideology of victims over several hundred years illustrates the evolution of society's responses to crime victims, and the socio-political perspective of each major time period is described to explain the defining factors that determined the way in which victims received support and whether they were treated with legitimacy. This historical overview illustrates how much work is still needed to ensure that remedies for crime victims are inclusive to all victims.

Chapter 5 presents the landmark legislation that have marked the Victims Rights' Movement, starting with the 1982 Presidential Task Force on Victims of Crime and traces the movement to the present. Select legislation and case-law are discussed, based on their impact in the development of victimology and more importantly on the growth of the field of victim services. Each of which were essential in helping to establish victim rights, victim related laws, the reintegration of victims into the criminal justice system, and the development of the field of victim services.

Chapter 6 guides the reader through each stage of the criminal justice system to help them better understand each phase of the criminal justice proceeding. In the late 1990s, for the first time victims' rights dictated that the criminal justice system allow victims to be integrated into the various stages of the criminal justice process. Thus, it is essential that victim service providers acquire a sound understanding of the criminal justice process in order to better prepare the victim for the experience and reduce their likelihood of being retraumatized.

Chapter 7 presents contemporary legal remedies available to victims to support them through the complex legal proceedings and guide them toward their recovery. The chapter is divided into three parts; the first part describes the restorative model of justice and its role in repainring the harm caused by criminal behavior. It describes the complex roles of the victim, offender, and community in the restorative justice approach, and provides a summary of the many approaches currently used to provide reparation, as well as support services available to assist victims through the criminal justice process. The second part discusses the relationship of the media to crime victimization, and how the media can be utilized for victim advocacy and community awareness. And, the final section describes the use of technology to support crime victims and victim service providers, particularly through its ability to facilitate the networking and sharing of services, knowledge, and expertise. Several examples are provided to illustrate how technology has benefited victims and contributed to the advancement of the collection and preservation of evidence.

Chapter 8 provides a comprehensive summary of model programs and best practices in victim services in context with the contemporary needs of victims, survivors, their families, and the community. This chapter demonstrates how far the field of victim services has evolved and the complexity of the service industry that has been designed specifically to address the critical care and support needed by a widely diverse victim population. The range of services presented may not capture all the resources available to victims, but it captures several of the most multifaceted and complex categories of support essential to the recovery of many of the most serious forms of victimization.

Chapter 9 provides an overview of vicarious traumatization, also known as secondary trauma, which is caused by the indirect exposure to traumatic events through the firsthand account or narrative of that event. Vicarious traumatization also referred to as "compassion fatigue" is a very real outcome for victim service providers. They experience this form of secondary trauma when working with crime victims and listening to their traumatic victimization experiences day after day. This chapter provides various resources and tools to support victim service providers struggling with vicarious traumatization, and lends guidance for how to avoid secondary trauma, and on-the-job burnout.

Chapter 10 provides an overview of the diverse and complex field of victim services and traces its efforts at professionalizing the field. The chapter summarizes the standards that have been established, and provides an overview of model trainings, certifications, and educational programs that help victim service providers, programs, and agencies put those standards into practice. The chapter concludes by providing a roadmap for how victim services should move forward in the 21st Century to achieve the level of professionalization it requires to better meet the needs of all crime victims.

Conclusion

Although the role of the crime victim was a focus of research for more than fifty years (1920s–1960s), it wasn't until the 1970s that a *rediscovery* of crime victims occurred. American society finally began to recognize that the indifference toward the plight of victims was directly related to the preceding research that held them "responsible" for their own victimization. Although many find the early victimology research offensive because of its undertones of victim blaming, its basis is critical to understanding the long and arduous evolution of Victimology and society's slow acceptance of crime victims. Had it not been for the large number of victims and their advocates speaking out in the 1960s and 1970s, revealing the full impact of victimization, society may not have turned its sights toward the plight of the victim, and the field of Victimology may not have evolved, at least not as we know it today. Most importantly, the momentum and energy has continued to increase over the past fifty plus years, and the support from advocates, victims and survivors, legislators and politicians, and concerned citizens grows each year.

Discussion Questions

1. Describe the major events in the evolution of victimology.
2. Discuss the impact of the various social movements on the development of victims' rights and victim services.
3. Select one of the noted challenges facing the field today, and explain how we may overcome the challenge.

References

Craven, D. (1996, December). *Female victims of violent crime* [NCJ-162602]. Washington, DC: U.S. Department of Justice, Office of Justice Programs, Bureau of Justice Statistics.

Davis, R.C. (1987, May/June). Crime victims: Learning how to help them. *National Institute of Justice, Report No. 203,* Washington, DC: National Institute of Justice.

Elias, R. (1986). *The politics of victimization: Victims, victimology, and human rights.* New York: Oxford University Press.

Fattah, E.A. (1991). *Understanding criminal victimization: An introduction to theoretical victimology.* Scarborough, Ontario: Prentice Hall.

Hoffman, H. (1992). What did Mendelsohn really say? In S.B. David & G. F. Kirchhoff (Eds.) *International Faces of Criminology.* Monchengladbach: WSV Publishing.

Kelly, D.P., & Erez, E. (1997). Victim participation in the criminal justice system. In A. Lurigio, W. Skogan, & R. Davis (Eds.), *Victims of crime: Problems, policies, and programs* (2nd ed.). Thousand Oaks, CA: SAGE Publishing.

Koss, M.P., & Harvey, M.R. (1991). *The rape victim.* Thousand Oaks, CA: SAGE Publishing.

Mendelsohn, B. (1956). Une nouvelle branche de la Science BioPsycho-Sociale: La victimologie. *Revue Internationale de Criminologie et de Police Technique, X,* 2, 95–109. (1974) The Origin of the Doctrine of Victimology. I. Drapkin et E. Viano (eds.), *Victimology* (pp.3–12). Lexington, MA: Lexington Books.

National Center on Child Abuse and Neglect. (1996). *Fact sheet.* http://www.acf/ dhhs.gov/ALFPrograms/NCCAN/abuse.txt

National Organization for Victim Assistance. (2019). A chronology of the victims' rights movement. *NOVA Newsletter, 17*(4).

Office for Victims of Crime. (1998). *New directions from the field: Victims' rights and services for the 21st Century.* Washington DC: Office of Justice Programs, U.S. Government Printing Office.

Office for Victims of Crime. (2013) *Vision 21: Transforming victim services* [NCJ 239957]. Washington, DC: Office of Justice Programs, U.S. Government Printing.

Pagelow, M.D. (1992). Adult victims of domestic violence: Battered women. *Journal of Interpersonal Violence, 7,* 87–120.

Parent, D.G., Auerbach, B., & Carlson, K. E.. (1992). *Compensating crime victims: A summary of policies and practices.* Washington, DC: U.S. Department of Justice.

Pfohl, S. (1984). The discovery of the child abuse. In D. Kelly (ed.), *Deviant Behavior,* (pp. 50–60). Thousand Oaks, CA: SAGE Publishing.

President's Task Force on Victims of Crime. (1982). *Final report.* Washington, DC: U.S. Government Printing Office.

Sengstock, M.C. (1976) *Culpable victim in Mendelsohn's typology.* Presentation at the Annual Meeting of the Midwest Sociological Society. St. Louis, Missouri.

United States Department of Justice. (1993). *Highlights from 20 years of surveying crime victims: The National Crime Victimization Survey, 1973–92.* Washington, DC: U.S. Government Printing Office.

Van Ness, D., & Strong, K. H. (1997). *Restoring justice.* Cincinnati, OH: Anderson Publishing Company.

Von Hentig, H. (1948). *The criminal and his victim: Studies in the sociobiology of crime.* New Haven, CT: Yale University Press.

Young, M.A. (1997). Victim rights and services: A modern saga. In A. Lurigio, W. Skogan, & R. Davis (Eds.), *Victims of crime: Problems, policies, and programs* (2nd ed.) (pp.194-210). Thousand Oaks, CA: SAGE Publishing.

Young, V. (1992). Fear of victimization and victimization rates among women: A paradox. *Justice Quarterly, 9*(3), 419–442.

CHAPTER 2

Measuring Crime Victimization – What The Data Tells Us

Objectives

Upon completion of this chapter, you will be able to:

- understand different measurements of crime victimization,
- think critically about differences in measures and conceptualization of the victmization in official and unofficial statistics, and
- discuss the intersection of data, politics, and media and how it influences public perception of crime and fear of victimization.

Introduction

Believe it or not, we all utilize statistics on a daily basis. However, the data we often use and interpret in victimology and crime victimization come from many different sources, including news media and governmental officials. In fact, the common perception about crime and deviance, offenders and their victims, is largely shaped by the news and popular media. The proliferation of technology in our daily lives, such as the increasing use of surveillance cameras in public spaces, provides the media with an unprecedented access to images of crimes as they happen. The media also provides the public a front-row seat to the criminal justice system when cameras are allowed in the courtroom. While this has helped to increase the public's awareness about crime and victims' experiences, the stories we hear from the popular media, as well as from our elected officials, do not always present an objective portrait of crime or victimization. Both the popular media and politicians are very selective about what crime victimization stories they highlight, typically focusing on only those crimes that are currently viewed as a threat to law, order, morality, and social control. Consequently, they socially construct the image and magnitude of the crime problems and victimization for the general public. Yet, the data derived from governmental agencies like the Federal Bureau of Investigation's Uniform Crime Reports (UCR) arrest data, and the Bureau of Justice Statistics' National Crime Victimization Surveys (NCVS), as well as other unofficial surveys do not always align with what popular media and elected officials are telling us. So, it is critical for the public to educate themselves by reviewing actual crime and victimization data to get a more accurate picture. This chapter provides the reader with an overview of crime and victimization statistics drawn from official data and national surveys, covering a wide-range of types of crime and demographics.

The chapter is divided into two sections. The first part provides an overview of how crime victimization is measured in the United States, and examines what the data from each source seems to tell us about the crime rate, the scale of victimization, and its trends over time. It highlights some of the differences in measures and conceptualization of the offenses in official and unofficial statistics, and points out their limitations. The second section examines the intersection of politics, media, and data; and, discusses how politicians and popular media's portrayal of crime statistics and/or victims' stories can affect the public's attitudes towards victims, as well as increase their fear of crime.

Measuring Crime and Crime Victimization

What is crime and crime victimization? How is crime measured? How much crime is committed in different geographic locations or over different time periods? What approaches and methods are available for measuring crime and crime victimization? These and other questions must be asked to gain information about crime prevalence, crime victims, and consequences of crime; and enable us to compare crime and victimization rates over time and across different jurisdictions.

One of the starting points for those who are interested in the measurement of crime and crime victimization involves defining the phenomena. Without a specific definition of crime, a precise measurement of crime and crime victimization is impossible. In general terms, the legal definition of crime is any wrongdoing classified by the state or federal government as a violàtion against a public law. In reality, however, the legal definition of crime has proven to be more fluid. Laws vary from jurisdiction to jurisdiction, and sometimes change over time causing some behaviors to become a part of our legal statutes and language, while others are eliminated from legal lexicon. Hence, many scholars argue that crime is a socially constructed phenomenon and is created by social forces in society that may change our responses to such behavior.

This malleable nature of the legal definition of crime may lead to an unrealistic picture of the scope, nature, and causes of crime. Thus, the change in what constitutes a crime has an impact on our perception of the crime rate and scale of crime victimization. While it is almost impossible to accurately measure the scope and change in crime, some national programs have been developed to track the extent of crime and crime victimization over time and place.

Uniform Crime Report

The gathering of police arrest data into a centralized data system managed by the Federal Bureau of Investigation is referred to as the Uniform Crime Report (UCR). The UCR was initiated in 1930 as a uniform way to collect, publish, and house crime data for law enforcement administration and management. Today, over

16,000 city, county, state, tribal, and federal law enforcement agencies (99 percent of all law enforcement agencies in the U.S.) voluntarily participate in the program each year (FBI, 2018). The UCR collects official crime data on crimes reported to the police, as well as arrests, and then categorizes it into two parts. Part I, often referred to as the *Index Offenses*, is comprised of eight serious crimes: homicide, rape, robbery, aggravated assault, burglary, larceny-theft, motor vehicle theft, and arson (FBI, 2018). Part II offenses of the UCR include data for 21 additional types of offenses, and are comprised of low-level offenses, including: simple assault, forgery and counterfeiting, curfew offenses and loitering, embezzlement, disorderly conduct, driving under the influence, drug offenses, fraud, gambling, liquor offenses, offenses against the family, prostitution, public drunkenness, runaways, sex offenses, stolen property, vandalism, vagrancy, and weapons offenses.

The UCR statistics are reported in two main formats: crime *volume* and crime *rate*. Crime volume is a simple way to report a count of the number of crimes that occurred and is known to law enforcement agencies in a specific jurisdiction in any given year. Crime rate is a relative number, and is generally reported in terms of rates per 100,000 people in the population. The crime rate is often used for comparison among jurisdictions even though the FBI warns against comparing crime rates and ranking jurisdictions into "safe" and "unsafe" categories. Other factors such as poverty, urbanization, and population density, unemployment, and other social and economic factors may influence law enforcement agencies and consequently influence the crime rate.

One of the benefits of the UCR is that researchers are able to use the data to identify patterns and trends in crime over time, as well as across jurisdictions. For example, as illustrated by Figure 2.1, one can quickly discern that the majority of crimes reported to law enforcement involve property crimes, and that overall, crime has been largely declining for the past 15 years. Looking more closely at the data, however, we can see two notable trends. First, the number of property crimes reported to the police have consistently dropped every year, for the past five years (see Figure 2.2). However, a different trend is observed with violent crime. As illustrated in Figure 2.3, the number of violent crimes reported to the police actually started to increase in 2015, and then began to decline in 2017. Some of the reasons offered for the temporary rise in violent crime is believed to be attributed to the spike in homicides in a handful of large cities (e.g., Chicago, Baltimore, St. Louis, etc.), as well to what some researchers have asserted is a "crisis in police legitimacy," particularly among disadvantaged minority communities following a number of high-profile police brutality and use-of-force cases (Lartey & Li, 2019). Thus, individuals who fall victim to a violent crime in such communities may be more reluctant to report such incidents to the police. Fortunately, the number of violent crimes have once again dropped for the past two years, and researchers have noted that current levels of violent crime are more than 50% lower since their peak in the 1990s (Lartey & Li, 2019).

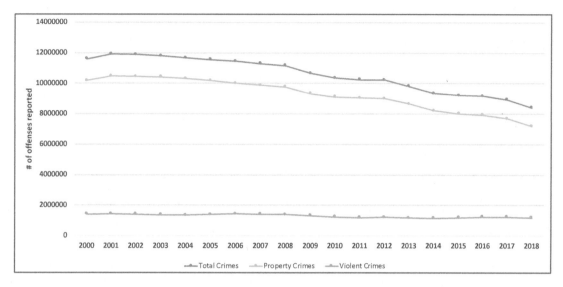

Source: Federal Bureau of Investigation. (2018). Uniform Crime Report, 2018.

FIGURE 2.1 Part I Offenses Reported to Law Enforcement, 2000-2018

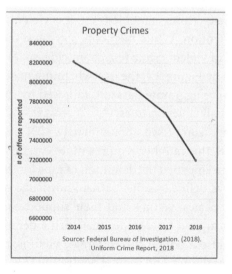

FIGURE 2.2 Property Crimes Reported to Law Enforcement, Five Year Trend

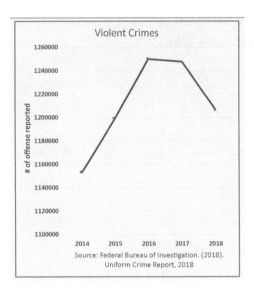

Source: Federal Bureau of Investigation. (2018). Uniform Crime Report, 2018

FIGURE 2.3 Violent Crimes Reported to Law Enforcement, Five Year Trend

Other notable patterns emerge when examining the data for the most recent year. In 2018, a total of 8,402,881 serious crimes were reported to law enforcement, of which approximately 86% (n = 7,196,045) were for a property crime and 14% (n = 1,206,836) were for a violent crime (FBI, 2018). Thus, approximately six times as many property crimes were reported to the police than violent crimes. The majority of the property crimes reported were for larceny-theft (see Figure 2.4). In fact, the number of larceny-thefts reported to police were four times greater than *all* of the violent crimes combined. Yet, it is violent crime that receives the greatest amount of attention. While the public's greatest concern center around the most serious types of violent crime (e.g., homicide, rape), both are relatively rare events. As illustrated by Figure 2.4, the overwhelming majority of violent crimes reported to police involve aggravated assault, followed by robbery. Homicides, in contrast, only up 1% of all violent crimes.

While rape comprised approximately 10% of all violent crimes reported to police in 2018, this number requires more careful attention. In 2013, the Department of Justice amended the definition of rape for the UCR. For the previous eighty years, rape was defined as the "carnal knowledge of a female forcibly and against her will." Advocates, victims and their supporters, as well as many law enforcement officials argued for decades that such a definition artificially suppressed the statistics because it only included female victims, required the use of force in the commission of the act, and vaginal pentration (FBI, 2014). Thus, it excluded a long list of other sexual offenses that would defined as a serious felony in most other jurisdictions, as well as excluded male victims. Finally, in 2013, the definition was

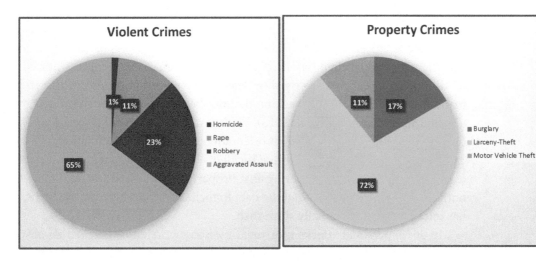

Source: Federal Bureau of Investigation. (2018). Uniform Crime Report, 2018.

FIGURE 2.4 Crimes Reported to Law Enforcement, By Type and Percentage, 2018

amended to now state, "penetration, no matter how slight, of the vagina or anus with any body part or object, or oral penetration by a sex organ of another person, without the consent of the victim" (FBI, 2014). Consequently, since the adoption of the new definition, the number of rapes reported in the UCR have increased by roughly one-third each year (see Figure 2.5).

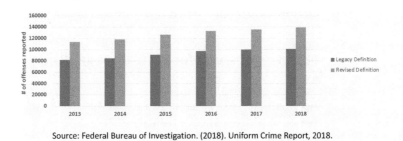

Source: Federal Bureau of Investigation. (2018). Uniform Crime Report, 2018.

FIGURE 2.5 Impact of Change of Rape Definition in Reporting Data, 2014-2018

The FBI also releases a few supplemental reports each year that focus on specific crimes – a supplemental homicide report, a report on the number of law enforcement officers killed and assaulted, the number of reported hate crimes, and the national incident based reporting system. In 2009, Congress passed the Matthew Shepard and James Byrd, Jr. Hate Crimes Prevention Act, which in part mandated the FBI to begin tracking the number of hate crimes commited by or directed against juveniles (FBI, 2018). Victims of hate crimes are targeted for either their race or ethnicity, their sexual orientation, their religious affiliation, or physical and/or mental disabilities. These incidents can involve crimes against persons (e.g., assault, homicide), crimes against property (e.g., vandalism, arson, etc.), or both. In 2013, the FBI expanded the data to include victims over the age of 18, and has released a report annually since then.

In 2018, personal attacks motivated by bias or prejudice reached an all-time high FBI, 2018). A total of 7,120 incidents of hate crimes were reported involving 8,819 victims (see Figure 2.6). The overwhelming majority of these incidents were single-bias (e.g, only one type of victim was the focus of the crime) and the majority were based on racial or ethnic bias. Approximately 1 out of every 2 of the victims of these types of hate crimes were Black (see Figure 2.7), and White victims were the next largest group. However, another group that has been targeted at increasing rate in the past few years are Hispanics and Latinos.

- Total of 7,120 hate crimes involving 8,646 victims were reported to law enforcement

- 98% of reports were for a single-bias incident

- Approximately 60% of victims were targeted because of their race, ethnicity; 19% were targeted because of their religious affiliation; 17% were targeted because of their sexual orientation; and, 2% were targeted because of either a physical or mental disability

Source: Federal Bureau of Investigation. (2018). Hate Crimes, 2018.

FIGURE 2.6 Number of Hate Crimes Reported to Law Enforcement, 2018

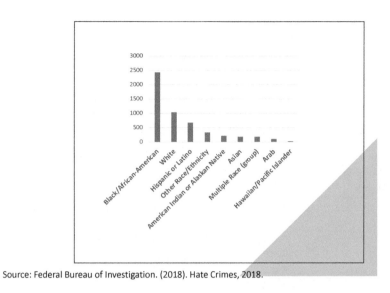

Source: Federal Bureau of Investigation. (2018). Hate Crimes, 2018.

FIGURE 2.7 Number of Hate Crimes Reported to Law Enforcement, By Race and Ethnicity, 2018

The second most prevalent type of hate crime reported to law enforcement were for religious bias. In 2018, a total of 1,617 victims were targeted because of their religious affiliation (see Figure 2.8). In 2018, the religious group most often targeted were Jewish victims, with approximately four times as many incidents recorded among this group as for the second most populous group, Muslims.

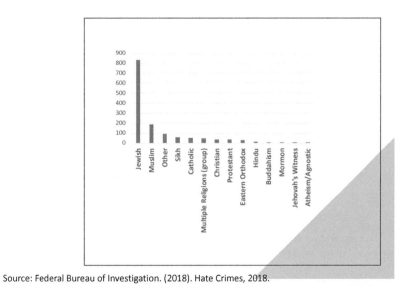

Source: Federal Bureau of Investigation. (2018). Hate Crimes, 2018.

FIGURE 2.8 Number of Hate Crimes Reported to Law Enforcement, By Religious Affiliation, 2018

Unfortunately, these numbers are a reflection of a broader, more disturbing trend. Law enforcement officials have noted the number of anti-Semitic hate crimes in the nation's three largest cities (e.g., New York, Los Angelos, Chicago) were poised to reach their highest level in 2019.

Muslims have also been disproportionately victimized by hate crimes. This pattern is markedly different from what researchers observed in the immediate aftermath following the terrorist attacks on September 11, 2001, when there were 93 reported hate crimes against Muslims. While those numbers dropped precipitously in the years that followed, they spiked again in 2016 to 127 and have been trending upwards since (Kishi, 2017).

The third most prevalent hate crime reported to law enforcement involved individuals who were targeted because of either their sexual orientation or gender identity. In 2018, a total of 1,634 victims experienced this type of hate crime (see Figure 2.9). Over 50% of these victims were gay males. Lesbian women and transgender individuals experienced similar rates of victimization. Interestingly, the second most prevalent incident reported to law enforcement involved a group of LGBTQ individuals.

National Incident Based Reporting System

Although the UCR provides law enforcement and the public with the largest measure of official crime statistics annually, it is not without significant limitations. First, and foremost, it only includes those crimes that are reported to law

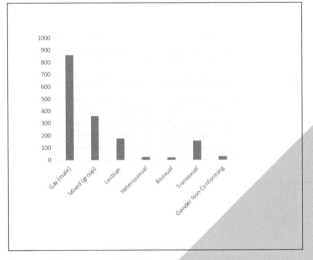

Source: Federal Bureau of Investigation. (2018). Hate Crimes, 2018.

FIGURE 2.9 Number of Hate Crimes Reported to Law Enforcement, by Sexual Orientation or Gender Identity (2018)

THE 21ST CENTURY TRANSFORMATION OF VICTIMOLOGY

enforcement. Many crimes, particularly inter-personal crimes, are never reported. Many victims of domestic violence, child abuse, elder abuse, and sexual assault never come forward because they may be struggling with feelings of shame, or they may fear retaliation from their abuser, or both. Thus, the estimates of these crimes have historically been artificially low. Another limitation is that the UCR utilizes a method of reporting in which only the most serious offense is reported for each crime incident (e.g., 'hierarchy rule'). For example, if during the commission of a robbery, the victim is murdered, only the homicide would be recorded for the UCR. This is problematic because often, multiple offenses are committed simultaneously, thus the less serious crimes will not be reflected in the data. Finally, the UCR presents a fairly narrow scope of crime, as a limited number of offenses are included and measured for Part I and Part II.

To improve the overall quality of crime data by law enforcement, the Bureau of Justice Statistics and the FBI sponsored a study of the UCR Program in 1982 with the objective of revising it to meet law enforcement needs in the 21st century (FBI, n.d.). Over the next five years, the agencies worked collaboratively to redesign how crime data would be recorded and reported by law enforcement. These efforts led to more comprehensive and detailed crime statistics being collected on each reported crime incident, and the official launch of the National Incident-Based Reporting System (NIBRS).

NIBRS differs significantly from the UCR in a number of ways. Currently, under the summary system for the UCR, law enforcement authorities aggregate the number of incidents by offense type monthly and report these totals to the FBI. Under incident-based reporting, agencies provide an individual record for each crime reported. Another significant difference between the two systems is the scope of offenses it collects information on. Currently, the UCR collects offense information on the eight Part I crimes of homicide, rape, robbery, aggravated assault, burglary, larceny-theft, motor vehicle theft, and arson; and arrest data for 21 additional crime categories (lower-level offenses). Under NIBRS, law enforcement authorities provide information to the FBI on each criminal incident involving 52 specific offenses, including the 8 Part I crimes, and 10 additional offenses for which only arrest data is provided. Each offense is classified into one of three categories: crimes against persons, crimes against property, or crimes against society (FBI, 2012)[1]. And finally, and arguably, the greatest difference between NIBRS and the UCR is the level of detail it collects about each incident. For each incident, NIBRS includes incident date and time, whether reported offenses were attempted

---

[1] Crimes against persons involve victims who are always indivdiuals; crimes against property are intended to obtain money or property; and, crimes against society represent society's prohibition against engaging in certain types of activity; they are typically victimless crimes in which property is not the object (FBI, 2012).

or completed, expanded victim types, relationships of victims to offenders and offenses, demographic details, location data, property descriptions, drug types and quantities, the offender's suspected use of drugs or alcohol, the involvement of gang activity, and whether a computer was used in the commission of the crime (FBI, n.d.). Thus, it is able to provide law enforcement with more information about circumstances and context for each crime incident.

In 2018, approximately 44% of the law enforcement agencies that participated in the UCR program submitted data to NIBRS (FBI, n.d.). These agencies reported 5.4 million incidents, which included 6 million criminal offenses and approximately 4.5 million victims (FBI, 2018). Sixty-one percent of the incidents involved property crimes, 23% involved crimes against persons, and 16% involved crimes against society (e.g., animal cruelty, gambling, prostitution, etc.). Over one-half of the victims were female, and approximately one-quarter of the victims were betweeen the ages of 21-30. Most notably, over 50% of the victims knew at least one of their offenders, and 24% of the victims were related to their perpetrator. Nearly two-thirds of the perpetrators identified by the victim were male, and the majority (42%) of perpetrators were between the ages of 16-30 (FBI, 2018).

The benefit to this level of detail about each incident is that provides law enforcement with greater context to specific crime problems (e.g., sex offenses, identity theft, drug offenses, etc.), and allows them to see many more facets of crime, and the relationships and connections between those facets. Armed with such information, law enforcement can better define the resources it needs to fight crime, as well as use those resources in the most efficient and effective manner. Therefore, to aid law enforcement agencies in this endeavor, the FBI has committed to the nationwide implementation of NIBRS by 2021 and discontinuing the UCR program (FBI, n.d.).

National Crime Victimization Survey

The National Crime Victimization Survey (NCVS) was introduced in 1973 as an attempt to address the limitations of the UCR data, and is the primary source of national crime victimization data (National Crime Victims' Rights Week [NCVRW], 2017). Every year, household survey data is collected by the U.S. Census Bureau for the Department of Justice, Bureau of Justice Statistics (BJS). Interviews are conducted either in person or over the telephone. In 2018, approximately 151,000 households were randomly selected, and each individual living in the home who is over the age of twelve was interviewed (Morgan & Oudekerk, 2019). Overall, 73% of eligible households completed an interview, and 82% of the eligible persons within the household (n = 242,928) completed an interview. These participants will remain in the sample for three years, and be re-interviewed every six months (NCVRW, 2017).

The interviews rely on self-reported victimization of: aggravated and simple assault, robbery, rape, sexual assault, household burglary, trespassing, theft, and motor vehicle theft (NCVRW, 2017), and gathers information on crimes both reported and not reported to law enforcement, and describes the reasons victims gave for reporting or not reporting; and includes questions about the victim's experiences with the criminal justice system. The NCVS also collects demographic information about both victims and offenders (e.g., age, sex, race/ethnicity, marital status, income, relationship between victim and offender), as well as details about the incident, including time and place, use of weapons, nature of injury, and economic impact. In addition, the NCVS will periodically collect supplementary information about specific crimes, such as stalking and school crime, and release it with its annual report (NCVRW, 2017).

In 2018, a total of 19,888,360 victimizations were reported in the NCVS, of which 68% involved a property crime and 32% involved a violent crime (see Figure 2.10)[2]. Over three-quarters of the property crimes reported were for theft (n = 10,329,210). Approximately 3.3 million individuals age 12 and older reported 6.4 million violent crimes, of which 63% were a victim of simple assault (see Figure 2.11).

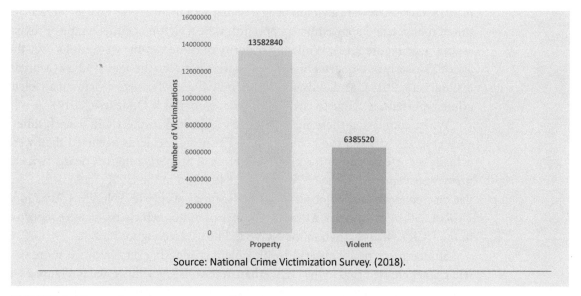

Source: National Crime Victimization Survey. (2018).

FIGURE 2.10 Number of Property v. Violent Victimizations, 2018

[2] Approximately 9 million households reported 13.5 million incidents of property victimization. The NCVS does not include a count of the number of *individuals* who were a victim of a property crime, as it does with violent crime. Rather, if any respondent states they had been a victim of a property offense in the prior year, the incident is classified as a crime againstthe entire household (Morgan & Oudekerk, 2019).

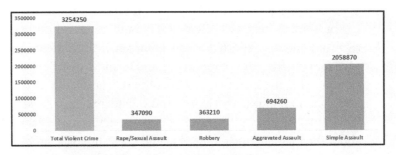

Source: National Crime Victimization Survey. (2018).

FIGURE 2.11 Number of Victims of Violent Crime, by type of crime (2018)

Unfortunately, 1.3 million individuals were a victim of a serious violent crime in 2018. Over 50% were a victim of aggravated assault, over one-quarter were a victim of robbery, and approximately one-fifth were a victim of either a rape or sexual assault[3] (see Figure 2.12). While the majority of these victims were adults over the age of 25, nearly one-quarter of the victims were between the ages of 12-24 (Morgan & Oudekerk, 2019). And, only 43% of the indivduals who were a vicim of a violent crime reported the crime to law enforcement (Morgan & Oudekerk, 2019).

When comparing these figures to those reported in the UCR, a stark difference emerges between the two measures. Far more incidents occurred than were actually reported to law enforcement. In terms of property offenses, nearly twice as many were reported in the NCVS (13,582,840) than in the UCR (7,196,045). Similar discrepancies can be observed for residential burglaries (NCVS: 1,724,720 v. UCR: 1,230,149), however, a greater number of motor vehicle thefts were reported in the UCR (748,841) than in the NCVS (534,010) (see Figure 2.13).

Similar patterns are observed with violent crimes. In every instance, more violent crimes are reported in the NCVS than in the UCR. As illustrated in Figure 2.14, nearly five times as many rapes and twice as many robberies were reported in the NCVS than in the UCR. While the number of aggravated assaults reported in the

---

[3] In addition to rape and attempted rape, the NCVS also asks respondents if they had been a victim of a sexual assault, which includes attacks or threatened attacks, involving unwanted sexual contact between the victim and offender. Sexual assault may or may not include the use of force (Morgan & Oudekerk, 2019).

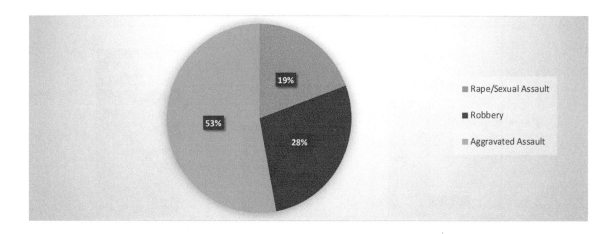

Source: National Crime Victimization Survey. (2018).

FIGURE 2.12 Percentage of Persons Who Were Victims of Serious Violent Crime (2018)

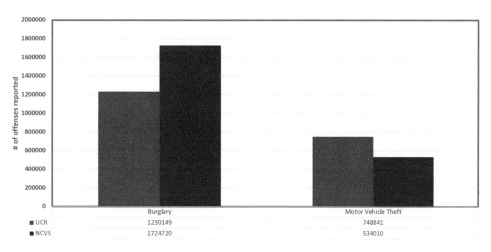

*NCVS reports sexual assault and rape as one measure; UCR does not include sexual assault   Source: National Crime Victimization Survey. (2018).

FIGURE 2.13 Number of Property Victimizations Reported, by type of crime, UCR vs. NCVS (2018)

NCVS similarly exceed what was reported in the UCR, the disparity between the two numbers is not as significant. These differences, however, may be somewhat distorted due to the lack of continuity between the two measures.

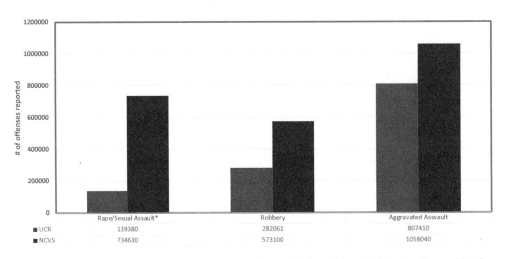

Source: National Crime Victimization Survey. (2018).

FIGURE 2.14 Number of Violent Victimizations Reported, by type of crime, UCR vs. NCVS (2018)

One of the major reasons for such differences is that the NCVS reports both crimes that are and are not reported to law enforcement, whereas the UCR is based exclusively on crimes known to law enforcement. Moreover, both measures do not collect data on the same crimes. The UCR includes murder, non-negligent manslaughter, and commercial crimes (including burglary of commercial establishments), while the NCVS excludes these crimes; and the NCVS includes sexual assault while the UCR does not (Morgan & Ouderkerk, 2019). The NCVS' estimates are also based on interviews with persons from a nationally representative sample, whereas the UCR's estimates are based on counts of crimes reported by law enforcement. And finally, the NCVS uses different definitions of certain crimes. For example, the UCR defines burglary as the unlawful entry or attempted entry of a structure to commit a felony or theft. The NCVS, not wanting to ask victims to ascertain offender motives, defines burglary as the entry or attempted entry of a residence by a person who had no right to be there (FBI, 2017). And, as noted previously, the NCVS includes sexual assault along with rape and attempted rape, which the UCR excludes.

While the NCVS has successfully addressed several weaknesses of the UCR and helped shine a light on the 'dark figure of crime' researchers often talk about, it too has several limitations. First, the NCVS does not measure crimes against children 11 and younger, nor does it measure crimes against persons who are homeless, incarcerated, or in a health care facility; all of which, are highly vulnerable populations for victimization. It also does not include households on military bases. And similar to the UCR, the NCVS does not include victimization data involving

THE 21ST CENTURY TRANSFORMATION OF VICTIMOLOGY

white-collar and corporate crimes. To address these limitations, the NCVS is currently undergoing a major redesign (NCVRW, 2017). Over the next few years, it hopes to provide sub-national estimates so researchers will be able to compare victimization estimates across the 22 largest states. It is also working to moderninize the socio-demographic information it collects from participants to reflect victimization by sexual orientation, gender identity, veteran status, and citizenship; and, expand the information collected about formal and informal help-seeking behavior, issues related to fear of crime, and perceptions of neighborhood disorder and police performance. And finally, it is going to expand the type of crimes collected in the survey to include stalking and fraud.

National Intimate Partner & Sexual Violence Survey

In 2010, the Centers for Disease Control and Prevention published the first National Intimate Partner and Sexual Violence Survey (NIPSV) to better describe and monitor the magnitude of intimate partner violence (IPV)[4] in the United States (Centers for Disease Control [CDC], 2010). It is now an ongoing, nationally representative telephone survey that collects detailed information on IPV, sexual violence, and stalking victimization of adult men and women ages 18 and older in the U.S; and, collects data on past-year and lifetime experiences for each type of violence and asks respondents about the impact of their experiences (e.g., type of injury suffered, being fearful or concerned for one's safety, if experienced any symptoms of PTSD, missing days of school or work, etc.) (CDC, 2010)[5]. The estimates presented in the 2015 report are based on a total of 10,081 completed interviews.

Lifetime and one-year estimates for IPV, SV, and stalking are alarmingly high for adults in the United States, with IPV alone affecting more than 12 million people each year (CDC, 2018). As illustrated in Figure 2.15, women are disproportionately affected by IPV, SV, and stalking when compared to men. Over the course of their lifetime, approximately 44 million women have been victims of intimate partner violence, over 52 million were victims of some form of contact sexual violence, and approximately 19 million were victims of stalking. Men also experienced high rates of IPV, SV, and stalking over the course of their lifetime. According to the 2015 data, 1 out of every 10 men have been a victim of IPV, 1 out of 14 had experienced a completed or attempted rape, and 1 out of 17 had been stalked during his lifetime (see Figures 2.16 and 2.17)

---

[4] NISVS defines initimate partner violence to include physical violence, sexual violence, stalking, and psychological aggression (including coercive tactics) by a current or former intimate partner (e.g., romantic or sexual partner) (CDC, 2010).
[5] In addition to its standard report, the CDC has also released special and supplemental reports to the NIPSVS on victimization by sexual orientation, and the consequence of IPV on health outcomes and impact on public health and social services.

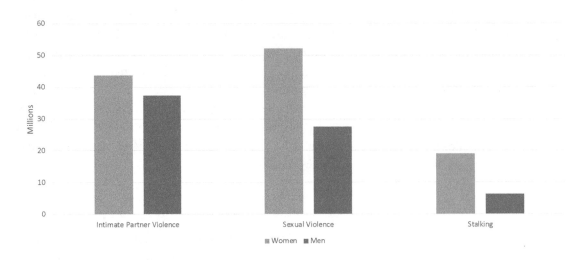

Source: National Intimate Partner & Sexual Violence Survey (2015)

FIGURE 2.15 Lifetime Prevalence of IPV, SV, and Stalking, by Gender (2015)

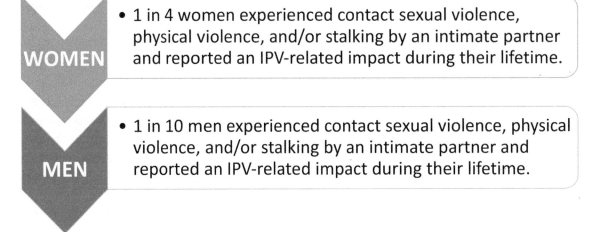

WOMEN
- 1 in 4 women experienced contact sexual violence, physical violence, and/or stalking by an intimate partner and reported an IPV-related impact during their lifetime.

MEN
- 1 in 10 men experienced contact sexual violence, physical violence, and/or stalking by an intimate partner and reported an IPV-related impact during their lifetime.

Source: National Intimate Partner & Sexual Violence Survey. (2015).

FIGURE 2.16 Prevalence of Intimate Partner Violence (IPV) in Lifetime, by Gender (2015)

THE 21ST CENTURY TRANSFORMATION OF VICTIMOLOGY

- 1 in 5 women experienced completed or attempted rape during her lifetime

- 1 in 14 men was made to penetrate someone (completed or attempted) during his lifetime

Source: National Intimate Partner & Sexual Violence Survey. (2015).

FIGURE 2.17 Prevalence of Sexual Violence in Lifetime, by Gender (2015)

Unfortunately, the data also revealed that majority of this victimization starts early in life (CDC, 2018). Among female victims of IPV, nearly 26% reported that they first experienced this type of violence before the age of 18; and, approximately 15% of male victims of IPV reported to have experienced this type of violence for the first time prior to the age of 18 (CDC, 2018). More disturbing patterns emerge from the data that addresses age of onset for sexual violence. Among female victims of completed or attempted rape, over 43% reported that it first occurred prior to the age of 18, and approximately 13% reported that it first occurred at the age of 10 or younger (CDC, 2018). Similar patterns are found among male victims of completed or attempted rape. Approximately 51% reported that it first occurred prior to the age of 18, and approximately 26% reported that it first occurred at the age of 10 or younger (CDC, 2018).

While the NIPSVS is considered to be one of the most comprehensive sources of information on intimate partner violence and sexual violence, it does have a few limitations. First, since it is a telephone-based survey in which participants are selected by random-digit dialing, not everyone who was called agreed to participate. For this most recent survey, only about 1 in every 4 individuals contacted by phone agreed to participate (CDC, 2018). While this reflects a low response rate, nearly 90% of those who agreed to participate completed the survey. Second, the NISVS is designed as a household survey, similar to the NCVS; therefore, individuals who are institutionalized, residing in shelters, or living on military bases are excluded. Third, given the reliance on self-reports, the estimates presented are likely to be underestimate the true prevalence of IPV, SV, and stalking. Many victims choose not to disclose these experiences out of fear, shame, or stigma. Others may not be able to recall accurately incidents from their past. And finally, the survey can not capture every type of victimization. For example, the questions about unwanted sexual experiences does not include noncontact unwanted sexual experiences (e.g., sexual harassment).

National Survey of Children's Exposure to Violence

In 2007, the Office of Juvenile Justice and Delinquency Prevention and the Centers for Disease Control and Prevention launched a national survey to document the incidence and prevalence of children's exposure to violence, with particular attention to domestic and community violence (Crimes Against Children Research Center (CACRC), n.d.). In addition to measuring the incidence and prevalence of children's exposure to violence in the United States, the survey collects data on the rates of exposure by demographic characteristics (e.g., gender, race/ethnicity, age, family structure), the characteristics of each incident (e.g., severity of event, child's relationship to perpetrator), the co-occuring nature or 'clustering' of violence exposure, the impact of varying levels and types of violence exposure on a child's mental health, the extent to which children disclose incidents of violence to different individuals, and the nature and source of assistance or treatment the child received (CACRC, n.d).

Phone interviews are conducted with a nationally representative sample of 4,500 households with children ages birth to 17. One target child is randomly selected from each eligible household, and permission is secured from the child's caregiver. If the child selected is younger than 10, a proxy interview is conducted with the adult in the household who is most familiar with the child's activities. Interviews are conducted in both English and Spanish.

In 2014, nearly 2 out of 3 children under the age of 17[6] were exposed to violence within the past year, either directly (as victims) or indirectly (as witnesses) (Child Trends Data Bank, 2016). As illustrated in Figure 2.18, over the course of their lifetime, 50% of children had been physically assaulted, 25% suffered some form of maltreatment, 8% had been sexually assaulted, 38% had witnessed violence in their homes and communities, and 20% had witnessed an incident of IPV by a family member. The researchers also found that children who were exposed to one type of violence were significantly at higher-risk of experiencing other types of violence, illustrating the potential for chronic exposure to violence for many of these youth (Child Trends Data Bank, 2016)

Except for physical assault, all types of exposure to violence was more common among older children (ages 14-17). The greatest incidence of physical assault was

---

[6] To capture more high-risk children, households from high-risk communities are oversampled (CACRC, n.d.)

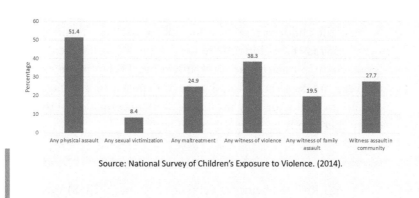

Source: National Survey of Children's Exposure to Violence. (2014).

FIGURE 2.18 Children's Lifetime Exposure to Violence, by Type (2014)

most common among children between ages of 6 – 9 (Child Trends Bank, 2016). A few notable differences were also observed by gender. Males were more likely to be physically assaulted and to witness violence in the community; whereas, females were more likely to be sexually assaulted and witness an incident of IPV by a family member (see Figure 2.19) (Child Trends Bank, 2016).

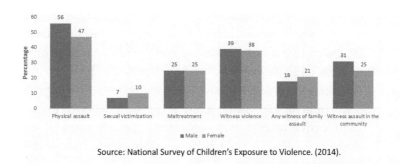

Source: National Survey of Children's Exposure to Violence. (2014).

FIGURE 2.19 Children's Lifetime Exposure to Violence, by Gender (2014)

While this survey captures critical information about children's exposure to violence in the United States, these findings likely understate their actual exposure because the children may be reluctant to disclose certain incidents out of fear or shame, or may have difficulty remembering a specific incident (Child Trends Data Bank, 2016). Similarly, for youth under age 11, family members may not be aware of every incident their child has been exposed to, or may be reticent to disclose certain incidents (or may minimize particular incidents) that implicate their own or another family member's involvement.

National Youth Risk Behavior Surveillance System

The Youth Risk Behavior Surveillence System (YRBSS) was developed in 1990 by the Centers for Disease Control and Prevention to monitor health behaviors that contribute significantly to the leading causes of death, disability, and social problems among youth and young adults in th United States (CDC, 2018). The purpose of the survey is fourfold: to describe the prevalence of health-risk behavior among youth; assess trends in health behaviors over time, as well as examine the co-occurrence of said behaviors; provide comparable national, state, territorial, tribal, and local data, as well as data among subpopulations of youth; and, to evaluate and improve health related policies and programs. While it may seem unusual that this data has been used to measure victimization among youth, violence has been declared to be a significant public health concern. Since 1965, homicide and suicide have consistently been among the top 15 leading causes of death in the United States (CDC, 2009). Moreover, the data shows the risk of each of these specific causes of death is disproportionately higher among youth and members of minority groups, particularly among young African-American males. Therefore, in 1979, the Surgeon General of the United States released a report that classified violence as a public health crisis, and mandated it to be one of the 15 priority areas to focus on to improve the nation's overall health and well-being (CDC, 2009).

The survey is conducted every two years with a representative sample of students in grades 9 – 12 in public and private schools in the United States. Since its introduction in 1991, it has collected data from more than 4.4 million high school students (CDC, 2018). In 2017, approximately 15,000 high school students participated in the survey.

In 2017, the most common form of victimization high students reported was bullying – 19% reported to have been bullied at school, and 15% reported to have been bullied electronically (see Figure 2.20). Six percent of students surveyed reported to have been threatened or injured with a weapon at school, and approximately 7% reported they stayed home from school at least once because they feared for their safety (see Figure 2.21).

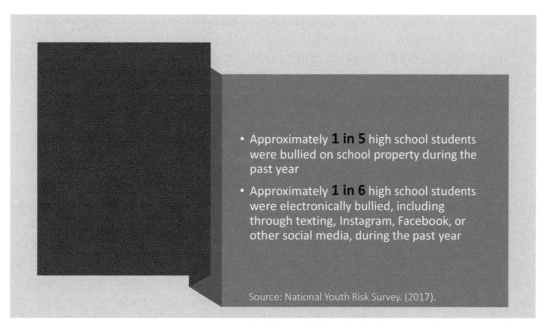

FIGURE 2.20 Prevalence of Bullying among 9th-12th Grade Students (2017)

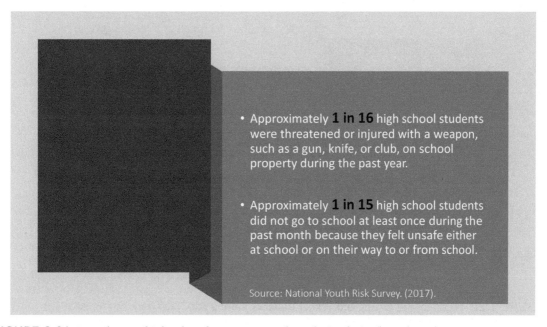

FIGURE 2.21 Prevalence of School Violence among 9th-12th Grade Students (2017)

A small but significant number of students also reported being a victim of intimate partner violence. Eight percent reported being a victim of physical dating violence, and 7% reported being a victim of sexual dating violence (see Figure 2.22). And, over 7% of students reported they had been physically forced to have sexual intercourse when they did not want to.

As with the other surveys that have had to rely on participants self-reporting their experiences with victimization, particularly those incidents involving intimate partner violence and sexual violence, researchers generally believe these estimates are underreported. Youth, in particular, are much more reticent about reporting IPV and sexual violence than adults (O'Grady & Matthews-Creech, 2020). A youth may blame him or herself for the incident, may fear retaliation from their perpetrator and/or their peers, may be struggling with feelings of extreme shame, or all of the above. Hence, they may perceive it to be safer to remain silent. Another limitation is that the survey only includes youth who attend school, and are enrolled in high-school. Thus, the estimates can not be generalized to all youth. To address this gap, the CDC has administered a number of supplemental surveys with specific subpopulations that are excluded from the YBRSS. These include a survey of middle school students (grades 6-8) in interested states, territories, tribal governments, and large urban school districts; a nationally representative survey of students in alternative high schools; and, a nationally representative survey of undergraduate students (CDC, 2018).

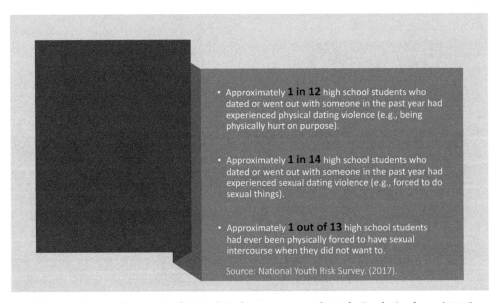

- Approximately **1 in 12** high school students who dated or went out with someone in the past year had experienced physical dating violence (e.g., being physically hurt on purpose).

- Approximately **1 in 14** high school students who dated or went out with someone in the past year had experienced sexual dating violence (e.g., forced to do sexual things).

- Approximately **1 out of 13** high school students had ever been physically forced to have sexual intercourse when they did not want to.

Source: National Youth Risk Survey. (2017).

FIGURE 2.22 Prevalence of Dating and Sexual Violence among 9th-12th Grade Students (2017)

National Child Abuse and Neglect Data

The National Child Abuse and Neglect Data System (NCANDS) was established in 1988 in response to the Child Abuse and Prevention and Treatment Act (Children's Bureau, 2018). The purpose was to create a central database to collect information on the number of incidents of child maltreatment reported to Child Protective Services agencies across the United States, as well as in Washington DC and the U.S. territories (Children's Bureau, 2018). Each year, the Children's Bureau submits a report to Congress that summarizes the incidence and prevalence of child abuse and neglect in the nation and its territories. This data allows researchers and lawmakers to assess for patterns and trends of child abuse and neglect.

Although each state has its own defintions of child abuse and neglect that are based on standards set by federal law, the minimum standard states "any recent act or failure to act on the part of a parent or caretaker which results in death, serious physical or emotional harm, sexual abuse or exploitation; or an act or failure to act which presents an imminent risk of serious harm" (Children's Bureau, 2018, p.viii). The data included in NCANDS therefore reflects all referrals received by Child Protective Services (CPS) for an allegation of abuse and neglect. Once a referral is made, CPS screens the case and makes a determination whether to file a formal report or to dismiss (Children's Bureau, 2018). If a report is filed, CPS then makes a determination whether the case requires a formal investigation to determine if a child was maltreated or is at-risk of maltreatment, and establishes whether an intervention is needed. The majority of reports are forwarded for investigation, however some reports receive alternative responses, which focus primarily upon the needs of the family rather than focus on a determination if the child was maltreated (Children's Bureau, 2018).

NCANDS collects case-level data on all children who had a report filed with CPS. The data includes information about the characteristics of screened-in referrals (e.g., reports) of abuse and neglect that are made to CPS agencies, the children and perpetrators involved, the types of maltreatment they suffered, the dispositions of the CPS responses, the risk factors of the child and the caregivers, and the services that are provided (Children's Bureau, 2018).

In 2018, CPS agencies received a total of 4.3 million referrals alleging abuse and neglect involving 7.8 million children (see Figure 2.23) (Children's Bureau, 2018). Among those referrals, approximately 56% were screened-in and approximately 45% of the children received either an investigation or an alternative response. In sum, approximately 19% of those children were found to be victims of abuse and neglect. Over three-quarters (78%) of the perpetrators of such incidents were the child's parent (Children's Bureau, 2018).

- **4.3 million REFERRALS** alleging maltreatment to CPS involving 7.8 million children
- **56% referrals SCREENED IN; 2.4 million REPORTS** received a disposition
- **3.5 million children** received either an investigation or an alternative response
- **678,000 victims of child maltreatment** were substantiated

Source: National Child Abuse and Neglect Data System (2018)

FIGURE 2.23 Official Reports of Child Abuse and Neglect (2018)

The majority of children (85%) suffered from a single maltreatment type. Over three-quarters of the children were found to be neglected, 18% had been physically abused, and approximately 9% had been sexually abused (Children's Bureau, 2018). Children in their first year of life were at the highest risk for maltreatment, and females were moderately more at risk than males. Sadly, in 2018, 1,770 children died from abuse and neglect, with nearly one-half of those fatalities involving a child under the age of 1.

Many of the limitations noted previously in regard to estimates drawn from other sources of official data, such as the UCR, are similarly applicable to NCANDS. First, and foremost, a referral has to made to CPS to start the process in determining whether a child has been abused or neglected. If no one reports it to authorities, it can not be captured in the data. Sadly, many incidents of child maltreatment remain in the shadows. Additionally, even when such cases do come to the attention of the authorities, not all of them are investigated. Due to limited resources, typically it is the most serious cases that garner the most attention. Therefore, some children may be screened out despite the fact they have suffered some form of maltreatment. Thus, researchers assert that the true estimates of child maltreatment are likely to be much larger than what is reflected in the official data.

National Public Survey on White Collar Crime

Although the public generally believes that the greatest threat to their person and property comes from street crime, many will fall victim to a white-collar crime.

White collar crime has been defined as the "illegal or unethical acts that violate fiduciary responsibility and public trust for personal or organizational gain." (National White Collar Crime Center, 2010). Such a definition covers both individual and organizational offenders; and encompasses a wide range of offenses, such as embezellment, money laundering, insurance fraud, identity theft, internet fraud. Unfortunately, many of these crimes involve significant financial losses for their victims. For example, a survey conducted on behalf of the Federal Trade Commission on the prevalence of identity theft in the United States revealed 3.7% of adults (est. 3 million) reported they had been a victim of identity theft in the previous year, resulting in over $15.6 billion in financial losses for these victims (Synovate, 2007). And on an organization level, researchers and lawmakers now know the global financial crisis in 2008 was linked to the fraudulent lending activities by the mortgage industry (National White Collar Crime Center, 2010).

There are numerous forms of white-collar crime, and the FBI divides these crimes into categories such as money laundering, securities and commodities fraud, bank fraud and embezzlement, environmental crimes, fraud against the government, election law violations, copyright violations, and telemarketing, healthcare, and financial institutions fraud (Federal Bureau of Investigation, n.d.). However, the UCR figures does not collect socioeconomic or occupational characteristics of offenders, thus the UCR data are limited about the information it makes available on white-collar crime. Consequently, the scope of white-collar crime is largely unknown, and what information is available is often presented by different agencies that vary in their purpose, methodology, and definitions of the said crimes.

To try to fill in these gaps, the National White Collar Crime Center created a National Public Survey on White Collar Crime (NPSWCC) to capture information on the prevalence of victimization of white collar crimes among the public, patterns of reporting behaviors, and their perceptions of crime seriousness. The data was collected from a nationally representative sample of over 2,500 adult participants by telephone interviews conducted in English and Spanish. Participants were asked about experiences within their households, as well as their own personal experiences concerning any of the following white collar crimes within the past 12 months - mortgage fraud, credit card fraud, identity theft, unnecesseary home or auto repairs, price misrepresentation, losses due to false stockbroker information, fraudulent business ventures, and Internet scams (National White Collar Crime Center, 2005; 2010). The first report was published in 2005, and a subsequent survey was conducted five years later, and a second report was published in 2010.

According to the data, 24% of households and 17% of individuals reported experiencing at least one type of white-collar crime victimizations (National White Collar Crime, 2010). The most common form was credit card fraud, with approximately 40% of the survey respondents reporting that someone in their household had their credit card compromised (National White Collar Crime Center, 2010) (see Figure 2.24). Nearly 16% reported losing money to an Internet scam and 12% reported be a victim of Identity Theft.

Similar to reporting trends observed with other victims, very few of the respondents who stated they had been a victim of a white-collar crime in the previous year reached out to law enforcement. Approximately, only 1 out of 5 of these vctims did so (National White Collar Crime Center, 2010). The most common reporting trend reported was they had called the credit card company (31%).

As with other surveys that are reliant on self-reports, the NPSWCC has a number of limitations (National White Collar Crime Center, 2010). Respondents can only report on crimes that they are aware of (e.g., they may have been a part of a fraudulent scheme at the time of the survey but thought it was legitimate, or included as part of large class-action lawsuit but do not realize they were an actual victim). Similarly, they mistakenly think a particular behavior (e.g., being billed for work not completed by a contractor they hired) is a civil rather than a criminal matter. Or, they realize they were a victim of some kind of fraudulent act and choose not to disclose it. Hence, the researchers assert the actual rate of white collar crime victimimzation is likely higher than what is reflected in this report.

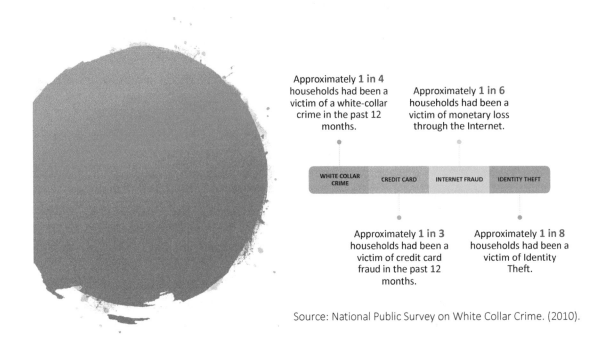

Source: National Public Survey on White Collar Crime. (2010).

FIGURE 2.24 Household Victimization by White Collar Crime (2010)

The Future of Crime and Victimization Research

While all of these measures of crime victimization, along with countless other studies on crime victims, has helped us begin to understand the nature and scope of this phenomena in our society, none are able to capture all of the information that we need. Gaps still exist, particularly for emerging crimes, such as human trafficking, Internet crimes, and mass casualty crimes, as well as those involving interpersonal violence, such as elder abuse, intimate partner violence, or child abuse. Research has found that the victim-offender relationship is one of the major factors to affect a victim's willingness to disclose and to report the crime to authorities. Studies show that an increased social distance between the victim and the offender results in an increased reporting of victimization to the police (Gartner & Macmillan, 1995; Kaukinen, 2002). Bachman (1998) for example, found that victims of rape were more likely to report victimization events to the police when the perpetrator was unknown to them. However, research shows that most sexual assaults, including rape, are committed by someone known to the victim, which tells us that a great number of violent crimes (e.g., rape and sexual assault) go unreported. Thus, researchers must continue to refine their methodology and definitions of victimization to capture larger and more diverse populations of crime victims. But, information alone is still not enough. We have to know how to use this data to help craft policies and practices that will aid crime victims. Unfortunately, as the next section lays out, sometimes this data can be mispresented or manipulated to influence the public's perception of crime and attitudes about particular victims of crime.

The Art of Spinning Statistics: The Intersection of Data, Politics, and the Media

Mark Twain was infamously quoted as saying, "There are three kinds of lies – lies, damned lies, and statistics." In this quote, he expertly captures the persuasive power of numbers, and how people often will use statistics to try to bolster a weak argument. This is commonly referred to as 'spinning statistics.' Nowhere is this more evident than in the media and politics, particularly when it comes to crime. As noted in the introduction of this chapter, the public conception of crime is often influenced by media and politics. According to Robinson (2011) the public generally believes that the nature of crime tends to be violent; people fear more street crime rather than white-collar and corporate crime, and even though the violent crime rate is declining, the public perceives it as widespread and out of control. This is largely because the public's primary source of information for what's happening in their community comes from news organizations and social media. And sadly, much of what dominates the news cycle are stories about crime, particularly violent crime. There is an old saying in journalism, "if it bleeds, it leads." Thus, many of the lead stories on broadcast news or placed on the front page of the local newspaper involve some kind of violent crime - a homicide, a shooting, a sexual assault. It permeates our psyche and convinces us that violent crime is rampant in our society. Yet, as illustrated by the data presented in this chapter, there are far fewer violent crimes than non-violent crimes. This trend is supported by both official and unofficial statistics. In 2018, there were more than seven times as many property crimes reported to law enforcement than violent crimes (FBI, 2018). And, of the nearly 8.5 million serious crimes reported to the police, homicides made up less than 0.1 percent, and rape made up less than 2 percent. This pattern is also observed in unofficial crime statistics. Of the nearly 20 million crimes reported in the National Crime Victimization Survey, less than one-third (32%) were a violent crime; and, of the violent crimes reported, approximately 12 percent were a rape or sexual assault (NCVS, 2018). Moreover, because the media typically focuses on those crimes that occur within urban city centers, the public's perception about *who* is a victim of a crime is similarly distorted. More often than not, stories that involve homicides involve a minority youth or young adult. While African-Americans are disproportionately represented as victims of homicide, there were roughly equal numbers of White and African American homicide victims in 2018 (FBI, n.d.).

However, it is not just the media that influences the public's perception of crime and who are the victims of crime, politicians often use stories presented in the media, or a random crime statistic, to generate fear of crime in their community. As a political pundit once said, "Fear is candy to politicians because it is easy to harness, and it plays on the primal parts of human nature." (Cuomo, 2020). Thus, some politicians will use official statistics derived from governmental agencies like the Federal Bureau of Investigation's Uniform Crime Reports (UCR) arrest data to draw comparisons across states, cities, and counties in order to identify which jurisdictions are "safe" or "unsafe," or what type of crimes we should be most worried about. They then use those statistics to ask the public to fund more resources or to support a specific policy they want to enact. A recent example of this can be seen in how some politicians are responding to the immigration issue. In 2019, President Trump passed an Executive Order limiting the number of migrants seeking asylum at the U.S.-Mexico border, and asked Congress to reallocate funds to help build more segments of the wall between the United States and Mexico to serve as deterrent to individuals who are seeking to cross the border illegally. The justification he has consistently offered for such actions is that the majority of these individuals are serious, and violent criminals, thus pose a serious threat to the United States. Yet, the data does not support his claims (Zatz & Smith, 2014). In one of the most comprehensive studies to date, Light and Miller (2018) analyzed criminal, socioeconomic, and demographic data from all 50 states and Washington, DC, from 1990 to 2014, and found that undocumented immigration does not increase violence; rather, the relationship between undocumented immigration and violent crime is generally negative. Meaning, cities that had higher proportions of immigrants actually had lower crime rates. Moreover, Bersani and Piquero's (2016) review of arrest records confirmed that immigrants commit less crime compared to documented immigrants and native-born Americans. But it is not just undocumented immigrants risk of offending that is being mis-portrayed. Data also shows that undocumented immigrants are at greater risk of victimization than native-born people, given their vulnerable status (McDonald, 2018; Zatz & Smith, 2014).

None of this is intended to discount the seriousness that violent crime poses to our communities, or the harm it causes for victims and their families. This discussion merely illustrates how our perceptions of the prevalence of crime, and our conceptions about who can be a victim of a crime, can be distorted if we only rely on what we hear from the media or listen to what politicians tell us. There is an abundance of research and data available that can help to create a more realistic portrait of crime and victimization in the United States, and ultimately, to guide us when developing responses to crime and creating solutions to assist those who have been a victim of a crime.

Conclusion

All of the official and unofficial data on crime victimization profiled in this chapter are valuable sources of information to help us build estimates on the nature and scope of victimization in the United States. However, each of these measures has limitations, thereby impeding our ability to understand the true reality of crime victimization. With emerging types of victimization (e.g., human trafficking, Internet crimes, etc) and underserved populations that are more reluctant to come forward (e.g., elder abuse victims, LGBTQ victims, undocumented immigrant victims, etc.), researchers must refine their definitions and methodologies in order to fill in these missing gaps. But it is not enough to focus on the incidence and prevalence of crime victimization, we must also devote equal attention to studying the impact of victimization on the health and well-being of crime victims if we want to create policy and programs that will effectively aid them with their recovery. Thus, victimology is still a young field, and it must continue to evolve and grow in the 21st century.

Discussion Questions

1. What are the two largest official data sources of crime and victimization and what is the difference between them?
2. What are some other national surveys conducted on a regular basis to help measure crime victimization?
3. What are some limitations of both official and unofficial crime and victimization data that we use to create policy?
4. How do media depictions of crime influence public attitudes toward crime, victimization, and criminal justice policy?

References

Bachman, R. (1998). The factors related to rape reporting behavior and arrest: New evidence from the national crime victimization survey. *Criminal Justice and Behavior, 25*(1), 8–29.

Bersani, B. E., & Piquero, A. R. (2016). Examining systematic crime reporting bias across three immigrant generations: Prevalence, trends, and divergence in self-reported and official reported arrests. *Journal of Quantitative Criminology, 33*, 835-857.

Centers for Disease Control and Prevention. (2010). *An overview of intimate partner violence in the United States – 2010 findings*. Atlanta, GA: Author.

Centers for Disease Control and Prevention. (2018). *Youth Risk Behavior Surveillance System (YRBSS) overview*. Retrieved from: https://www.cdc.gov/healthyyouth/data/yrbs/overview.htm

Centers for Disease Control and Prevention. (2009). *The history of violence as a public health issue*. Retrieved from: https://www.cdc.gov/violenceprevention/pdf/history_violence-a.pdf

Child Trends Data Bank. (2016, May). *Children's exposure to violence – Indicators on children and youth*. Retrieved from: https://www.childtrends.org/wp-content/uploads/2016/05/118_Exposure_to_Violence.pdf

Children's Bureau. (2018). *Child maltreatment, 2018*. Washington, DC: U.S. Department of Health & Human Services, Administration for Children and Families, Administration on Children Youth and Families.

Crimes Against Children Research Center. (n.d.). *National Survey of Children's Exposure to Violence* (NatSCEV). Durham, NH: University of New Hampshire.

Cuomo, C. (2020, March 4). *Let's get after it* [Audio podcast]. Potus Channel, Sirus Radio.

Federal Bureau of Investigation. (2012). *National Incident Based Reporting System: Crimes against persons, property, and society*. Retrieved from: https://ucr.fbi.gov/nibrs/2012/resources/crimes-against-persons-property-and-society

Federal Bureau of Investigation. (2014, December). *Frequently asked questions about the change in the UCR definition of rape*. Retrieved from: https://ucr.fbi.gov/recent-program-updates/new-rape-definition-frequently-asked-questions

Federal Bureua of Investigation. (2018). *Hate crimes - Victims*. Retrieved from: https://ucr.fbi.gov/hate-crime/2018/topic-pages/victims

Federal Bureau of Investigation. (2018). *Uniform Crime Reports*. Retrieved from http://www.fbi.gov/about-us/cjis/ucr/ucr

Federal Bureau of Investigation. (n.d.). *NIBRS: National Incident Based Reporting System*. Retrieved from: https://www.fbi.gov/services/cjis/ucr/nibrs

Federal Bureau of Investigation. (n.d.) *White-collar crime*. Retrieved from https://www.fbi.gov/investigate/white-collar-crime

Gartner, R., & Macmillan, R. (1995). The effect of victim-offender relationship on reporting crimes of violence against women. *Canadian Journal of Criminology, 37*(3), 393–429.

Kaukinen, C. (2002). The help-seeking decisions of violent crime victims: An examination of the direct and conditional effects of gender and the victim-offender relationship. *Journal of Interpersonal Violence, 17*(4), 432–456.

Lartey, J., & Li, W. (2019, September 30). *New FBI data: Violent crime still fading.* Retrieved from: https://www.themarshallproject.org/2019/09/30/new-fbi-data-violent-crime-still-falling

Light, M. T., & Miller, T. (2018). Does undocumented immigration increase violent crime? *Criminology, 56*(2), 370-401.

McDonald, W., (2018). The criminal victimization of immigrants: A meta survey. In *The criminal victimization of immigrants* (pp.29-45). Palgrave MacMillian.

Morgan, R. E., & Oudekerk, B. A. (2019, September). *Criminal victimization*, 2018. Washington, DC: U.S. Department of Justice, Office of Justice Programs, Bureau of Justice Statistics.

National Crime Victims' Rights Week. (2017). *Crime & victimization in the United States.* Retrieved from: https://www.ncjrs.gov/ovc_archives/ncvrw/2017/images/en_artwork/Fact_Sheets/2017NCVRW_CrimeAndVictimization_508.pdf

National White Collar Crime Center. (2005). The 2005 *National Public Survey on White Collar Crime.* Retrieved from: https://www.nw3c.org/docs/research/2005-national-public-survey-on-white-collar-crime.pdf?sfvrsn=8

National White Collar Crime Center. (2010). *The 2010 National Public Survey on White Collar Crime.* Retrieved from: https://www.nw3c.org/docs/research/2010-national-public-survey-on-white-collar-crime.pdf

O'Grady, R. L., & Matthews-Creech, N. (2020). *Why children don't tell.* Retrieved from: https://lacasacenter.org/why-child-abuse-victims-dont-tell/

Smith, S., Zhang, X., Basile, K. C., Merrick, M.T., Wang, J. Kresnow, M., & Chen, J. (2018). *The National Intimate Partner and Sexual Violence Survey (NISVS): 2015 data brief – Updated release.* Atlanta, GA: National Center for Injury Prevention and Control, Centers for Disease Control and Prevention.

Synovate. (2007). *Federal Trade Commission – 2006 identity theft survey report.* Retrieved from: https://www.ftc.gov/sites/default/files/documents/reports/federal-trade-commission-2006-identity-theft-survey-report-prepared-commission-synovate/synovatereport.pdf

Zatz, M. S., & Smith, H. (2014). Understanding immigration, crime and victimization in the United States. In S. Pickering & J. Ham, *The Routledge handbook on crime and international migration.* Retrieved from: https://www.routledgehandbooks.com/doi/10.4324/9780203385562.ch2

CHAPTER 3

Typologies of Crime Victimization

Objectives

Upon completion of this chapter, you will be able to:

- understand different typologies of victimization and their limitations,
- understand and recognize the multidimensional role of the victim in a crime event,
- discuss the theoretical paradigms for crime victimization, and
- describe how data and research can be used to assist in evidence-based decision making to ensure better outcomes for victims of crime.

Introduction

The field of criminology has spent decades explaining criminal behavior in order to propose a variety of ways to control criminals. Because crime is as old as mankind, theories of crime used to be exclusively offender-oriented. It is only very recently that the attention of scholars, researchers, and practitioners began to focus on victims of crime. The earliest studies focused on the relationship between perpetrators and their victims, and more specifically, how characteristics of the victim (e.g., personality, temperament, decision-making) could explain criminal behavior (Wemmers, 2010). Thus, victims of crime were not portrayed as individuals harmed by a criminal act, but rather as persons who contribute to crime.

This paradigm began to shift, however, in the early 1970s when the rhetoric of criminal justice shifted towards crime victims' rights and welfare, and the foundation for support services were established (Maguire, 1991). Under the influence of the victims' movement, contemporary criminology similarly began to shift its focus from predominantly offender-oriented theories to crime opportunity theories and victim-oriented theories, thus laying the foundation for victimology to evolve into its own discipline (van Kersteren, 2015). As a scientific discipline, victimology strives to address four questions—Who is a victim of crime? Why are some people more likely to become a victim of crime? How does the experience of being a victim of a crime effect an individual? And, what is the most effective way to aid a victim of crime in their recovery?

To answer the first question, researchers use a variety of official and unofficial measures of crime victimization to identify the nature and scope of victimization in the United States. Some of these measures were presented in the previous chapter. Each provides information on the number and types of victims, as well as data that enables researchers to examine for trends across jurisdictions, by type of victim, as well as over time. From this data, researchers are then able to create victim typologies (i.e., classification model).

To answer the second question, researchers focus on how victimization is distributed across society. The data has consistently shown that select demographic and social characteristics may place some individuals at higher risk for victimization (Landau & Freeman-Longo, 1990; Spalek, 2006). Thus, victimologists try to decipher how these variables interact, construct a series of theoretical statements that articulate specific causal relationships to explain such phenomena, and then test their assumptions with the data. This is undoubtedly one of the most challenging aspects of research. Yet, without theory testing, researchers can not develop strategies to help prevent victimization, explore the impact of victimization, or identify the most effective strategies to help mitigate the harm victims suffer and aid in their recovery.

This chapter provides an overview of existing typologies of victimization and their potential limitations, and discusses the intersection of demographic and social characteristics with criminal victimization. It then provides a summary of the theoretical paradigms that have been forwarded to explain victimization patterns and trends; and, concludes with a discussion on how researchers, practitioners, and policymakers can use all of this data to design a tailored approach for victim assistance and services.

Early Crime Victim Typologies

As victimology emerged in the middle of the twentieth century, a small number of scholars began to study crime victims, develop theories of victimization and construct typologies of victims (Tobolowsky, Beloof, Gaboury, Jackson and Blackburn, 2016). Because large-scale data was not available at that time, these early scholars relied on anecdotal observations to formulate their typologies. The first of these scholars was Hans Von Hentig. In his book, *The Criminal and His Victim: Studies in the Sociobiology of Crime* (Von Hentig, 1948), he asserted that some of the same characteristics that produce crime also produce victimization. In his research, he specifically focused on the relationship between the victim and the offender, and looked at charcteristics of the victim that may increase their risk of victimization. He proposed that some victims provoke victimization because they possess certain individual characteristics, thus making them attractive targets for offenders. His typologies for crime victims are presented in Table 3.1.

While Von Hentig's theory received significant attention when first introduced, it was the research of Benjamin Mendelsohn (1930; 1948) that helped to establish the study of crime victims as its own science. As noted in chapter one, Mendelsohn was the first to empirically explore personality attributes of victims

Table 3.1 Hans von Hentig's Victim Typology

Characteristic	Why at Greater Risk of Victimization?
The young	Children and infants: physically weaker, less mental prowess, fewer legal rights, economically dependent.
Female	All women: physically weaker than men, culturally conditioned to men's authority, financially dependent, conditioned to believe that their value is associated with their bodies—sexuality.
The old	The elderly: many of the same vulnerabilities as children
The mentally defective and deranged	The feeble-minded, the "insane", drug addicts, and alcoholics: have an altered perception of reality.
Immigrants	Foreigners unfamiliar with the culture: gaps in communication and comprehension
Minorities	The racially disadvantaged: groups in which there is some amount of bias and prejudice
Dull normal	The simple minded persons: same type of exposure as the mentally defective
The depressed	Persons with various psychological maladies: they can expose themselves to all manners of danger
The acquisitive	The greedy, those looking for quick gains: may suspend their judgement or put themselves in dangerous situations in order to achieve their goals
The wanton	The promiscuous persons: they engage themselves in indiscriminate sexual activities with different partners
The lonesome or heartbroken	The widows, widowers, those in mourning: they are prone to substance abuse and become easy prey
The tormentor	The abusive parents: they expose themselves to the harm they inflict, the resulting angst, and the degree to which their victims fight back
The blocked, exempted, or fighting	Victims of blackmail, extortion, and scams: they are exposed to continual financial loss or physical harm, or must suffer the consequences that come from bringing the police in to assist

Adapted from Doerner, W.G., and Lab, S.P. (2011). *Victimology*, 6th edition, Cincinnati, OH: Anderson Publishing Company.

and develop the first *victim typologies*. Mendelsohn was an attorney who became interested in the relationship between the victim and the criminal after years of observing the dynamics between the two parties in the courtroom. So, he began interviewing victims and witnesses, and discovered that the victim often shared a relationship with his or her offender. Based on his observations, he categorized

Table 3.2 Mendelsohn's Victim Typology

Level of Culpability	Description
Completely innocent victim	No provocative or facilitative behavior
Victim with minor guilt	Inadvertently places him/herself in a compromised situation
Victim as guilty as offender	Engages in vice crimes and is hurt; Includes victims of suicide
Victim more guilty than offender	Provokes or instigates the causal act
Most guilty victim	Starts off as the offender and in turn is hurt
Imaginary victim	Pretends to be a victim

Adapted from Doerner, W.G., and Lab, S.P. (2011). *Victimology*, 6th edition, Cincinnati, OH: Anderson Publishing Company.

victims into one of six typologies to help ascertain their level of culpability (see Table 3.2). He used this information to create a classification system for victims that he and his fellow defense attorneys would use to aid in their preparation for criminal court cases. Under his classification scheme, only children and individuals who were not conscious during their assault were deemed 'innocent.' In all other instances, the victim shared some level of responsibility for their victimization. The level of culpability varied depending on how much the victim's behavior could be considered provocative, ignorant, paranoid, and/or hysterical (Landau & Freeman—Longo, 1990).

Once again, these typologies portrayed crime as a product of the victim's personality or behavior, rather than the action of the offender. Hence, it reinforced the narrative that victims were often to blame for their victimization, at least to some degree. In his later scholarship, Mendolsohn shifted his focus to the impact of victimization (e.g., feelings, responses victims have in reaction to their experience), and introduced the term "victimology" to describe the study of crime victims. Thus, earning him the title of the "father of victimology."

Stephen Schafer (1968) expanded upon Von Hertig and Mendolsohn's research and created a set of typologies that combined both social characteristics and behaviors of victims. In his book, *The Victim and His Criminal: A Study of Functional Responsibility*, Schafer argued that people have a functional responsibility not to provoke others into victimizing or harming them, and should take active steps to prevent either from occurring. In his classification scheme, he created seven victim typologies and identified the level of responsibility a victim shouldered for his or her victimization (see Table 3.3).

One of the methodological weaknesses of these early studies is that they relied exclusively on anecdotal information to create the typologies. Therefore, later scholars strove to expand the theoretical base of victim research by using empirical data

Table 3.3 Schaefer's Victim Typology

Level of Responsibility	Characteristic and/or Behavior
No responsibility	Unrelated victims
Share responsibility	Provocative victims
Some degree of responsibility	Precipative victims
No responsibility	Biologially weak victims
No responsibility	Socially weak victims
Total responsibility	Self-victiming
No responsibility	Political victims

Adapted from Daigle, L. E., and Muftic, L. R. (2016). *Victimology*. Thousand Oaks, CA: SAGE Publishing.

(van Kesteren, 2015). In 1957, Marvin Wolfgang developed another victim typology based on his analysis of Philadelphia police homicide data. Echoing the work of Mendelsohn, Wolfgang's classification primarily focused on the offender-victim relationship, and proposed a theory that victims share similar characteristics with their offenders (Wolfgang, 1957). For example, in his study, he noted approximately one-quarter of homicides were precipitated by the victim because the victim was the first to start a physical altercation with their offender, or was the first to display or use a weapon. Thus, Wolgang noted, these individuals were in part to blame for their own demise. He also found other common trends among the data. The majority of the victims knew their offender, many victims had a history of violence (as a perpetrator as well as a victim), and many of the events involved parties who were drinking alcohol.

A student of Wolgang's, Menachem Amir (1971), expanded on his research using Philadelphia Police Department data on forcible rape cases to construct a similar classification scheme. Echoing Wolfgang's theory, Amir asserted that some rape victims were in part responsible for their own victimization. In his review of the police reports, he classified 1 out of every 5 forcible rapes to be victim precipated, advanced by the victim's own behavior (e.g., consumed alcohol, acted in a seductive manner, or engaged in other negligent or reckless behavior). Moreover, Amir argued the victim's intention was irrelevant, rather it was the offender's interpretation of the victim's actions in the situation that was important.

This concept of "victim precipitation" has been subsequently used in the criminal justice system to assign the victim's level of responsibility in the crime when considering mitigating circumstances for the offender during sentencing procedures and other legal rulings (Petherick, 2017). Typically, if a victim was

THE 21ST CENTURY TRANSFORMATION OF VICTIMOLOGY

perceived by the court to have facilitated in their own victimization by engaging in risky behavior, or using alcohol or drugs, the perpetrator has been treated more leniently. Such 'victim-blaming' has often been used in sexual assault cases, and has helped to support and promote rape-culture among the general public (Daigle & Mufitic, 2016).

While these early typologies have been met with consternation from advocates and contemporary victimology scholars for their portrayal of victims as someone who initiates or fosters the actions which lead to their harm or loss, they should not be discounted because they laid the foundation for the field of victimology as a scientific way to explain victimization as a phenomena. The scholarship that followed those early studies have since expanded the focus of the research to include a wider range of victimization experiences and explore the multidimensional role of the victim. As new victimology concepts arose, along with the introduction of the National Crime Victimization Survey in 1972 which made large survey data available to researchers, victimiologists began to create victim profiles that focused on the victim's individual attributes (e.g., demographics) and situational context of the crime (e.g., location, nature of relationship with offender, repeat victimization) without assigning any blame.

Demographic Characteristics Predicting Victimization

As noted in this chapter's introduction, historically, empirical research has focused predominantly on offenders. A number of criminological theories have relied on offenders' demographic characteristics to explain their involvement in crime. Only very recently, has empirical research and evidence suggest that certain individual characteristics also increase one's probability of one becoming a victim of crime. These demographic factors include gender, age, race and ethnicity, socio-economic status, marital status, religious affiliation, sexual orientation, being disabled, and citizenship status.

Gender

Males and females are not subject to the same crimes. Men are more likely to be victims of homicide, aggravated assault, and robbery, while females are at a greater risk for sexual assault and intimate partner violence (Lauritsen & Heimer, 2008; Lauritsen & Carbone-Lopez, 2011; see Appendix A). According to official data, males comprise the majority of perpetrators as well as victims of violent crimes. In 2018, 77% the victims were male (FBI, 2018). However, while the vast majority of murder victims are men, women are far more likely to be killed by those closest to them. According to the CDC, more than half of all female homicide victims were killed by an intimate partner (Petrosky et al., 2017); and 94% of victims of a murder-suicide involving intimate partners were female (National Coalition Against Domestic Violence [NCADV], n.d.).

While males are also more likely to experience physical violence than females, and most often assaulted by another male, females are more likely to experience domestic violence at the hands of their male partner. Females are twice as likely to experience IPV during their lifetime as males, and are twice as likely to experience severe intimate partner physical violence (NCADV, n.d.). According to NCADV, women are significantly more likely than men to be injured during an assault, and among female victims of rape and physical assault the risk of injury increases significantly when the perpetrator is their current or former spouse, partner, boyfriend, or date (Tjaden & Thoennes, 2000).

Significant gender differences are also observed for sexual violence. Females are significantly more likely than males to be sexually assaulted. According to RAINN (2020), six times as many females have experienced sexual assault in the lifetime than males, and 90% of all rape victims are female. Moreover, 1 in 10 females have experienced being sexually assaulted by an intimate partner (NCADV, n.d.)

Age

Age is another important variable when predicting risk of victimization. In general, individuals under the age of 25 and adults over the age of 65 experience higher rates of victimization then the rest of the population. However, the type of victimization each of these two age-groups experiences varies.

As discussed in chapter two, younger children are especially at risk for maltreatment. Nationally, more than one-quarter of victims of child maltreatment are under the age of 3 (Children's Bureau, 2018). Children in their first year of life have the highest rate of victimization, and are particularly vulnerable when it comes to child fatalities. Nearly 45% of child fatalities recorded in 2018 involved a child under the age of 1, and 80% involved a child under the age of 4 (Children's Bureau, 2018). A disproportionate number of young children are also exposed to intimate partner violence in their homes. Approximately 1 in every 15 children are exposed to IPV each year, and 90% of those were a direct witness of such violence (Child Trends Databank, 2016).

As children get older, research indicates that the type of violence they are exposed to tends to increase in severity (Child Trends Databank, 2016). This is particularly true for sexual violence, intimate partner violence, and gun violence. Females, ages 16-19, are four times more likely to be a victim of rape, attempted rape, or sexual assault then the general population (RAINN, 2020). And females between the ages of 18-24 have the highest incidence of intimate partner violence

(NCADV, n.d.) Sadly, nearly one-quarter of those victims reported to have first experienced IPV between the ages of 11-17 (Smith et al, 2018).

Another type of violence youth have disproportionately affected by is gun violence. Approximately three million children witness gun violence every year, and it is now the leading cause of death among children and adolescents in the United States (Every Town, 2020). This type of violence has even infiltrated our schools. Over the past thirty years, there have been over 50 mass shootings at schools, involving children of all ages. For example, the shootings at Sandy Hook Elementary (Newtown, CT) in 2012 left 10 dead

© Gina Jacobs/Shutterstock.com

and injured 13; at Parkland High School (Parkland, FL) in 2018 left 17 dead and injured 17; and at Virginia Tech (Blacksburg, VA) in 2007 left 33 dead and 23 injured.

However, it isn't just the young who are disproportionately affected by victimization. The elderly are also at higher risk for certain types of victimization. Though we have a significantly large and growing population of senior citizens in the U.S., there is a serious lack of data on elder abuse, therefore researchers assert that we know less about this type of victimization than any other. For example, we know very little about victimization of those with dementia, those who reside in long-term care facilities, and who their perpetrators are. We do know this population is extremely vulnerable for abuse and exploitation because of their impairments in memory, cognitive functioning, and decline in physical ability. Despite that knowledge, signs of elder abuse may be missed by professionals who work with them. It may because of the victim's reluctance to report the abuse, or they lack the physical or cognitive ability to communicate. The studies that are available on elder abuse indicate 1 in 13 adults over 60 years of age have been victims either of financial exploitation; emotional, physical, and sexual abuse; or neglect (Lifespan of Greater Rochester, Inc. 2011); and, 47% of elders with dementia have been mistreated by their caregivers (Wiglesworth et al., 2010). Among those victims, 89% experienced psychological abuse, 20% experienced physical abuse, and 30% experienced neglect.

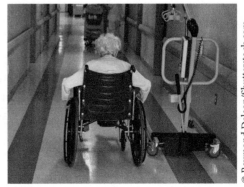

© Raymond Deleon/Shutterstock.com

Race/ethnicity

Racial and ethnic minorities consistently experience higher rates of violent victimization than Whites (see Appendix A); and, the type of violence they experience varies by age and gender. For child maltreatment, Native Americans have the highest rate among all children, followed by African Americans (Child Trends Databank, 2016). However, African American children are nearly three times as likely to suffer child fatality as the result of abuse than White children (Child Trends Databank, 2016).

Although every racial and ethnic group experiences intimate partner violence and sexual violence, Native American women and multiracial women experience the highest percentage of IPV among all races and sexes (OVC, 2018). African American women also experience a disproportionately high rate of IPV in comparison to other women. Similar patterns are observed among male victims of IPV with the highest rates being recorded among multiracial, Native American, and Black men (OVC, 2018). Similar disparities are evident among victims of sexual assault and rape. Once again, Native Americans are at greatest risk. They are twice as likely to experience rape and/or sexual assault compared to all other races (RAINN, 2020).

Another type of violence that disproportionately affects racial and ethnic minorities is gun violence. African Americans are most effected by this type of crime. Although Black males account for only 7% of the U.S. population, in 2018, they comprised 52% of all homicide victims (Every Town, 2020). And in general, Blacks are 10 times more likely than Whites to die by gun homicide, and 14 times more likely to be injured in gun assault (Giffords Law Center, 2018).

Lastly, racial and ethnic minorites are disproportionately targeted as victims of hate crimes. According to the FBI, in 2018, personal attacks motivated by bias or prejudice reached an all-time high. Of the total hate crimes reported to law enforcement for that year, approximately 47% of the victims were African Americans (FBI, 2018). Hispanic or Latinos were also victims (13%) of such crimes, and law enforcement has acknowledged this group is being targeted more frequently.

Socioeconomic status

Socioeconomic status is a vital factor in predicting human actions, including criminal and deviant behavior. Socio-economic status (SES) is measured in several different ways, but most often by household income or a combination of education, income, and occupation. Research in victimology suggests that SES is associated with victimization, and that victimization usually clusters in the poorest neighborhoods and among lower-income families (see Appendix A). Research indicates the relationship between measures of SES and violent victimization is much stronger than the correlation between SES and less serious offenses (Aaltonen, Kivivuori,

Martikainen, & Salmi, 2012; Menard, Morris, Gerber, & Covey, 2011). For example, gun violence is consistently found to be heavily concentrated in poor, urban communities (Giffords Law Center, 2018), and similarly, homicide rates are highest among low-income neighborhoods.

Low-income households also experience higher rates of IPV and child maltreatment. While IPV occurs in every socioeconomic bracket, households earning between $15,000 and $24,999 experienced slightly more intimate partner than other households (OVC, 2018). Child maltreatment has also been found to be more prevalent among low-income communities (Ekenrode, Smith, McCarthy, & Dinnen, 2014), and the disparities are particularly pronounced for child fatalities related to child maltreatment. In a retrospective study examining 15 years of national data of child fatalities, researchers found such fatalities were three times higher in counties with the highest poverty rates than counties with low poverty rates (Farrell et al., 2017)

Marital Status

Research has also found that individuals who are single, separated, or divorced are at greater risk of victimization than married couples (Lauritsen & Carbone-Lopez, 2011) (see Appendix A). Young adults who are single are particularly at higher-risk for victimization than single adults who are older. The prevalence of sexual violence and rape is significantly greater among young women between the ages of 18–24 (RAINN, 2020). Approximately 42% of women who have reported being raped in their lifetime reported the first incident happened prior to age 18 (National Domestic Violence Hotline, n.d.). Similarly, intimate partner violence is more prevalent among individuals who are not married but who are in a dating relationship. Approximately 1 out of 10 teens reported being physically abused by their dating partner in the past year, and 1 out of 3 college-aged women reported to have been in an abusive dating relationship (NDVH, n.d.).

In terms of homicide, males between the ages of 15–29 are at greatest risk of being a victim of homicide (United Nations Office of Drugs and Crime, 2015). Given the younger nature of this cohort, most of these victims are not married. A similar pattern is not observed among females however. Interestingly, researchers have not found a significant difference in risk levels between single women and married women, however, divorced women were 55% more likely to be a victim of homicide than married women, even after controlling for other known risk factors (Breault & Kpowsa, 1997).

Religious Affiliation

While one's religious affiliation may not seem to be an expected risk factor for victimization, it has sadly become a reason why some individuals are targeted. In

2018, there were 1,617 individuals who were a victim of a hate crime because of their religious affiliation (FBI, 2018). Over half of these victims were Jewish. While the majority of these crimes involved property crimes, there has been an increasing number of violent crimes directed at Jews, including the mass shooting at the Tree of Life synagogue in Pittsburgh where the assailant killed 11 and wounded 6 others during Shabbat morning services. Moreover, anti-Semitic hate crimes have been on the rise for the past three years, and law enforcement officials are predicting the number to surpass the previous record (Hassan, 2020).

Another religious group disproportionately targeted as victims of hate crime are Muslims. In 2018, they comprised approximately 12% of the victims of hate crimes due to religious bias. While the most recent data show that their numbers are below what they experienced in the immediate aftermath of 9-11, they rose dramtically in 2016 and have been trending upwards since (Kishi, 2017).

Sexual Orientation

Individuals from the LGBTQ community are similarly targeted for bias crimes. Members of the LGBTQ community experience violent victimization at a dispro-portionately high rate, and experience victimization at school, in the workplace, and in the community. In the 2017 National Youth Risk Survey, LGBTQ students reported significantly higher incidents of bullying (33%) and cyberbullying (27%) than their heterosexual peers (17% and 13%). Moreover, 4 out of 5 LGBTQ students reported being harassed for their appearance and/or their perceived sexual orientation (GLAAD, n.d.). Even among students who reported they are 'unsure' of their sexual orientation, were more likely to report being bullied then their hetero-sexual peers (Stopbullying, n.d.). Unfortunately, these experiences continue into adulthood.

In 2018, over 1,600 LGBTQ individuals reported being a victim of a hate crime, either because of their sexual orientation or gender identity (FBI, 2018). Gay males appear to be the primary targets of such crimes, many of which involve violence.

THE 21ST CENTURY TRANSFORMATION OF VICTIMOLOGY

One of the most horrific examples was the 2016 Pulse Nightclub mass shooting in Orlando, when an assiliant killed 46 and wounded 56 individuals inside the gay club.

However, the threat to LGTBQ individuals is not exclusive from members outside of their community; they are also more likely to experience violence at the hands of an intimate partner (CDC, 2010).

© Mia2You/Shutterstock.com

In 2010, the CDC released the first report on the prevelance of intimate partner violence, sexual violence, and stalking among the LGBTQ population. Findings from this survey indicate that individuals who self-identify as lesbian, gay, or bisexual have an equal or higher prevelance of experiencing all forms of IPV compared to self-identified heterosexuals (see Figure 1). Bisexual men and women, however, reported the highest rates of rape, physical violence, and/or stalking by an intimate partner. Nearly half of bisexual women and bisexual men reported to have been raped at some point in their lifetime.

Transgender individuals have also been found to be at greater risk for sexual violence. In a recent survey, 21% of transgender young adults reported to have been sexually assaulted at school, in comparsion to 18% of gender-conforming females and 4% of gender-confirming males (RAINN, 2020)

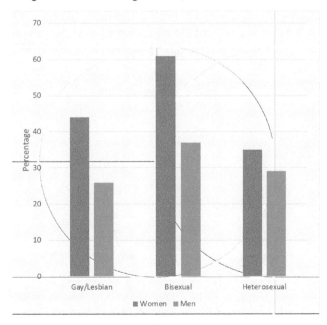

FIGURE 3.1 Lifetime Prevalence of Rape, Physical Violence and/or Stalking by an Intimate Partner

Individuals with a Disability

There are approximately 40 million Americans living with a disability—this can be any kind of cognitive, physical (e.g., ambulatory), or sensory (e.g., sight, hearing) limitation that makes it difficult for them to care for themselves and/or live independently. Approximately 13 percent of the U.S. population living outside an institution have at least one of the aforementioned disabilities (Kraus, Lauer, Coleman, & Houtenville, 2018). Over three-quarters of these individuals are over the age of 65, however approximately 6% are under the age of 18 (Bialik, 2017). Given their challenges, individuals who have a disability are more vulnerable to victimization.

The National Victimization Survey has also similar disparities. The data has consistently found that individuals with disabilities are significantly at greater risk for victimization (Harrell, 2017). They are approximately three times more likely to have been a victim of violent crime than individuals without a disabilty, and nearly one-half of those who are disabled have been a victim of a serious violent crime (see Tables 3.4 and 3.5) (Harrell, 2017). The most common type of victimization as been robbery and aggravated assault, however, over one-third of the individuals who were disabled reported they had been sexually assaulted. The risk for victimization is even higher for individuals who have has multiple disabilities (see Table 5). Most notably, the rate of sexual assault nearly doubled when the individual had more than one disability (Harrell, 2017).

Children with disabilities are also disproportionately at risk for victimization. Research has found they are three times more likely to be abused or neglected than children without a disability, and are more likely to suffer serious injury or harm

Table 3.4 Rate of violent victimization against persons with and without disabilities by victim characteristics, 2011–2015

Victim characteristics	Persons with disabilities	Persons without disabilities
Total	32.3	12.7
Sex		
Female	32.8	11.4
Male	31.8	14.1
Race		
White	30.8	12.0
Black	30.8	18.2
Hispanic	29.3	13.0
Other	28.2	6.4

Adapted from: Harrell, E. (2017). *Crime Against Persons with Disabilities*, 2033.609-2015—Statistical Tables. U.S. Department of Justice, Office of Justice Programs, Bureau of Justice Statistics, July 2017, NCJ 250632.

THE 21ST CENTURY TRANSFORMATION OF VICTIMOLOGY

Table 3.5 Percent of violent victimization against persons with disabilities by type of crime and number of disability types, 2011–2015

Type of Crime	Single disability type	Multiple disability types
Total	46.4%	53.6%
Serious violent crime	45.4%	54.6%
Rape/sexual assault	34.6 %	65.4%
Robbery	48.4%	51.6%
Aggravated Assault	46.7%	53.3%
Simple Assault	47.0%	53.0%

Adapted from: Harrell, E. (2017). *Crime Against Persons with Disabilities*, 2033.609-2015—**Statistical Tables. U.S. Department of Justice, Office of Justice Programs, Bureau of Justice Statistics, July 2017, NCJ 250632**

from maltreatment (Child Welfare Information Gateway, 2018). They are also three times more likely to be sexually abused (Smith & Harrell, 2013). Children who have a cognitive or mental health disability are at an even higher risk; they are nearly five times as likely to be a victim of sexual abuse than other children.

Citizenship status

The United States has more immigrants than any other nation in the world. In 2018, there were an estimated 45 million immigrants residing in the U.S., accounting for approximately 13% of the country's population (Radford, 2019). The majority are here legally, but approximately one-quarter are undocumented (Radford, 2019). The greatest proportion of the immigrant population in the U.S. are of Hispanic or Latino origin (44%) (Migration Policy Institute, 2017).

Estimates of crime against immigrants are difficult to determine, especially for undocumented immigrant victims of crime, because many of these individuals do not report incidents of victimization out of fear that they will be deported. However, the National Crime Victimization Survey does include rates of violent victimization by citizenship status (see Table 3.6). In the NCVS, non-citizens is composed of individuals with undocumented status, visa holders, permanent residents (green card holders), and others. Interestingly, the data indicates that immigrants experience a lower rate of violent victimization than native-born citizens. However, researchers caution these estimations may be artificially low. Conditions surrounding the immigration process and status, particularly for undocumented immigrants, may make them less willing to participate in surveys such as this, or to report any victimization they experience to law enforcement. Moreover, language and cultural barriers may further complicate the situation (Ricks, 2017). In fact, other studies have found that undocumented immigrants are especially vulnerable for victimization. They are more likely to be trafficked (labor or sex), financially exploited

Table 3.6 Number and rate of violent victimization by victim's citizenship status, 2017–2018

Citizenship Status	2017		2018	
	Number	Rate per 1,000	Number	Rate per 1,000
U.S. citizen	5,304,470	20.8	6,163,570	23.9
U.S. born citizen	5,106,650	21.9	5,900,190	25.1
Naturalized U.S. citizen	197,820	9.1	263,380	11.6
Non—U.S. Citizen	260,320,	16.2	196,350	12.5
U.S. born	5,106,650	21.9	5,900,190	25.1
Foreign—born	458,140,	12.1	459,730	11.9

Adapted from: Morgan, R.E. & Oudekerk, B.A. (2018). *Criminal Victimization, 2018*. U.S. Department of Justice, Office of Justice Programs, Bureau of Justice Statistics, September 2019, NCJ 253043.

by employers (e.g, low-paying jobs, wage theft, etc.), and physically and sexually assaulted in the community (Ricks, 2017).

Immigrants of Hispanic or Latino origin, both documented and undocumented, are also at greater risk of being a victim of a hate crime. In 2018, Hispanic or Latino victims made up 13% of the hate crimes reported (FBI, 2018). Many of these victims have been targeted because of their presumed immigration status, and law enforcement has reported an uptick in the number of hate crimes involving Latinx victims in recent years (Hassan, 2019).

Situational Context Variables Predicting Victimization

In addition to demographic risk factors, research have identified a number of situational context variables that may also increase an individual's risk of victimization; these include where a person lives, their prior history of victimization, as well as their relationship to the perpetrator.

Location

Research has established that crime is not equally distributed across all communities, rather it tends to cluster in metropolitan areas (FBI, 2018; OVC, 2015). This accounts for nearly all crimes, and is particularly true for violent crimes (see Table 3.7). For every type of violent crime, a greater proportion is reported in metropolitan and urban areas. Gun violence is is especially heavily concentrated in urban city centers, and tends to cluster among racially segregated and economically disadvantaged neighborhoods (Giffords Law Center, 2018). For example, nearly one-half of all gun homicides occur in metropolitan communities (Giffords Law Center, 2018). Thus, individuals who reside in these communities are more likely to be exposed to crime, and therefore, are at greater risk of becoming a victim of crime.

Repeat Victimization (multiple victimization)

Until recently, there was little discussion of the extent to which many people are victims of crime not just once, but several times during their lifetime. Moreover, there was little knowledge and understanding of how repeat victimization increases the risk of substance use, and mental and physical health problems, which in turn, contributes to repeat victimation. In some instances, the same pattern of victimization is repeated (e.g,. dating violence, then domestic violence); while other times, the individual experiences multiple forms of victimization (e.g., poly-victimization). Today, a body of literature and empirical research in victimology provides a better understanding of the extent to which victimization increases the risk of further victimization (Ruback, Clark, & Warner, 2014).

According to the NCVS, approximately 1 in 5 individuals who reported to have experienced a violent victimization in the prior survey, experienced at least one subsequent violent victimization in the current year (Bureau of Justice Statistics, 2017). Moreover, these individuals accounted for a disproportionate

Table 3.7 Crime Reported to Policy by Community Type, Rate per 100,000 (2014)

	Metropolitan Counties	Cities Outside Metropolitan Counties	Non-Metropolitan Counties
VIOLENT CRIME	395.7	376.0	179.5
Aggravated assault	239.8	271.2	133.8
Robbery	115.2	49.4	11.1
Rape	36.0	51.6	31.6
Murder/Manslaughter	4.7	3.9	3.0
PROPERTY CRIME	2678.5	3284.2	1315.6
Larceny-theft	1898.9	2475.9	795.2
Burglary	544.8	670.7	432.1
Motor Vehicle Theft	234.9	137.6	88.2

Source: Office for Victims of Crime. (2015). Urban and rural crime, 2014.

percentage of all violent victimizations that occurred that year. The 19% of individuals who had a history of repeat victimization, accounted for more than 50% of the total victimizations reported that year. Victims of IPV experienced the greatest percentage of repeat victimization (31%), compared to victims who did not share a close relationship with their perpetrator (see Table 3.8). Similarly sexual assault victims were significantly more likely to experience repeat victimization than other victims of non-fatal violent crimes (e.g., robbery, aggravated assault, simple assault).

Children are also at greater risk for revictimization than either adolescents or adults. Research has also found that the impact of such victimization often carries into their adulthood. Studies of victims of child sexual abuse have found that as many as 70 percent experience subsequent victimization, especially interpersonal victimization during adolescence and adulthood (Arata, 2002; Pittenger, Huit, & Hansen, 2016). Research has also found that if the abuse happens during adolescence, or is more severe in nature, it also increases their risk of re-victimization (Ford & Delker, 2017; Fortier et al. 2009; Matta Oshima, Jonson-Reid, & Seay, 2014).

Trauma associated with childhood victimization significantly increases a youth's risk of engaging in a range of high-risk behaviors, including substance use, running away, truancy, and participating in various deviant and criminal

Table 3.8 Percent of violent crime victims who experienced single or repeat victimization during the year by victim-offender relationship, 2005–2014

Victim-offender relationship	Intimate Partner	Well-known or Casual acquaintance	Relative	Stranger
Single Violent Crime Victims	66.7%	74.5%	75.4%	83.4%
Repeat Violent Crime Victims	33.3%	25.5%	24.6%	16.6%
Intimate Partner	26.2	1.5	2.3	0.8
Well-known or casual Acquaintance	4.3	18.6	3.6	3.9
Relative	1.5	0.8	16.7	0.6
Stranger	3.1	5.3	3.5	11.2
Average annual number of violent crime victims	372,300	1,036,600	239,900	1,420,200

Adapted from: Oudekerk, B.A. and Truman, J.L. (2017). *Repeat Victimization, 2005–2014*. U.S. Department of Justice, Office of Justice Programs, Bureau of Justice Statistics, August 2017, NCJ 250567.

behavior. Many of these behaviors subsequently expose them to other offenders, thereby inadvertently but substantially increasing their risk of further victimization (Kaufman, 2009; Papachristos & Wildeman, 2014; Posick & Zimmerman, 2015).

Relationship between Victim and Offender

While some individuals grew up being warned of 'stranger danger,' the reality is that you are far more likely to be victimized by someone you know than by a stranger. For every type of crime reported to the police, the most common perpetrator was either a family member or an acquaintance of the victim (see Table 8). In fact, of the 1.5 million victims that experienced some type of violent crime in 2018, less than 10% were committed by a stranger (FBI, 2018). Children, in particular, are typically victimized by someone they know. Among victims of child abuse, in approximately 7 out of every 10 cases the perpetrator is the child's parent(s) (Child Trend Databank, 2016). Similar patterns are found among individuals who are disabled. Over forty percent of these victims were abused by a caregiver or family member (Harrell, 2017). Thus, the data has thoroughly debunked the myth of 'stranger danger.'

Theoretical Paradigms of Crime Victimization: Positivist vs. Critical Victimology

As noted in the introduction of this chapter, victimologists strive to understand the nature and scope of victimization in society, and in turn, develop typologies from the data. They then use the data to try to uncover the reasons why some individuals are at greater risk of victimization than others. This part of the exercise requires careful thought and a lot of trial and error.

There are two primary schools of thought that have been forwarded to explain crime victimization—Positivist and Critical Criminology. Victimologists who subscribe to a Positivist theoretical framework focus on why some people are more prone to victimization than others by concentrating on the individual's actions and behaviors (Fattah,1991; Miers,1990). To aid in their research, these scholars use conventional state and local crime statistics and victimization surveys to explain the distribution of victimization and its varying patterns across society (Finkelhor & Hashima, 2001). Two of the more well-known theories within this paradigm are Hindelang, Gottfredson, and Garofolo's (1978) lifestyle theory of criminal victimization and Cohen and Felson's (1979) routine activities theory.

The lifestyle theory proposes a set of propositions to describe the connection between personal victimization and lifestyle that provides a possibility for offender-victim interactions. The theorists argue that the demographic and socioeconomic characteristics of individuals, as well as their lifestyle patterns, determine their exposure to personal victimization (Hindelang et al, 1978). Hindelang et al argue personal victimization is not random, but varies by the individual's socioeconomic status, age, race, and geographical location, employment, and marital status. Specifically, the likelihood of personal victimization increases as the amount of time a person spends outside of family increases. Moreover, the ability of individuals to isolate themselves from potential offenders varies by their individual characteristics. For example, those with higher income are more likely to isolate themselves from potential offenders because they live in communities with lower crime rates. Similarly, those who are married are less likely to be alone when venturing out into the community. Thus, the theory is based on the assumption that a combination of vocational and leisure activities, as well as demographic characteristics, is linked with personal crime and one's risk of victimization.

The routine activity theory, articulated by Lawrence Cohen and Marcus Felson (1979), hypothesizes that one's daily routines influence one's likelihood of coming into contact with motivated offenders. Victimization occurs when the individual is perceived to be a suitable target by the offender (e.g., themselves or their property) and there is an absence of a capable guardian. The routine activity theory assumes the continual presence of a motivated offender, thus what is examined is "the manner in which spatial-temporal organization of social activities helps people to translate their criminal inclination into action" (Cohen & Felson, 1979). In other words, the theory does not offer propositions on how to change the motivation to offend, but rather suggests changes in the opportunities to offend; hence, it puts the onus of responsibility on the victim to either modify the target or to increase their level of guardianship.

While there is significant overlap between lifestyle and routine activity theories, the two differ in how they view the behaviors that put people at risk for victimization. The lifestyle theory asserts that the probability of one's likelihood to become a victim of crime is based on the type of activities one chooses to engage in. For example, a young college student is more likely to be a victim of crime than a middle-aged adult because their lifestyle often places them in high-risk times and places, and thereby are more likely to engage with high-risk people. Routine activity theory, in contrast, simply describes the victimization event. It focuses on the three factors (motivated offender, suitable target, presence of guardian) to see if they converge in time and space. If they do, a victimization occurs; if one of the elements is missing, victimization is avoided.

Given the focus the positivist theories have placed on the role or behavior of the victim in their victimization (e.g., drinking alchol or participating in late-night leisure activities), the paradigm has been been criticized by some in the field for victim blaming. Thus, a new paradigm started to emerge in the 1980s when some victimologists began to adopt the theoretical perspectives forwarded in Critical Victimology to explain patterns of victimization.

Critical Victimology

As opposed to positivist victimology, critical victimology is interested in the legalistic conception of crime and crime victims: how crimes are defined, as well as why some victims of crime are ignored by the criminal justice system, society, or both. The critical approach to victimization allows for an examination of forms of victimization both within and outside of law and legal statutes (Hilliard & Tombs, 2004). For example, critical victimology identifies victims of state crimes such as civilians and soldiers in war, individuals harmed by racism and sexism, prisoners, etc. Within this paradigm, government policies and legislative, societal, and structural patterns and relationships are viewed as contributing factors to the conditions under which certain segments of the population are more exposed to victimization, whereas others receive more protection and help through victim assistance programs (Long, 2015). For example, the poor, racial and ethnic minorities, and women are more often victims of crime because of their lower status, and limited power within society. Two schools of thought within this paradigm are conflict theory and feminist theory.

Conflict theorists focus on the inequities of power and wealth in society. They argue that in a capitalisitic society inequalities abound because its economic structure allows the wealthy to manipulate the system in order to protect their own interests. However, under a capitalistic society people are socialized to believe if they just 'work hard,' they too will be able to achieve the same levels of wealth. So, when people experience frustration over their inability to attain and/or maintain the desired level of financial stability, they may turn to illegitimate means to make ends meet, or may lash out violently at those around them. Thus, when more economic stressors are present, crime and victimization rates should rise.

Feminists theorists also focus on inequities as the root of crime and victimization, however, they attribute such inequities to the power differentials between males and females observed in society. Feminist theorists assert that gender is social rather than a biological construct. They argue people are socialized to believe in specific gender roles for males and females, which in turn, dictate how each is supposed to think and behave. Specifically, males are supposed to be strong and independent; whereas, females are supposed to be meek and subservient. This set of gender roles aligns with a patriarchal framework for relationships and family structure. In such a household, the man is the head of the family and the sole bread-winner, and his wife and children are completely dependent on him for their emotional and financial wellbeing. Thus, feminists theorists argue that when the man's position of authority is challenged either by his wife or his children, he must reassert his position of power and control. Because men have been socialized to believe that violence is an acceptable response to stress, when they perceive their authority has been challenged, they often will resort to violence to reestablish control (Witt, 1987). Thus, feminist theorists argue that it is only when we change the social narratives of the power arrangments between men and women (e.g., patriarchy) will we be able to eliminate domestic and family violence.

Evidence-Based Decision Making and Evidence-Based Practices in Victim Services

The third question victimologists are interested in answering is what is the impact of victimization, and how should we respond to help them in their recovery? In other words, what should do with all of the data and the research? In 2013, the Office for Victims of Crime released its report *Vision 21: Transforming Victim Services* that presented a call for action for a comprehensive, systemic, and evidence-based approach to addressing the needs of victims. The goal is to ensure better outcomes for victims, as well as to improve their safety and protect victims' rights. To accomplish this goal, OVC recommended the justice system and victim services adopt evidence-based decision making [EBDM]. EBDM is based on the belief that decisions made by policymakers and stakeholders should be informed by the best and most current research (Gibel, Carter, & Ramirez, 2017). Thus, all decisions should be driven by data and empirically sound research, and similarly, should also be used to inform every policy, practice, and intervention directed at victims of crime (e.g., evidence-based practices). By utilizing such a disciplined approach to decision-making, policymakers and stakeholders are in a better position to create sound policy to help reduce crime victimization, as well as to monitor programs' performance and effectiveness for improving outcomes for victims of crime.

Conclusion

Victimology is still a relatively young science, however over the past five decades it has created its own empirical research, institutions specializing in the study of victims and victimization, services and programs established to negate the consequences of crime and harm done to victims, and legislation and policies (Wemmers, 2010). However, there is still much to be learned. While there are some commonalities or intersections across the different typologies of vicims, they are not a monolithic group. And, how victims respond to their experiences is equally complex. Thus, we must continue to assess for risk factors that don't just explain the onset of victimization, but what may contribute to repeat victimization. Only by engaging in continual research will we gain the knowledge and a better understanding of victims' experiences and needs, thereby enabling us to develop evidence-based policies and practices that will aid them in their recovery.

Discussion Questions

1. What are the different typologies of victimization and their limitations?
2. What are the different predictors that increase the probability of becoming a victim of crime?
3. What is the role of victim in a crime event? Compare and contrast the lifestyle theory of criminal victimization with the routine activity theory. Explain why both theories have been criticized for promoting a philosophy of 'victim-blaming.'
4. Provide an example of how you could use data to create a new policy or practice to aid a specific type of crime victim.

References

Aaltonen, M., Kivivuori, J., Martikainen, P., & Salmi, V. (2012). Socio-economic status and criminality as predictors of male violence: Does victim's gender or place of occurrence matter? *British Journal of Criminology, 52*(6), 1192–1211.

Amir, M. (1968). Victim precipitated forcible rape. *Journal of Criminal Law and Criminology. Vol. 58*(4), 493–502.

Arata, C. M. (2002). Child sexual abuse and sexual re-victimization. *Clinical Psychology: Science and Practice, 9*(2), 135–164.

Bialik, K. (2017). *7 facts about Americans with disabilities.* Pew Research Center. Retrieved from: https://www.pewresearch.org/fact-tank/2017/07/27/7-facts-about-americans-with-disabilities/

Breault, K. D., & Kpowsa, A. J. (1997). Effects of marital status on adult femail homicides in the United States. *Journal of Quantitative Criminology, 13*(2), 217–230.

Child Trends Data Bank. (2016, May). *Children's exposure to violence—Indicators on children and youth.* Retrieved from: https://www.childtrends.org/wp-content/uploads/2016/05/118_Exposure_to_Violence.pdf

Child Welfare Information Gateway. (2018, January). *The risk and prevention of maltreatment of children with disabilities.* Washington, DC: U.S. Department of Health and Human Services, Children's Bureau.

Children's Bureau. (2018). *Child maltreatment, 2018.* Washington, DC: U.S. Department of Health & Human Services, Administration for Children and Families, Administration on Children Youth and Families.

Cohen, L.E., & Felson, M. (1979). Social change and crime rate trends: A routine activity approach. *American Sociological Review, 44*(4), 588–608.

Daigle, L. E., & Mufitic, L. R. (2016). *Victimology.* Thousand Oaks, CA: SAGE Publishing.

Doerner, W. G., & Lab, S. P. (2011). *Victimology* (6th ed.). Burlington, MA: Anderson.

Eckenrode, J., Smith, E. G., McCarthy, M. E., & Dineen, M. (2014). Income inequality and child maltreatment in the United States. *Pediatrics, 133*(3), 454-461.

Every Town For Gun Safety (2020). *Gun violence in America.* Retrieved from: https://everytownresearch.org/gun-violence-america/

Farrell, C. A., Fleeger, E. W., Monuteaux, M .C., Wilson, C. R., Cristian, C. W., & Lee, L. K. (2017). Community poverty and child abuse fatalities in the United States. *Pediatrics, 139*(5), 1–9.

Fattah E. A. (1991). *Understanding criminal victimization: An introduction to theoretical victimology.* Scarborough, Canada: Prentice Hall Canada.

Federal Bureua of Investigation. (2018). *Hate crimes-Victims.* Retrieved from: https://ucr.fbi.gov/hate-crime/2018/topic-pages/victims

Federal Bureau of Investigation. (2018). *Uniform Crime Reports.* Retrieved from http://www.fbi.gov/about-us/cjis/ucr/ucr

Finkelhor, D., & Hashima, P. (2001). The victimization of children and youth: A comprehensive overview. In S. O. White (Ed.), *Handbook of youth and justice* (pp. 49–78). New York: Kluwer Academic/Plenum.

Finkelhor, D., Ormrod, R. K. & Turner, H. A. (2007). Poly-victimization: A neglected component in child victimization. *Child Abuse & Neglect, 31*(1), 7–26.

Fortier, M., DiLillo, D., Messman-Moore, T., Peugh, J., DeNardi, K. A., & Gaffey, K. J. (2009). Severity of child sexual abuse and re-victimization: The mediating role of coping and trauma symptoms. *Psychology of Women Quarterly, 33*(3), 308–320.

GLAAD. (n.d.). *Violence and bullying*. Retrieved from: https://www.glaad.org/resources/ally/6

Gibel, S., Carter, M. M., & Ramirez, R. (2017). *Evidence-based decision making: A guide for victim service providers*. Prepared for the National Institute of Corrections. Retrieved from: https://info.nicic.gov/ebdm/sites/info.nicic.gov.ebdm/files/ebdm-users-guide-vsp.pdf

Giffords Law Center to Prevent Gun Violence. (2018). *Gun violence statistics*. Retrieved from: https://lawcenter.giffords.org/facts/gun-violence-statistics/

Grove, L. E. & Farrell, G. (2011). *Repeat victimization*. New York: Oxford Bibliographies, Oxford University Press.

Harrell, E. (2017, July). *Crime against persons with disabilities* [NCJ 250632]. Washington, DC: U.S. Department of Justice, Office of Justice Programs, Bureau of Justice Statistics.

Hassan, A. (2019, November 12). *Hate-crime violence hits 16-year high, F.B.I. reports*. New York Times. Retrieved from: https://www.nytimes.com/2019/11/12/us/hate-crimes-fbi-report.html

Hassan, A., (2020, January 3). *'A different era:' Anti-Semitic crimes, and efforts to track them, climb*. New York Times. Retrieved from: https://www.nytimes.com/2020/01/03/us/anti-semitism-hate-crimes.html

Hillyard, P., & Tombs, S. (2004), "Beyond criminology." In P. Hillyard, C. Pantazis, S. Tombs, & D. Gordon (Eds.), *Beyond criminology: Taking harm seriously* (pp. 10–29). London: Pluto Press.

Hindelang, M. J., Gottfredson, M. R., & Garofalo, J. (1978). *Victims of personal crime: An empirical foundation for a theory of personal victimization*. Ballanger Publishing.

Kaufman, J. M. (2009). Gendered responses to serious strain: The argument for a general strain theory of deviance. *Justice Quarterly, 26*(3), 410–444.

Kishi, K. (2017). *Assaults against Muslims in U.S. surpass 2001 level*. Washington, DC: Pew Research Center. Retrieved from: https://www.pewresearch.org/fact-tank/2017/11/15/assaults-against-muslims-in-u-s-surpass-2001-level/

Kraus, L., Lauer, E., Coleman, R., & Houtenville, A. (2018). *2017 disability statistics report*. Durham, NH: University of New Hampshire.

Landau, S. F. & Freeman-Longo, R. E. (1990). Classifying victims: A proposed multidimensional victimological typology. *International Review of Victimology, 1*(3), 267–286.

Lauritsen, J. L. & Carbone-Lopez, K. (2011). Gender differences in risk factors for violent victimization: An examination of individual-, family-, and community-level predictors. *Journal of Research in Crime and Delinquency, 48*(4), 538–565.

Lauritsen, J. L. & Heimer, K. (2008). The gender gap in violent victimization, 1973–2004. *Journal of Quantitative Criminology, 24*(2), 125–47.

Lifespan of Greater Rochester, Inc. (2011, May). *Under the radar: New York state prevlanece study of elder abuse.* Retrieved from: https://ocfs.ny.gov/main/reports/Under%20the%20Radar%2005%2012%2011%20final%20report.pdf

Long, M. A. (2015). Critical criminology. In W. Jennings (Ed.), *The Encyclopedia of Crime and Punishment* (pp.443-449). Malden, MA: Wiley.

Maguire, M. (1991). The needs and rights of victims of crime. *Crime and Justice,. 14,* 363–433.

Matta Oshima, K. M., Jonson-Reid, M., & Seay, K. D. (2014). The influence of childhood sexual abuse on adolescent outcomes: The roles of gender, poverty, and re-victimization. *Journal of Child Sexual Abuse, 23*(4), 367–386.

Menard, S., Morris, R. G., Gerber, J., & Covey, H. C. (2011). Distribution and correlates of self-reported crimes of trust. *Deviant Behavior, 32*(10), 877–917.

Miers, D. (1990). Positivist victimology: A critique part 2: Critical victimology. *International Review of Victimology, 1*(3), 219–230.

Migration Policy Institute. (2017). *United States demographics & social.* Retrieved from: https://www.migrationpolicy.org/data/state-profiles/state/demographics/US

Morgan, R. E. & Oudekerk, B. A. (2018, September). Criminal victimization, 2018 [NCJ 253043]. Washington, DC: U.S. Department of Justice, Office of Justice Programs, Bureau of Justice Statistics, Retrieved from: https://www.bjs.gov/content/pub/pdf/cv18.pdf

National Coalition Against Domestic Violence. (n.d.). *Domestic violence.* Retrieved from: https://ncadv.org/statistics

National Domestic Violence Hotline. (2019). *Get the facts and figures.* Retrieved from: https://www.thehotline.org/resources/statistics/

Office for Victims of Crime. (2015). *Urban and rural crime.* Retrieved from: https://ovc.ncjrs.gov/ncvrw2016/content/section-6/PDF/2016NCVRW_6_UrbanRural-508.pdf

Office for Victims of Crime. (2018). *Intimate partner violence.* Retrieved from: https://ovc.ncjrs.gov/ncvrw2018/info_flyers/fact_sheets/2018NCVRW_IPV_508_QC.pdf

Papachristos, A. V., & Wildeman, C. (2014). Network exposure and homicide victimization in an African American community. *American Journal of Public Health, 104*(1), 143–150.

Petherick, W. (2017). Victim precipitation: Why we need to expand upon the theory. *Forensic Research and Criminology International Research, 2*(2), 1–3.

Petrosky, M., Blair, J. M., Betz, C. J., Fowler, K. S., Jack, S. P. D. & Lyons, B. H. (2017). Racial and ethnic differences in homicides of adult women and the role of intimate partner violence—United States, 2003–2014, *Morbidity and Mortality Weekly Report, 66*(28), 741–746.

Pittenger, S. L., Huit, T. Z., & Hansen, D. J. (2016). Applying ecological systems theory to sexual re-victimization of youth: A review with implications for research and practice. *Aggression and Violent Behavior, 26*, 35–45.

Posick, C. & Zimmerman, G. M. (2015). Person-in-context: Insights on contextual variation in the victim-offender overlap across schools. *Journal of Interpersonal Violence, 30*(8), 1432–1455.

Radford, J. (2019, June 17). *Key findings about U.S. immigrants.* Pew Research Center. Retrieved from: https://www.pewresearch.org/fact-tank/2019/06/17/key-findings-about-u-s-immigrants/

RAINN. (2020). *Victims of sexual violence: Statistics.* Retrieved from: https://www.rainn.org/statistics/victims-sexual-violence

Ricks, A., (2017). *Latinx crime victims fear seeking help.* Urban Wire: Crime and Justice. Retrieved from: https://www.urban.org/urban-wire/latinx-immigrant-crime-victims-fear-seeking-help

Ruback, R. B., Clark, V. A., & Warner, C. (2014). Why are crime victims at risk of being victimized again? Substance use, depression, and offending as mediators of the victimization-re-victimization link. *Journal of Interpersonal Violence, 29*(1), 157–185.

Schafer, S. (1967). The victim and his criminal: A study of functional responsibility. *Criminology, 5*(3), 25-29.

Siegel, L. J. (2010). *Criminology: Theories, patterns, and typologies.* Boston: Cengage Learning.

Smith, N., & Herrell, S., (2013, March). *Sexual abuse of children with disabilities: A national snapshot.* New York, NY: Center on Victimization and Safety, Vera Institute of Justice.

Smith, S., Zhang, X., Basile, K. C., Merrick, M.T., Wang, J. Kresnow, M., & Chen, J. (2018). *The National Intimate Partner and Sexual Violence Survey (NISVS): 2015 data brief—Updated release.* Atlanta, GA: National Center for Injury Prevention and Control, Centers for Disease Control and Prevention.

Spalek, B. (2006). Crime victims: Theory, policy and practice. New York: Palgrave Macmillan.

Stopbullying.gov (n.d.). *LGBTQ youth.* Retrieved from: https://www.stopbullying.gov/bullying/lgbtq

Tjaden, P., & Thoennes, N. (2000). Full report of the prevalence, incidence, and consequences of violence against women: Findings from the National Violence against Women Survey [NCJ 183781]. Retrieved from: https://www.ncjrs.gov/PDFFILES1/NIJ/183781.PDF

Tobolowsky, P. M., Beloof, D. E., Gaboury, M. T., Jackson, A. L. & Blackburn, A. G. (2016). *Crime victim rights and remedies.* Carolina Academic Press.

United Nations Office on Drugs and Crime. (2015). *Homicides and gender.* Retrieved from: https://www.heuni.fi/material/attachments/heuni/projects/wd2vDSKcZ/Homicideand_Gender.pdf

van Kesteren, J. (2015). *Criminal victimization at individual and international level: Results from the international crime victims surveys.* Retrieved from https://pure.uvt.nl/ws/portalfiles/portal/8407046/Van_Kesteren_Criminal_02_10_2015.pdf

Von Hentig, H. (1948). *The criminal and his victim: Studies in sociobiology of crime.* New Haven, CT: Yale University Press.

Wemmenrs, J. A. (2010). A short history of victimology. In. O. Hagemann, P. Schäfer, & S. Schmidt (Eds.), *Victimology, victim assistance and criminal justice: Perspectives shared by international experts at the Inter-University Centre of Dubrovnik* (pp.33-42). Monchengladbach: Fachhochschule Niederrhein Verlag.

Witt, D. D. (1987). A conflict theory of family violence. *Journal of Family Violence, 2*(4), 291-301.

Wiglesworth, A., Mosqueda, L., Mulnard, R., Liao, S., Gibbs, L, & Fitzgerald, W. (2010). Screening for abuse and neglect of people with dementia. *Journal of the American Geriatric Society, 58*(3), 493-500.Wolfgang, M.F. (1957). Victim precipitated criminal homicide. *Journal of Criminal Law and Criminology, 48*(1), 1–11.

Rate of violent victimization, by type of crime and demographic characteristics of victims, 2017 and 2018 (rates per 1,000 persons' age 12 or older)

Victim demographic characteristic	Total violent victimization		Violent victimization	
	2017	2018	2017	2018
Total	20.6	23.2	7.3	8.6
Sex				
Male	20.4	22.1	7.0	7.5
Female	20.8	24.3	7.7	9.6
Race/Ethnicity				
White	20.8	24.7	6.9	8.2
Black	21.8	20.4	7.9	10.0
Hispanic	20.7	18.6	9.5	8.5
Asian	6.9	16.2	2.5	5.6
Other	45.5	49.2	15.4	20.5
Age				
12–17	33.5	34.2	10.4	10.1
18–24	34.7	35.9	18.3	16.3
25–34	26.3	31.8	8.5	11.3
35–49	20.1	25.2	7.4	9.8
50–64	16.3	18.3	4.4	6.4
65 or older	6.5	6.5	1.8	2.3
Marital Status				
Never married	31.2	33.5	12.1	12.9
Married	11.1	12.1	3.2	4.1
Widow/widower	11.5	12.5	5.0	4.3
Divorced	29.0	39.1	9.7	14.8
Separated	48.3	58.2	17.8	20.8

Household income				
Less than $25,000	32.0	40.8	12.6	19.0
$25,000–$49,999	21.1	23.5	8.5	9.3
$50,000–$99,999	17.8	16.5	5.3	4.7
$100,000–$199,999	15.1	19.2	4.9	5.8
$200,000 or more	9.7	16.3	2.2	3.0

Adapted from: Morgan, R.E., & Oudekerk, B.A. (2019). *Criminal victimization, 2018* [NCJ 253043]. Washington, DC: U.S. Department of Justice, Office of Justice Programs, Bureau of Justice Statistics.

CHAPTER 4

Remedies for Crime Victims in the United States: A Historical Overview

Objectives

Upon completion of this chapter, you will be able to:

- understand legal rights and services for victims of crime through history,
- discuss historical trends and repeated themes regarding remedies and responses to victims of crime, and
- understand the evolutionary processes by which victims of crimes were acknowledged and included by the major institutions.

Introduction

This chapter chronologically reviews legal remedies, rights, and services for U.S. victims of crime from the Revolutionary Era until the end of the 20th Century to provide the reader with an understanding of the evolutionary processes by which victims of crimes were acknowledged and included by the major institutions. The chapter is divided into four historical periods. Each section begins with a discussion of the socio-political climate of the period to provide a context for the official decisions and public sentiments that impacted victims of crime. The discussion highlights historical trends and repeated themes regarding remedies and responses to victims of crime. And, then provides an overview of legal remedies (e.g., laws and the enforcement of laws), rights, and services offered to victims during the time period. A more detailed discussion of landmark legislation that relates to victims rights and services is addressed in the subsequent chapter.

Rights vs. Laws

Rights and laws are not the same thing. Rights are protections that allow for an individual to exercise and enforce their right to a process or action (Beloof, 2012), whereas laws set forth criminal penalties for the violation of regulated behaviors. Throughout history, laws were created to address victimization before victims had the right to be protected under these laws. However, rights have given victims access to government-sponsored services (e.g., compensation) that criminal laws do not address.

Part 1 - American Revolution through the Civil War (1760s–1860s)

In the aftermath of the Revolutionary War, the forefathers of the nation grappled with the role of government in the private lives of citizens and as a more formalized administration of justice took root. Consequently, concepts of victimization and the role of the victim in legal proceedings were altered (Henderson, 1985; Tobolowsky, Beloof, Gaboury, Jackson and Black-burn, 2016). Many of the legal and social responses to victims were based upon factors such as the race, class, and/or gender of persons, as well as evolving public sentiment about the promotion of family values (Kann, 1999; Pleck, 2004). Overall, the nearly 100 years between the American Revolution and the Civil War saw crime victims lose their formal role in the administration of justice as the nation built its criminal justice system. In addition, discrimination and emerging ideals about family values guided public sentiment set the stage for years of struggle for many victims of crime.

Socio-political Context of the 1760s through 1860s

One of the most prominent socio-political factors to affect victims of crime was confusion and tension regarding the role of the government in the private lives of its citizens. During the Colonial Era, the Puritans promoted a system that relied upon community involvement to address family dysfunction, crime, and other social issues. However, by the late 1790s, conservative politics had emerged and the strength of the state was rising, creating the sentiment that communities could no longer rely exclusively on the family to confront social problems and there was a greater need for the law to resolve public and private disputes (Grossberg, 1988). Some of this shift in attitude can be attributed to an influential essay published by Cesare Beccaria, an Italian philosopher in the late 18th century, entitled *On Crimes and Punishment*. In his essay, Beccaria asserted that a system of law should serve society, not individuals. This notion resonated with the public at that time because it favored rationality and utilitarianism, and as a result provided the framework for our legal and criminal justice systems (Beloof, 2012). As a consequence of this shift in our approach to justice, a victim's right to initiate and participate in investigations, and the right to oversee (or at least guide) the punishment phase ended. Instead, crime was now viewed to be against the state, not the victim; therefore, it was the responsibility of police officers, prosecutors, and judges to oversee various stages in the criminal justice process.

Cesare Beccaria (1738–1794)

Another factor that has long affected crime victims is the intersectionality of race, class, gender, and victimization. Kann (1999) noted that revolutionary efforts during this era solidified the role of men as dominant over their wives. Much of public discourse during this time focused on family values. Concepts such as the sanctity of marriage, privacy, and the preservation of the family kept issues such as domestic violence and child abuse a personal matter (Pleck, 2004). For example, under the *law of coverture*, men had the right to govern the private and public lives of their wives; and , the *right of chastisement*, which was upheld by many court decisions in the early to mid-19th century, gave men permission to use corporal punishment on their wives as a means to maintain authority in the home (Siegel, 1995). This right similarly extended to abuses against children and servants. Thus, these victims were denied any sort of protection.

This era also saw the birth of three systems of justice: one for Whites, one for Blacks, and one for Native Persons, and these differing systems of justice extended to victims (Roth, 2010). For example, pre-Civil War sexual assault statutes based punishments on the race of the victim in relation to the race of the offender (Walker, Spohn & Delone, 2012). Block (2006) noted that White upper class women had more access to the protections than poor, immigrant, and/or Black women. Moreover, penalties assigned for harming White women were significantly higher than for women of color. Walker et al. (2012) noted that laws in Virginia, Georgia, and Kansas specified that penalties for raping White women were more severe, and in some cases the penalties for rape of a Black woman were implemented only at the court's discretion. In fact, Morris (1992) noted that in most instances when a victim was a slave, she "[was] outside the protection of common law" (p. 1290).

Legal Remedies and Rights

The emergence of a formal legal and criminal justice system during this era significantly impacted the role of the victim (Gitler, 1984; Tobolosky et al., 2010). On the one hand, it can be argued that victims' rights expanded as public prosecutors took on cases when indigent or unskilled citizens could not investigate their own cases and represent their interests; in this regard, the arbitrary application of rights was reduced. However, most scholars view this time as a period in which crime victims lost rights, as they no longer guided the investigation process or made recommendations about punishments. For example, in 1751, the Virginia courts ordered that victims consult with the deputy attorney general before filing a criminal complaint; by 1789, the deputy attorney general had complete control over prosecutions within his county (Cardenas, 1986). These changes also negated a victim's right to restitution; rather than monetary or other direct payments made directly to crime victims, any damages collected were deemed the property of the state (Derene, Walker, & Stein, 2010).

This shift in paradigm undoubtedly resulted in system-level transformations that negatively impacted victims; however, there are a few limited examples of specific rights or legal responses that had a positive impact on crime victims. In 1824, the Mississippi Supreme Court recognized that a husband does not have "unlimited license" to commit assault and battery on his wife; however they did not reject the husband's right to use corporal punishment altogether (Lentz, 1999). In the early 1840s, a number of state legislatures reconsidered married women's rights to contract, own property, or sue (Hasday, 2000); these rights afforded women legal standing, and ultimately opened the door for women to challenge men's rights to chastisement. By 1850, 19 states granted divorces on the grounds of marital cruelty (Pleck, 2004), and just prior to the Civil War, Tennessee and Georgia passed laws making wife beating a misdemeanor (Rutherford & MacKay, 2013).

Although there were no laws against child abuse until the mid-19th century, legislators also began to question the unchecked authority of parents in the lives of their children, allowing for individual child abuse cases to be heard. The rights of and legal responses to sexual assault victims also saw minor improvements. Prior to the mid-19th century, the age of consent was generally 10 years old; this age was increased throughout the 1800s to 16 or 18, and some states increased penalties for males who raped pre-pubescent girls (Oberman, 1994).

Victim Services

Very few services were available to victims of crime in the era between the Revolutionary and Civil Wars. The few services that were available appeared much later, and focused on child neglect. Anti-institutional child neglect responses began to emerge in early to mid-1800s. One of the first of these efforts was organized by a New York City minister, Charles Brace, who created a program that targeted children living in the city whom he feared were living in crime-ridden environments, and placed them in rural communities (Thomas, 1972). Scholars have subsequently argued that these efforts were less about the need to assist neglected children, and more about the public's fear of crime. Thus, interventions into the lives of neglected children were intended as a form of deterrence for the future criminal activity in which the children might engage.

In the 1820s, public authorities started to acknowledge a need to intervene in cases of child neglect. For example, in 1833 the Boston Children's Friend Society provided refuge for neglected and abused children (Boylan, 1990). Other cities such as New York, New Orleans, and Philadelphia opened similar programs; and laws soon began to be passed to authorize courts to commit neglected, destitute, and abandoned children to houses of refuge (Thomas, 1972, p. 306). Similarly,

Elizabeth Cady Stanton

THROUGH THE CONSTANT USE OF LIQUOR HE LOSES, AT TIMES, ALL CONTROL OF HIMSELF AND IN ONE OF THESE MOMENTS KILLS HIS WIFE.

Source: *The Bottle, 1847*

reformers and advocates during that time similarly condemned the mixing of children and adults in prisons and poorhouses. Thus, over the next few decades, children and adults were separated, leading to the creation of specialized services for children.

Another influential movement of this era that indirectly laid the foundation for services for domestic violence victims was the temperance movement (1830s – 1920s). The temperance movement, which focused on the social evils of alcohol, initiated public conversations about the connection between alcohol abuse and interpersonal violence (Siegel, 1995). Pleck (2004) noted that advocates within the temperance movement, such as Elizabeth Cady Stanton, pressured courts to consider wife abuse as a public harm, as it threatened family stability. Public campaigns against alcohol, such as the one illustrated below, were used to show the dangers of alcohol use.

The temperance movement ultimately became intertwined with the women's movement, and provided a platform to discuss women's economic dependency on their husbands, and physical abuses experienced in the home. Leaders of the movement, like Elizabeth Cady Stanton, similarly fought for a women's right to divorce as a mechanism to end domestice violence. While these women did not organize any formal programming *per se* for victims of domestic violence, they laid the groundwork for the creation of support groups and advocacy centers.

Part 2 - Reconstruction through the early Women's Rights Movement (1860s–1960s)

In era between the Civil War and the late 1960s, the government and public realized that personal rights were fundamental in a democracy. The ratification of the 13th, 14th, and 19th amendments suggested the government's acknowledgement that exploitation and oppression, the cornerstones of victimization, needed to be addressed. In addition, this period saw the beginning of official recognition that crime victims' rights, laws, and services were necessary. Child abuse interventions and burgeoning domestic violence laws were among the first efforts to address criminal victimization. However, these advances were situated in the backdrop of post-Civil War notions of American social order, and "the war was a determining factor in the structure of race, class, and gender relations in the United States" (Stutzman, 2009). Therefore, although rights and services were provided to many in need, they were not provided to all. The system of excluding certain victims or placing parameters around responses was solidified.

Socio-political Context of the 1860s through 1960s

The period between the Civil War and the Victims' Rights Movement saw numerous social and political changes that impacted the development of victims' rights directly or indirectly. The formal abolishment of slavery, the incorporation of persons under the 14th Amendment, women's suffrage, the formal recognition of child and domestic abuse, and the civil and women's rights movements are some of the changes that influenced public and government views on individual rights.

In addition to the above widely known but indirect advances, the temperance and social work movements during this era directly impacted responses to victims of crimes. The temperance movement, which was discussed previously, initiated public conversations about the violence associated with alcohol abuse, particularly family violence (Siegel, 1995). The social work movement also helped to raise public awareness, mainly in the area of child neglect and abuse. The movement was initially a middle-class effort to encourage poor parents to better care for their children by encouraging a stronger work ethic and morals. However, McGowan (2005) noted that the movement quickly realized that social forces (e.g., neighborhood conditions and work shortages) beyond the control of the parents were a factor.

The reform movements of late 1800s and early 1900s helped to change public attitudes and bring attention to the plight of certain crime victims; however, it also solidified notions of victimization based upon race, class, gender, and other socio-political issues. For example, the temperance movement opened discussions on wife abuse, but at the expense of reinforcing social prejudices against the lower class. In addition, Jimenez et al. (2014) noted that the early child welfare efforts strove to improve the lives of White children, while doing little to benefit Native, African American, and Latino or Hispanic children. Moreover, emerging tensions in the 1960s between liberals and conservatives within the American public further complicated how crime victims were viewed and treated. Henderson (1985) noted that whereas liberals focused on isolating and addressing perceived social causes of crime, conservatives focused on individuals wrongdoings as the cause of crime (e.g., victim-blaming). Hence victimization was politicized, and the "anguish of victims [was] reformulated or mistranslated into support for a particular ideology" (p. 1020).

Legal Remedies and Rights

The decades immediately following the Civil War saw numerous changes to state laws. In 1866, a Massachusetts law authorized judges to intercede when "by reason of orphanage or of the neglect, crime, drunkenness or other vice of parents," a child was "growing up without education or salutary control, and in circumstances exposing said child to an idle and dissolute life" (Myers, 2008, p. 450). By 1867, nearly all states had laws ensuring the protection of children to government agencies, and mandating doctors to report suspicions of abuse to the police.

Laws directed at protecting adults also began to emerge. By 1871, Alabama and Massachusetts both rescinded a man's right to beat his wife. Other states soon followed, and by 1920 wife beating was illegal in every state (Robbins, 1999). Divorce, as a legal remedy, was also available in nearly all states by the early 1900s. Minor advances were also made in terms of sexual violence. During the last two decades of the 19th century, every state increased the age of sexual consent from 10 to either 16 or 18, thus beginning a discussion that acknowledged that "the legal definitions of coercion and resistance in the existing law of forcible rape were unrealistic and harsh" (Larson, 1997, p. 4). Finally, between the 1890s and 1930s, 16 states passed anti-lynching laws to prevent mobs from enacting vigilante violence; however, these laws were rarely enforced (Levin, 2002).

In addition to state laws, the federal government also addressed victimization. In 1912, President William Howard Taft signed into law legislation establishing The Children's Bureau to investigate and report "upon all matters pertaining to the welfare of children and child life among all classes of our people." (Social Security Administration, n.d.). This legislation was the culmination of a nearly decade long grass-root efforts led by two early social reformers, Lillian Wald of New York's Henry Street Settlement House, and Florence Kelly of the National Consumer League. The Bureau was largely funded by the Social Security Act of 1935 (Meyers, 2008), and officially became a part of the Social Security Administration in 1946. And in 1958, Amendments to Title V in the Social Security Act gave the Bureau equal status with the unemployment compensation and old-age provisions of the Act (Social Security Administation, n.d.). Today, it is a part of the Department of Health and Human Services' Administration for Children and Families.

Example of public awareness campaign produced by The Children's Bureau 1918

A number of key court cases also impacted the legal standing of crime victims during this period. In 1869, the Illinois Supreme Court ruled in *Fletcher v. People* that child abuse could be illegal, stating that authority must be exercised within the bounds of reason and humanity. Specifically, the court noted "If the parent commits wanton and needless cruelty upon his child, either by imprisonment of his character or by inhuman beating, the law will punish him" (Myers, 2008, p. 450). In 1891, the Mississippi Supreme Court ruled in *Hewlett v. Georgia* that although a child cannot obtain civil redress as a result of abuse, "The state, through its criminal laws, will give the minor child protection from parental violence and wrongdoing, and this is all the child can be heard to demand." Similar protections were extended to victims of domestic violence. In 1874, *The State of North Carolina v. Oliver* (1874, 70 N.C. 60) ruled that "the old doctrine, that a husband had a right to whip his wife, provided he used a switch no larger than his thumb, is not law in North Carolina. Indeed, the Courts have advanced from that barbarism until they have reached the position, that the husband has no right to chastise his wife, under any circumstances."

Victim Services

During this era, the most prominent remedies for victims came in the form of child abuse intervention and welfare services. Although there are no exact dates regarding the creation of informal community services, many historical documents agree that the case of Mary Ellen Wilson in 1874 spurred the development of child welfare services. Mary Ellen was a child left in the care of a foster family; records indicated years of abuse and neglect at the hands of her foster mother, Mary McCormick . At approximately age 10, her mother was brought to court and found guilty of felonious assault (Thomas, 1972). The case ignited public outcry and thus the compelled the founder of the Society for the Prevention of Cruelty to Animals, Elbridge T. Gerry, to develop the New York Society for the Prevention of Cruelty to Children (NYSPCC).

Thomas (1972) noted that by 1922 there were 300 non-governmental child protection societies. However, by the 1930s many reformers were calling for government intervention and control; this overlapped with the increasing role of state and federal governments in social services, such as departments of welfare, social services, health, and labor. By the time of the Great Depression, the role of nongovernmental societies, dependent on charitable contributions from the community, nearly vanished; they were replaced by official government-controlled programs created under the signing of the Social Security Act of 1935. By 1967, nearly all states had laws placing responsibility for child protection in government hands (Thomas, 1972). Government-controlled services included interventions and

Mary Ellen's Court Statement

"My name is Mary Ellen ____. I don't know how old I am. My mother and father are both dead. I call Mrs. C____ momma. I have never had but one pair of shoes, but can't recollect when that was. I have no shoes or stockings this winter. I have never been allowed to go out . . . except in the night time, and only in the yard [to use the outdoor privy]. My bed at night is only a piece of carpet stretched on the floor underneath a window and I sleep in my little undergarment with a quilt over me. I am never allowed to play with other children. Momma has been in the habit of whipping me almost everyday. She used to whip me with a twisted whip — a rawhide. The whip always left black and blue marks on my body. I have now on my head two black and blue marks which were made by momma with the whip, and a cut on the left side of my forehead which was made by a pair of scissors in momma's hand. She struck me with the scissors and cut me. I have no recollection of ever having been kissed and I have never been kissed by momma. I have never been taken on momma's lap or caressed or petted. I never dared speak to anybody, because if I did I would get whipped. I have never had . . . any more clothing than I have on at present. . . . I have seen stockings and other clothes in our room, but I am not allowed to put them on. Whenever momma went out, I was locked up in the bedroom . . . I don't know for what I was whipped. Momma never said anything when she whipped me. I do not want to go back to live with momma because she beats me so." The New York Society for the Prevention of Cruelty to Children (NYSPCC).

removals, foster placements, medical and therapeutic services, and services for addressing family issues (e.g., poverty and substance abuse).

Evidence of advances to services for battered women can similarly be found at the beginning in the late 19th century. The first battered women's shelter, or refuge as it was called, operated between 1875 and the 1890s in Belton, Texas (Miller, 2000); and in 1887 a local chapter of the Women's Christian Temperance Union (WCTU) in San Diego opened a refuge for wives who had been abandoned by their husbands (Pleck, 2004). These two programs seem to be isolated examples, as the shelter movement and associated services, such as court advocacy and counseling, did not emerge until the latter part of the 1960s.

However, the paradigm really began to shift towards the end of the 1960s. In 1967, a landmark report released by President Johnson's Commission on Law Enforcement and Administration of Justice, titled *The Challenge of Crime in Free Society*, publically acknowledged for the first time that one of the most neglected subjects in the study of crime was its victims. This report laid the foundation for the creation of the National Crime Victimization Survey, which then enabled researchers to really measure the extent of crime victimization in the United States.

Part 3 - The Crime Victims' Rights Movement (1970s–1980s)

The Victims' Rights Movement of the 1970s and 1980s saw the recognition of victims of certain crimes through the development of legal responses and services, as well as the recognition that victims' rights were equally important as rights for the accused. At the federal level, in 1982, President Reagan's Task Force on Victims of Crime examined the impact of victimization and the disregard for crime victims by the criminal justice system. The Task Force recommended the creation of the Victims of Crime Act (VOCA) of 1984. (Chapter 5 discusses the Task Force outcomes in greater depth.) The country similarly witnessed an attempt to add a constitutional amendment that specifically addressed the rights of crime victims. State level efforts were also abundant; laws to protect the rights of victims were being created, and community services, such as shelters, child abuse programming, and court services emerged. Furthermore, media attention to landmark cases and evolving victimization research further supported the need for responses to victims of crime. However, as is the case with any period of rapid growth, tensions and political turmoil also manifested. Tension between victims' advocates and law enforcement began to emerge over how the 'war on crime' of the 1980s was to be handled, which resulted in some disruptions to the progress made during this era (Dubber (2002)).

Socio-political context of the 1970s and 1980s

The Victims' Rights Movement arose from and drew some of its strength from other social movements, such as the civil and women's rights movements. Each of these movements acknowledged the need to expose inequities, while also recognizing the complex nature of change; as a result, the depth and breadth of criminal victimization was brought to light. Books such as Friedan's (1963) *Feminist Mystique* opened the door for discussions about relations in the home, and Brownmiller's (1976) *Against our Will*, and Del Martin's (1973) *Battered Wives*, exposed the realities and social construction of victimization. In addition, research uncovered additional layers within victimization. Burt's (1980) work on rape myths exposed public attitudes about rape myths and the acceptance of violence against women. Lenore Walker's (1979) work on Battered Women's Syndrome and Dr. Henry Kempe's (1962) work on Battered Child's Syndrome uncovered the trauma and effects of domestic violence and child abuse, respectfully. Furthermore, media attention given to high-profile cases, such as *Oregon v. Rideout* (1978) and *Thurman v. Torrington* (1984), addressed the apathy of the criminal justice system toward victims of domestic violence; and, the 1981 abduction and murder of Adam Walsh brought public attention to child abduction.

Although the increased attention on cases like these spurred a number of positive advances for many victims, a number of criticisms emerged in how services were delivered. For example, the child welfare system experienced increasing criticism over the cost of foster care, the impact of removal has on the child, the varied structure and organization of services between the states, the qualifications of workers, and the inability to reach underserved populations (McGowan, n.d.). In addition, activists and scholars began to call attention to services that excluded women of color and the poor. Activists such as Schechter (1982) pointed out that while federal dollars helped to increase services, the monies also quelled the social change aspect of the women's movement. Schechter argued that because Title XX funding could not be used for community education, only programming that focuses on the victims' immediate needs, no significant change could be made to the social or political structures that help to perpetuate violence against women.

Conflict also arose between advocates who worked on behalf of crime victims, and agents of the criminal justice system (Toblowsky, 2016) . For example, prosecutors wanted to increase victims' participation in the process to increase convictions, whereas advocates wanted victims to be independent participants in the process and increase access to services. Although these positions are not mutually exclusive, the reality is that if victims of crime were not being treated well within the criminal justice system, they were less likely to cooperate, and prosecutions were less likely to be successful (Lee, 2019).

Even the intentions of the President's Commission's Task Force on Victims of Crime were questioned. The Task Force was charged with reviewing policies and programs for victims of crime, and offer solutions (Hook & Seymour, 2004). The Task Force completed their charge and presented a *Final Report* that outlined shortcomings and puts forth recommendations. However, in the opening statement by the Chairman, there are numerous references to victims of violent crimes. Critics noted that the attention given to victims of violent crime by many politicians in the administration was a method to garner support for the "War on Crime". And they argued the "War on Drugs" was not about helping innocent victims of violent crime, but rather about incarcerating persons who committed drug-related offenses (Dubber, 2002).

Legal remedies and rights

The 1970s and 1980s saw numerous state-level legislative initiatives that addressed victimization. By the early 1970s, every state made child abuse and spousal abuse a punishable offense, and some states also created laws to establish enforcement standards. For example, in 1977, Oregon became the first state to pass a mandatory arrest law that mandated arrests in domestic violence cases (NCVRW, 2016). Additionally, Michigan passed the first rape shield law in 1974, which prevented a rape victim's sexual history from being used as evidence to discredit the victim at trial (Kello, 1987). Other states soon followed (Kello, 1987). Similarly, marital rape exemptions were being removed from state's sexual assault statutes, which had permitted rape within marriage, by defining rape as an act that occurs in situations in which the perpetrator is not a current or former spouse (Ross, 2015). Throughout the 1970s and 1980s, and state courts used judicial review to rule marital exemptions unconstitutional (Ross, 2015). And, in 1980, Wisconsin was the first state to enact a Bill of Rights for Victims and Witnesses of Crime, and three years later passed the first Child Victim and Witness Bill of Rights (Wisconsin Department of Justice, 2016). This is particularly notable, given that both pieces of legistlation predate the President's Commission and Task Force on Victims of Crime.

While state laws expanded the legal conceptualization of criminal victimization, federal legislation and initiatives expanded possible remedies and shaped responses to crime victims. For example, the U.S. Department of Justice's Office of Justice Programs was the first federal agency to allocate funds to victim-witness programs (1974); the Child Abuse Prevention and Treatment Act (CAPTA) (1974) provided states with assistance to develop child abuse and neglect identification and prevention programs, and the Indian Child Welfare Act (1978) established standards for the placement of Native American children in foster and adoptive homes and to prevent the breakup of Native American families (Child Welfare Information Gateway, 2015). In addition, the Victim and Witness Protection Act of 1982 brought "fair treatment standards" to victims and witnesses in the federal criminal justice system; Congress passed the Family Violence Prevention and Services Act in 1984, which earmarked federal funding for domestic violence programming (NCVRW, 2016).

As previously noted, the most prominent federal initiative was the 1982 President's Commission; the *Final Report* proposed 68 recommendations which led to rights and remedies for crime victims. Two of the 68 are particularly noteworthy as they led to major initiatives for victims' rights and remedies. One of the most significant outcomes led to the establishment of the Office for Victims of Crime (OVC), and the passage of the Victims of Crime Act of 1984 (VOCA). VOCA initially established funding streams that would support state victim compensation programs; by 1986, 35 states had compensation programs (NCVRW, 2016). A second major recommendation of the President's Commission was the creation of a Federal Constitutional Amendment, "to give teeth" to other recommendations (Hook & Seymour, 2004). Although the federal amendment did not pass, state level efforts were underway. California was the first state to address the interests of crime victims by establishing a constitutional right to victim restitution in their constitution. In 1986, Rhode Island passed a victims' rights constitutional amendment that granted victims the rights to restitution, to submit victim impact statements, and to be treated with dignity and respect (NCVRW, 2016). Numerous states drafted state constitutional amendments in the years to follow.

In addition, to state laws and federal initiatives, legal remedies came in the form of court cases. *Thurman v. Torrington* 595 F.Supp. 1521 (1984) compelled police departments to re-evaluate their responses to victims of domestic violence. The U.S. District Court for the District of Connecticut ruled "that official behavior that reflects an on-going pattern of deliberate indifference to victims of domestic assault violates the Equal Protection Clause of the Fourteenth Amendment" (Frisch, 1992). Additionally, *State v. Ciskie* 751 P.2d 1165 (1988) was the first case to permit the use of expert testimony to explain the reactions of a rape victim who did not immediately contact the police after repeated physical and sexual assaults by an intimate partner.

Victim Services

This period saw the creation of numerous direct services for victims of crime[1], most notably for victims of interpersonal violence. Early grassroots efforts by advocates and survivors were the catalyst; the History of Battered Women's project outlines many of these advances (citation). In 1971, Women's Advocates in Minneapolis/St. Paul, MN becomes one of the first groups to provide services, and in 1974 a number of battered women's shelters were founded across the country. Throughout the 1970s and 1980s sexual assault and domestic violence services increased dramatically. In 1976, there were 400 independent rape crisis centers that provided self-defense courses, support groups, and counseling. Services provided to victims of sexual assault and domestic violence included individual counseling, support

---

[1] This time period saw the creation of thousands of services for victims of crime; this chapter can only present a sample of such services. For a chronological list of emerging services see the NCVRW Resource Guide (2013). Also, see Young and Stein (2004) and the Children's Bureau Timeline.

groups, court advocacy, child/family counseling, shelter, and safe houses. In addition, these services were growing increasingly aware of the need to be inclusive; thus, programs for lesbians, immigrants, and persons of color emerged.

Dr. Kempe's research on child abuse in the 1960s and 70s, and the creation of CAPTA (1974) and the federal Administration of Child, Youth and Families in 1977, were catalysts in the development of child abuse/neglect detection and intervention services. Early services focused on public awareness campaigns. Eventually intervention efforts included home visitation programs for new at-risk mothers to teach basic caregiving skills and encouraged a healthy home environment (Child Welfare Information Gateway, 2017). After 1980, every state established services to serve children in their homes, prevent foster placements, and facilitate reunification (McGowan, n.d.).

In addition to services for victims of interpersonal violence, programming to meet the needs of other victims was being developed. Much like domestic violence and sexual assault services, these early programs were generally grassroots efforts led by survivors and their advocates. Many of these grass-roots approach were spearheaed by parents who lost children. In 1978, Robert and Charlotte Hullinger founded Parents of Murdered Children, Inc. (POMC) after their 19-year-old daughter, Lisa, was murdered by her boyfriend. Frustrated by the justice system's failure to hold their daughter's assailant accountable, they wanted to change how initimate partner homicide was treated in the criminal justice system, and help other parents who have lost a loved one to homicide through the grief process. What started as a small gathering of five parents in the basement of a church has now grown into a national organization that offers over a variety of services for survivors of homicide, as well as hosts a national conference each year (National Organization of Parents of Murdered Children, Inc., 2018).

Two other grass-roots initiatives launched around this same time helped to change legislation at the federal level. In 1980, Candace Lightner and Cindi Lamb founded Mothers Against Drunk Driving (MADD) after each lost a child to a drunk driver (Tucker Davis, 2005). In both instances, the person responsible for their child's death had been arrested multiple times for driving under the influence, however, had never received any substantive punishment. Candace, Cindi, and their supporters spent the next two years pressuring lawmakers to change drunk-driving laws and enact tougher sanctions on repeat offenders (MADD, 2019). As a result of their efforts, President Ronald Reagan created the Presidential Commission on Drunk Driving in 1982, and in the subsequent year successfully lobbied to lower the minimum BAC (blood alcohol content) for driving to .08%, as well as raise the minimum drinking age to 21 nationwide. Today, there is at least one MADD office in every state, and their efforts have saved over 380,000 lives (MADD, 2019).

A Mothers Against Drunk Driving (MADD)sign is posted during a sobriety checkpoint.

In 1986, Howard and Connie Clery created Security on Campus, Inc. (now the Clery Center for Security on Campus) following the assault and murder of their 19-year-old daughter Jeanne in her dorm room at Lehigh University. The Clery's were angered by the failure of university and college administrators to share information about crimes on campus with the students and their families, and argued the failure to do so violated Title IX of the Education Amendements (Clery Center, 2019). Their persistant lobbying efforts resulted in the passage of the Jeanne Clery Disclosure of Campus Security Policy and Crime Statistics Act (aka, The Clery Act) in 1990. The law requires any college or university that received federal funding to prepare, publish, and distribute information about their security policies and crime statistics on and near their respective campuses each year (Clery Center, 2019).

While many early victims service efforts, such as those highlighted previously, were informally organized at the community-level, survivors and their advocates pressed for more formal services to be made available.. To address this issue the National Organization for Victim Assistance (NOVA) partnered with the Office for Victims of Crime (OVC) to put forth the Model Victim Assistance Program Brief (1986-1988). This brief articulated eight basic services that victim service programs should provide: crisis intervention, counseling, and advocacy; support during criminal investigations; support during prosecution; support after case disposition; crime prevention; public education; and training of allied professions (Young & Stein, 2004). Services were further formalized by the injection of VOCA funding. By 1984, there were 2,000 community-based programs that focused on services in law enforcement, prosecution, courts, community corrections and institutional corrections agencies, and the juvenile justice system (Hook & Seymour, 2004). And the number of programs have kept growing. By 2014, more than 7 million crime victims natiowide were served by a VOCA-funded assistance program, and programs and service continue to expand today (*See Table 4.1 - Type and Number of victims serviced by VOCA funding*)

Part 4 - Post Crime Victims' Rights Movement (1990s to mid-2000s)

The last four decades have seen the continued development of legal remedies, rights, and services, as well as progress in the form of expanded views on who is a victim

Table 4.1 Type and Number of victims serviced by VOCA funding

Victims served by voca assistance programs in FYs 2013 and 2014, by type of victimization

Crime Category	Total Number of Victims Served (FY 13 + FY 14)	Percentage of Total Victims
Child physical abuse	364,314 (182,277 + 182,037)	5.0 (5.16)
Child sexual abuse	788,862 (416,592 + 372,270)	11 (11.18)
DUI/SWI	110,385 (55,947 + 54,438)	2 (1.56)
Domestic violence	3,254,926 (1,637,052 + 1,617,874)	46 (46.12)
Adult sexual assault	394,813 (193,700 + 201,113)	6 (5.59)
Elder abuse	77,201 (39,404 + 37,797)	1 (1.09)
Adult molested as children	96,613 (50,644 + 45,969)	1 (1.37)
Survivors of homicide victims	153,962 (77,978 + 75,984)	2 (2.18)
Robbery	377,678 (198,299 + 179,379)	5 (5.35)
Assault	579,478 (299,552 + 279,926)	8 (8.21)
Other	858,754 (365,914 + 492,840)	12.17
Total	**7,056,986 (3,517,359 + 3,539,627)**	**100**

Currently there are numerous programs for various types of victims of crime, supported by VOCA funding. According to OVCA, in 2013 and 2014 a total of 7,056,986 crime victims nationwide benefited from $655,441,166 in VOCA-funded assistance.

Source: https://www.ovc.gov/pubs/reporttonation2015/VOCA-compensation-and-assistance-statistics.html

and a more inclusive approach in the delivery of services. Important legislation such as the 1994 Violence Against Women Act (VAWA), the 2003 Prison Rape Elimination Act, and the 2004 Justice for All Act, have created concrete and enforceable responses to crime victims. In addition, research has been used to expand the reach and quality of services provided. Again, with advances come tensions. The last four decades have seen political posturing between liberals and conservatives, and the realization that White, middle-class views of victimization and victims' needs often differ from those from historically disenfranchised groups. Thus, for as a far as we have come in our understanding of and response to criminal victimization, we still have a long way to go.

Socio-political context of the 1990s through mid-2000s

The critique that the Victims' Rights Movement and the War on Crime were one and the same continued to grow throughout the 1990s (Dubber, 2002; Henderson, 1985). Many scholars argued that victimization was politicized to increase harsh penalties, such as lengthy prison sentences. While this statement may be true, it is also true that victims of crime received legitimate services and increased rights. One example of this dual reality is the 1994 Violence Against Women Act (VAWA). VAWA allocated funding to expand services and provide training for law enforcement; however, it was also part of the Omnibus Crime Act, which increased funding for prisons. Therefore, while victim services grew so did the incarceration epidemic (see: 13th the documentary). In addition, the 1994 version of VAWA was critiqued for excluding many groups, including immigrants, Native Americans, and members of the LGBTQ community (Whittier, 2016). Subsequent reauthorizations have addressed many of these issues.

Socio-political forces and research efforts prompted the expansion of the concept of victimization. Victims of bullying, human trafficking, identity theft, and cyber crimes are now recognized. Moreover, greater levels of public discourse evolved around sexual harrassmet and sexual assault in the workplace as the result of the #MeToo movement. Originally introduced on social media in 2006 by Tarana Burke, a sexual assault survivor, the movement aimed to empower women through empathy and strength in numbers, by visibily demonstrating how many women have survived sexual harassment and sexual assault, especially in the workplace (MeToo, 2018). However, the movement did not garner the national spotlight until 2017, following the exposure of widespread allegations of sexual abuse by Harvey Weinstein, a high-powered Hollywood producer. Soon after, other high-profile media and political figures were exposed for similar behaviors; and, millions of women and men began to share their story via social media using the hashtag, #MeToo (MeToo, 2018). On February 24, 2019, a jury in New York found Harvey Weinstein guilty of two counts of sexual

Women's march protesters in San Francisco, January 20, 2018.

THE 21ST CENTURY TRANSFORMATION OF VICTIMOLOGY

assault (e.g., third degree rape and first degree sexual assault), capping a landmark trial of the #MeToo era (Arkin & Reiss, 2020).

In addition, changing socio-political sentiments during this era have called for the inclusion of all victims, including male victims of interpersonal violence, the LGBTQ population, the elderly, and persons affected by intersectionality (e.g., race, class, age, disability). This inclusion did not come without struggle. Cresnshaw (1991) and Allard (1991) noted that advocates and programs for victims of domestic violence and sexual assault often excluded the perspectives and needs of persons of color. Furthermore, while expanded services for child welfare benefited many children, it also created a burden on poor communities and/or communities of color (Roberts, 2002). Finally, this period saw victims' advocates struggle to address some unintended consequences, such as dual arrests. Dual arrests occur when both the victim and perpetrator of domestic violence are arrested in states that have mandatory arrest polices[2]. As a result, advocates pushed for the creation of primary aggressor laws, which mandates that law enforcement arrest the primary physical aggressor.

Finally, these past few decades have been affected by evolution of technology, both positively and negatively. The proliferation of social media, in particular, has played a significant role. For example, the Steubenville sexual assault case in 2012 involved cell phone recordings of an unconscious girl being sexually assaulted; however, the victim was unaware of the sexual assault until viewing social media sites that publicized the assault. Recordings of the assault, and of bystanders and classmates mocking and blaming the victim, were made public on social media sites. This case exposed the reality of victim blaming, but it also highlighted the role that technology can play in both fueling and verifying victimization. Technology

---

The Steubenville Sexual Assault Case

On the evening of August 11, 2012, at a high school party in Steubenville, Ohio an intoxicated teenage girl was sexually assaulted by two teenage boys; the boys were convicted. The investigation revealed more than the facts necessary to convict the perpetrators; it also brought to light the use of technology and social media to capture, distribute, and commentate on the assault, as well as taunt and blame the victim. This news clip describes many details of the case: http://abcnews.go.com/2020/video/steubenville-partys-18795344

---

[2] Mandatory arrest policies require an officer to make arrest when responding to a domestic violence call, if there is probable cause.

has increased access to victims, in cases such as cyber-bullying, stalking, and child pornography. However, it has also led to advances in evidence collection and preservation in criminal trials.

Legal Remedies and Rights

Two of the most significant federal initiatives that have been passed during this era are the 1994 Violence Against Women Act (VAWA) and the 2004 Crime Victims' Rights Act. In further support of crime victims, Senator Joe (D-Delaware) initiated legislation in 1990 for the enactment of a bill to address the crisis of violence against women (domestic violence, dating violence, sexual assault, and stalking). In 1994, President Bill Clinton signed the Violence Against Women Act (VAWA) (Title IV of the Violent Crime Control and Law Enforcement Act) in response to the needs of victims of domestic violence, dating violence, sexual assault, and stalking. The Act created funding and assistance to develop federal and state programs, policies, services, training, and research directed at ending violence against women. The Act has been reauthorized three times since 1994; over time, language was changed to address the needs of previously ignored populations (e.g., Native Americans, elders, the LGBTQ community, and persons with disabilities).

The 2004 Crime Victims' Rights Act, part of the 2004 Justice for All Act, enumerated specific rights to be afforded to all victims of federal crimes, including the right to be included in all criminal justice proceedings, the right to restitution, and the right to give a victim impact statement. The Act provides over $1.6 billion annually toward investigation and prosecution of violent crimes against women, imposed automatic and mandatory restitution on those convicted, and allowed civil redress in cases prosecutors chose to leave unprosecuted. The Act led to the establishment of the Office on Violence Against Women (OVW) within the Department of Justice. In 2013, VAWA extended protections to same-sex couples and added provisions allowing battered undocumented immigrants to claim temporary visas. In 2019, new provisions were added to protect transgender victims and to ban individuals convicted of domestic abuse from purchasing firearms.

Other less publicized but equally important initiatives include The 1990 Victims of Child Abuse Act incorporated reforms to make the federal criminal justice system less traumatic for child victims; the Identity Theft and Deterrence Act of 1998 made identity theft a federal crime; and the Victims of Trafficking and Violence Protection Act of 2000 created the framework for the federal response to human trafficking. Other federal legislative initiatives passed during this time strengthened laws to reduce drunk driving, campus sexual assault, and child abduction[3].

---

[3] For a comprehensive list of federal initiatives see the National Center for Victims of Crime, Landmarks in victims' rights and services: https://victimsofcrime.org/docs/ncvrw2013/2013ncvrw_5_landmarks.pdf?sfvrsn=0)

In addition to federal initiatives, a number of state laws were enacted to expand victims rights and services. By 1993, all states enacted anti-stalking legislation, and many states including Connecticut, Maine, Massachusetts, New Hampshire, and New Jersey have enacted laws regarding primary aggressors (Office of Legislative Research, 2015). States also increased efforts to reduce drunk driving. All 50 states have set legal limits for driving under the influence or while impaired to be .08% blood alcohol concentration (BAC) (Department of Motor Vehicles, 2017); as a result, 2015 data reveal that nearly 1.1 million drivers were arrested for driving under the influence of alcohol or narcotics (Department of Justice, 2016). And, as of 2014, 37 states have passed new human trafficking laws (Polaris Project, 2014).

Additionally, an important case decided by the U.S. Supreme Court advanced the collective rights of victims. In *Payne* v. *Tennessee* (501 U.S. 808), the Court ruled that the prosecution, in homicide cases, must be allowed to submit evidence regarding the "assessment of the harm caused by the defendant"; therefore, victim impact statements by survivors of the homicide victim are admissible at sentencing.

Victim Services

Following the passage of VAWA in 1994 services for victims of crime rapidly expanded. The National Network to End Domestic Violence (2016) estimates that there are currently 1,894 domestic violence programs in the U.S. These programs offer individual/group counseling, medical attention, legal/criminal advocacy, victim assistance, emergency shelter, casework assistance, and education. Many of these programs are also involved in advocating for victims in public policy (National Network to End Domestic Violence, 2016). Sexual assault programming is also funded in every state through the Office on Violence Against Women (OVM) Sexual Assault Services Program (SASP); services include intervention and advocacy services, especially accompaniment when victims interact with the medical and criminal justice systems. In addition, child maltreatment programs expanded from state-run intervention programs to community-based family and child treatment and intervention programs (Department of Health and Human Service, Children's Bureau). Currently, every state utilizes community-based programs to implement services such as parent education, parent support groups, family resource centers, and school-based programs[4].

Outreach and intervention programs, and community education programs, have also expanded to reach underserved victims that have been previously overlooked, such as trafficking victims, victims who are also military personnel, victims on college campuses, elderly victims, immigrants who are victimized, and victims

---

[4] For more information about child abuse and neglect prevention programs see the Department of Health and Human Services, Children's Bureau.

of financial crimes. For example, the Clery Act requires that all college campuses record and report acts of victimization. This Act also ensures that campuses provide prevention education and access to counseling and legal services, and ensure that disciplinary proceedings are conducted by trained personnel. The federal government has also created protections for legal and undocumented immigrants who have been victims of a crime. In the 2000 Reauthorization of The Violence Against Women Act (VAWA), Congress created two new categories of visas for undocumented immigrants who are victims of crime. The first was the U-visa which provides temporary legal (nonimmigrant) status, work authorization to the victims and certain members of their families, and opportunities to obtain permanent residency status (green cards) after three years under certain conditions. Congress authorized that the visa can be granted yearly for up to 10,000 victims of eligible crime; if the cap is reached before all U nonimmigrant petitions have been adjudicated, a waiting list is created. The second visa created was the T visa, which was specifically for undocumented immigrants who are victims of a severe form of trafficking in persons. The T visa also allows victims to remain in the United States and assist federal authorities in the investigation and prosecution of human trafficking cases.

Federal and state mandates also created court services such as victim compensation programs, victim impact statements, and restitution programs (National Center for Victims of Crime, 2012). Victim compensation programs could now reimburse victims (and in some instances family members) for out-of-pocket expenses, such as medical and dental expenses, funeral costs, counseling costs, and lost wages that were the direct result of their victimization. Victim impact statements afford victims the opportunity to present an oral or written statement to the court during the sentencing hearing that explained how the crime impacted them. Finally, courts could now order an offender to pay restitution directly to his or her victim to cover any damanges they may have incurred. In one-third of the states, restitution can be ordered to cover medical, counseling, therapy, or prescription charges. It can also be used to cover lost wages, crime scene cleanup, and lost or damaged property. It differs from compensation in that the costs come directly from the offender, rather than the state. (*More about these programs will be discussed in chapter 8 and 10.*)

In addition, Trauma-Informed Approaches (TIAs) were prioritized after research uncovered that trauma can trigger biologically-driven survival strategies within a person, creating them to respond in a manner that may seem odd (e.g., a sexual assault victim laughing during an interview or a victim who does not "fight back"). TIAs recognize that trauma affects how victims see themselves and react to their victimization. The Office of Victims of Crime states that TIAs reduce the stress on victims, reduce the risk of advocates and law enforcement re-traumatizing the victim, and increase cooperation with law enforcement[5].

Service providers were forced to recognize the need to deliver culturally competent services. The Office for Victims of Crime sponsored the development and implementation of a cultural competence assessment tool (Anand & Rious, 1999) for victim services providers and offered training to increase cultural competency among service providers. In addition, states recognized the need for victim service providers to co-advocate for victims with cultural organizations (e.g., immigrant rights groups, LGBTQ advocacy groups). As a result, services such as multilingual counseling, court advocacy, and hotlines emerged, as did counseling that recognized that impact of intersectional issues such as race, immigration status, class, and sexuality.

The field also recognized the need to increase technological efforts to serve victims. Hotlines were one of the first technology-based services to be introduced and were utilized at both the national and local levels. The National Domestic Violence Hotline reported that between its inception in 1996 and 2016, it has received more than 20 million calls. In 1994, the Victim Information and Notification Everyday (VINE) system was created so that victims could call a toll-free number to obtain information about their cases and receive advance notice about inmates' release schedules. Today, VINE is available in 48 states. Advocates and allied professionals across the nation continue to utilize technology every day to facilitate professional development and advance the field of victim services, as well as to expand community education on issues related to crime victims.

---

[5] Office for Victims of Crime, Training and Technical Assistance Center: https://www.ovcttac.gov/taskforceguide/eguide/4-supporting-victims/41-using-a-trauma-informed-approach/

Conclusion

This chapter presented an overview of legal remedies, rights, and services for U.S. victims of crime, from the Revolutionary Era through the mid-21st Century. The discussion was not meant to be exhaustive; rather, it was meant to summarize the evolution of responses to victims of crime. In addition, the chapter sought to impress upon the reader two important realities. First, the creation of services has always been connected to legal remedies and rights; and second, the socio-political climate of the period similarly shaped official responses to victims of crime. As such the needs of certain victims, namely White, middle-class victims, were prioritized. However, the journey has not yet been completed. The victims' rights movement must continue to ensure that the rights of *all* victims are valued, and their needs are equally met.

© Uncle Leo/Shutterstock.com

Discussion Questions

1. How are laws a reflection of social sentiments? Use at least two examples of social movements that preceded the creation of laws that impacted victims of crime.
2. Laws are often enacted after highly publicized media cases spark public outrage. Discuss an example of a highly publicized media case that resulted in the passage of a new law. Also discuss how this case impacted the development of related services.
3. The Victims' Rights Movement of the 1970s and 1980s was spurred by grassroots efforts in many sectors. Present three examples of grassroots efforts that improved official responses to victims of crime.

4. The evolution of responses to victims of crime in the United States has been plagued by discriminatory official and public sentiment. Explain how issues of racism, classism, sexism or other prejudices have impacted responses to victims of crime.

References

Allard, S. A. (1991). Rethinking battered woman syndrome: A Black feminist perspective. *UCLA Women's Law Journal, 1*, 191.

Anand, R. & Rious, S. (1999). *Cultural competence assessment tool for victim service providers.* Retrieved from: http://victimsofcrime.org/docs/Information%20 Clearinghouse/Cultural%20Competence%20Assessment%20Tool%20for%20 Victim%20Service%20Providers.pdf? sfvrsn=0

Arkin, D., & Reiss, A. (2020, February 24). Harvey Weinstein found guilty of rape but acquitted of top criminal charges. Retrieved from: Beccaria, C. (2009). *On crimes and punishments and other writings.* Toronto: University of Toronto Press.

Beloof, D.E. (2012). *Victims' rights: A documentary and reference guide.* ABC–CLIO.

Block, (2006). *Rape and sexual power in early America.* Chapel Hill, NC: Univeristy of North Carolina Press.

Boylan, A. (1990). Women and politics in the era before Seneca Falls. *Journal of the Early Republic, 10*(3), 363–382. doi:10.2307/3123393

Bowman, C. G., & Altman, B. (2002). Wife murder in Chicago: 1910–1930. *Cornell Law Faculty Publications.* Paper 132. Retrieved from: http://scholarship.law.cornell.edu/facpub/132

Brownmiller, S. (1976) (2013 reprint). *Against our will: Men, women and rape.* New York: Open Road Media.

Burt, M. R. (1980). Cultural myths and supports for rape. *Journal of Personality and Social Psychology, 38*(2), 217-230.

Cardenas, J. (1986). The crime victim in the prosecutorial process. *Harvard Journal of Law & Public Policy, 9*, 357-359.

Child Welfare League of America. *Timeline of major child welfare legislation.* Retrieved from: http://www.cwla.org/wp- content/uploads/2014/05/TimelineOfMajorChildWelfareLegislation.pdf

Child Welfare Information Gateway. (2015). Retrieved from: https://www.childwelfare.gov/pubPDFs/majorfedlegis.pdf

Child Welfare Information Gateway. (2017). *Child maltreatment prevention: Past, present, and future.* Washington, DC: U.S. Department of Health and Human Services, Children's Bureau.

Clery Center. (2019). *At the heart of campus safety*. Retrieved from: https://clerycenter.org

Crenshaw, K. (1991). Mapping the margins: Intersectionality, identity politics, and violence against women of color. *Stanford Law Review, 43*(6), 1241–1299.

Darene, W., & Stein (2010). *History of the crime victims' rights movement in the United States*. Retrieved from https://ce4less.com/Tests/Materials/E048R-Materials.pdf

Department of Motor Vehicles. (2017). *DUI & DWI*. Retrieved from: http://www.dmv.org/automotive-law/dui.php

Dubber, M. D. (2002). *Victims in the war on crime: The use and abuse of victims' rights*. New York: New York University Press.

Federal Bureau of Investigation. (2015). *Crime in the United States*.

Evans, W. N., Doreen N., & John D. G.. (1991). General deterrence of drunk driving: evaluation of recent American policies. *Risk Analysis, 11*(2), 279-289.

Fisher, B. S., Cullen, F. T., & Turner, M. G. (2000). *The Sexual Victimization of College Women*. Research Report.

Friedan, B. (1963). *The feminine mystique*. (Reprint 1983). New York: DeU.

Frisch, L. A. (1992). Research that succeeds, policies that fail. *Journal of Criminal Law & Criminology, 83*(1), 209-216.

Garcia, V. (2003). Difference in the police department: Women, policing, and doing gender. *Journal of Contemporary Criminal Justice,19*(3), 330-344.

Grossberg, M. (1988). *Governing the hearth: Law and the family in nineteenth-century America*. Charlotte, NC: University of North Carolina Press.

Hasday, J. E. (2000). Contest and consent: A legal history of marital rape. *California Law Review, 88*(5), 1373-1505.

Henderson, L. (1985).*The wrongs of victim's rights*. [Scholarly Works. Paper 871]. http://scholars.law.unlv.edu/facpub/871

History of the battered women's movement. Retrieved from: http://www.icadvinc.org/what-is-domestic-violence/history-of-battered-womens-movement/#slau

Hook, M., & Seymour, A. (2004). *A retrospective of the 1982 President's Task Force on Victims of Crime*. Retrieved from: https://www.ncjrs.gov/ovc_archives/ncvrw/2005/pg4d.html

Jimenez, J., Mayers Pasztor, E., Chambers, R. C., & Fujii, C. P. (2014). *Social policy and social change: Toward the creation of social and economic justice*. Thousand Oaks, CA: SAGE Publishing.

Kann, M. E. (1999). *The gendering of American politics: Founding mothers, founding fathers, and political patriarchy*. ABC-CLIO.

Kello, C. L. (1987). Rape shield laws – Is it time for reinforcement. *University of Michigan Journal of Law Reform, 21*(1-2), 317-354.

THE 21ST CENTURY TRANSFORMATION OF VICTIMOLOGY

Larson, J. E. (1997). Even a worm will turn at last: Rape reform in late nineteenth-Century America. *Yale Journal of Law & the Humanities, 9*(1), 1-73.

Lee, S. (2019, June). *Crime victim awareness and assistance through the decades.* Washington, DC: U.S. Department of Justice, National Institute of Justice.

Lentz, S. A. (1999). Revisiting the rule of thumb: An overview of the history of wife abuse. *Women & Criminal Justice, 10*(2), 9-27.

Levin, B. (2002). From slavery to hate crime laws: The emergence of race and status- based protection in American criminal law. *Journal of Social Issues, 58*(2), 227-245.

Martin, D. (1976). *Battered wives* (1981 reprint). Volcano, CA: Volcano Press.

Masson, M. E. (1997). The women's Christian temperance union 1874–1898: Combating domestic violence. *William & Mary Journal of Women and the Law, 3*(1), 163-188. Retrievedfrom: http://scholarship.law.wm.edu/wmjowl/vol3/iss1/7

McGowan, B. G. (2005). Historical evolution of child welfare services. *Child welfare for the twenty-first century: A handbook of practices, policies, and programs.* New York: Columbia Univesity Press.

MeToo. (2018). *History and vision.* Retrieved from: https://metoomvmt.org

Meyers, J. E. B. (2008–2009). A short history of child protection in America. *Family Law Quarterly, 42*(3), 449-464.

Miller, E. B. A. (2010). *Moving to the head of the river: The early years of the U.S. Battered Women's Movement.* Dissertation. University of Kansas.

Mothers Against Drunk Driving. (2019). *MADD: No more victims.* Retrieved from: https://www.madd.org

Morris, D. T. (1992). Slaves and the rules of evidence in criminal trials. Symposium on the law of slavery: Criminal and civil law of slavery, *Chicago Kent Law Review, 68,* 1209-1240.

National Center for Victims of Crime (2012). *Crime victim compensation.* Retrieved from: http://victimsofcrime.org/help-for-crime-victims/get-help-bulletins-for-crime-victims/crime-victim-compensation

National Network to End Domestic Violence. (2016). *Domestic violence counts 2015.* Retrieved from: http://nnedv.org/downloads/Census/DVCounts2015/DVCounts15_NatlReport.compressed.pdf

National Organization of Parents of Murdered Children, Inc. (2018). *History of POMC.* Retrieved from: https://www.pomc.com/index.html

National Crime Victims Rights Week. (2016). *Section 5: Landmarks in victim's rights and services.* Retrieved from: https://www.ncjrs.gov/ovc_archives/ncvrw/2016/pdf/2016NCVRW_5_Landmark s_FINAL-508.pdf

Oberman, M. (1994). Turning girls into women: Re-evaluating modern statutory rape law. *The Journal of Criminal Law and Criminology,*1, 15–79.

Office of Legislative Research. (2015). *Primary aggressor laws in Connecticut and neighboring states.* Retrieved from: https://www.cga.ct.gov/2015/rpt/pdf/2015-R- 0302.pdf

Pleck, E. H. (1987). *Domestic tyranny: The making of American social policy against family violence from colonial times to the present.* Chicago: University of Illinois Press.

Polaris Project. (2017). *State ratings on human trafficking laws, September* 2014. Retrieved from: https://polarisproject.org/resources/2014-state-ratings-human-trafficking-laws

Roberts, D. (2002). *Shattered bonds: The color of child welfare.* New York: Basic Civitas Books.

Robbins, K. (1999). No-drop prosecution of domestic violence: Just good policy, or equal protection mandate? *Stanford Law Review, 52*(1), 205-233.

Roth, M. P. (2010). *Crime and punishment: A history of the criminal justice system.* Boston: Cengage Learning.

Ross, J. M. (2015). *Making marital rape visible: A history of American legal and social movements criminalizing rape in marriage.* Dissertation. The University of Nebraska-Lincoln.

Rutherford, A., & McKay, J. (2013). From social purity to women's liberation: A history of violence against women in the United States. In J. A. Sigal and F. L. Denmark (eds.), *Violence against girls and women: International perspective* (Vol. 1), (pp.5–20). Santa Barbara, CA: Praeger.

Schechter, S. (1982). *Women and male violence: The visions and struggles of the battered women's movement.* Boston: South End Press.

Siegel, R. B. (1995). The rule of love: Wife beating as prerogative and privacy. *Yale Law Journal, 105*(8), 2117-2208.

Stutzman, M. (2009). *Rape in the American civil war: Race, class, and gender in the case of Harriet McKinley and Perry Pierson.* Retrieved from: http://www.albany.edu/womensstudies/journal/2009/stutzman.html

Thomas, M. P. (1972). Child abuse and neglect Part I—Historical overview, legal matrix, and social perspectives. *NCL Review, 50*(2), 293-349.

Tobolowsky, P. M., Beloof, D. E., Gaboury, M. T., Jackson, A. L., & Blackburn, A. G. (2016). *Crime victim rights and remedies.* Charlotte: Carolina University Press.

Tucker D. J. (2005). *The grassroots beginnings of the victims' rights movement.* Retrieved from: https://www.lclark.edu/live/files/6453-the-grassroots-beginnings- of-the-victims-rights

Walker, S., Spohn, C., & DeLone, M. (2012). *The color of justice: Race, ethnicity, and crime in America.* Boston: Cengage Learning.

Whittier, N. (2016). Carceral and intersectional feminism in Congress: The Violence Against Women Act, discourse, and policy. *Gender & Society, 30*(5), 791–818.

Wisconsin Department of Justice. (2016). *Wisconsin's history and the crime victims rights movement.* Retrieved from: https://docs.legis.wisconsin.gov/misc/lc/study/2016/1492/030_november_14_2016_9_00_a_m_room_411_south/1_karofsky_ppt

Young & Stein. (2005). *The history of the crimes victims movement in the United States.* Retrieved from https://www.ncjrs.gov/ovc_archives/ncvrw/2005/pdf/historyofcrime.pdf

SECTION II

THE IMPACT OF LAW AND POLITICS ON CRIME VICTIMS

Landmark Legislation, Cases, and Remedies

© Keith Homan/Shutterstock.com

Objectives

Upon completion of this chapter, you will be able to:

- discuss the evolution of responses to victims of crime, including lawmaking and policy development,
- summarize key recommendations from the President's Task Force on Victims of Crime, and
- discuss landmark legislation, such as the Victims of Crime Act (VOCA), the Violence Against Women Act (VAWA), the Crime Victims' Rights Act (CVRA), and explain how those laws expanded victims' rights and services.

Introduction

Chapter four provided a historical overview of responses to victims of crime, including lawmaking and policy development and the evolution of victims' rights and services in the United States. However, it did not provide a detailed explanation of the most significant legislative and policy advances. As such, this chapter examines these major milestones that have shaped the criminal justice system's responses to victims of crime.

The chapter begins with the President's Task Force on Victims of Crime and summarizes the recommendations it forwarded, and explains how their findings laid the foundation for landmark legislaton, including the Victims of Crime Act (VOCA), the Violence Against Women Act (VAWA), the Crime Victims' Rights Act (CVRA). The chapter also addresses landmark cases such as *Thurman v. Torrington* and *Payne v. Tennessee*, as well as other legal remedies that have since been adopted at the federal level.

The President's Task Force on Victims of Crime

In response to the growing strength of the women's and victims' rights movements, along with the access to new data from the National Crime Victimization Survey that revealed the nature and scope of crime victimization in the United States, President Ronald Reagan assembled a Task Force to examine the role of the victim in the criminal justice system. The Task Force was comprised of persons from all over the country who were directly or indirectly involved in the victims' rights movement. They represented varying levels within the criminal justice system, the victims' services community, and law- and policy-makers. The members interviewed victims, reviewed state policies, reviewed research, held public meetings, and met with professionals who work with victims or the topic of victimization, such as persons in the criminal justice system, victims' services, law, medicine, mental health, research, the press. and politicians.

The Task Force found that crime victims were often ignored, mistreated, or blamed; and were often excluded from the process and retraumatized by those who were supposed to assist them. Consequently, many victims harbored feelings of resentment and distrust of the justice system, and vowed to never seek the assistance of the system again. The Task Force recognized that not only was the treatment of crime victims to be unjust, it was also counterproductive to the mission of our justice system. They acknowledged that the criminal justice system is dependent upon the cooperation of citizens to report crime to the authorities, and then to assist them in their investigation. Without the help of crime victims, the system can not hold offender's accountable, which in turn enables crime to go unchecked. Thus, the safety and well-being of entire communities is jeopardized.

In their final report, the Task Force recommended a series of federal- and state-level legislative actions and modifications to the criminal justice system, as well as recommendations to other organizations in the community that interact with victims of crime (e.g., hospitals, churches, schools) in order to assist victims of crime more effectively. They also proposed that the Sixth Amendment to the U.S. Constitution be modified to extend equal protection to victims of crime during judicial proceedings as are afforded to the accused. Given the length of this report, the following discussion will focus on the Task Force's recommendations for federal

"Victims have discovered that they are treated as appendages of a system appallingly out of balance. They have learned that somewhere along the way, the system has lost track of the simple truth that it is supposed to be fair and to protect those who obey the law while punishing those who break it. Somewhere along the way, the system began to serve lawyers and judges and defendants, treating the victim with institutionalized disinterest."
— PRESIDENT REAGAN'S TASK FORCE ON VICTIMS OF CRIME (DECEMBER 1982)

and state actions, and their proposal for a Constitutional Amendment to ensure victims' rights. Readers are encouraged to read the Task Force's entire report, and may download a copy from the U.S. Department of Justice, Office for Victims of Crime website.

Victim Related Recommendations for Federal and State Actions

In their report the Task Force put forth 12 recommendations for federal and state action; they are as follows:

Legislation should be proposed and enacted to address victims and witnesses who are not made public or available to the defense, absent a clear need as determined by the court.

Legislation should be proposed and enacted to ensure that designated victim counseling is legally privileged and not subject to defense discovery or subpoena.

Legislation should be proposed and enacted to ensure that hearsay is admissible and sufficient in preliminary hearings, so that victims need not testify in person.

Legislation should be proposed and enacted to amend the bail laws (see the Presidents' Task Force final recommendations for a description of the six bail related recommendations).

Legislation should be proposed and enacted to abolish the exclusionary rule as it applies to Fourth Amendment issues.

Legislation should be proposed and enacted to open parole release hearings to the public.

Legislation should be proposed and enacted to abolish parole and limit judicial discretion in sentencing.

Legislation should be proposed and enacted to require that school officials report violent offenses against students or teachers, or the possession of weapons or narcotics on school grounds. The knowing failure to make such a report to the police, or deterring others from doing so, should be designated a misdemeanor.

Legislation should be proposed and enacted to make available to businesses and organizations the sexual assault, child molestation, and pornography arrest records of prospective and present employees whose work will bring them in regular contact with children.

Legislation should be proposed and enacted to accomplish the following:
    a. Require victim impact statements at sentencing;
    b. Provide for the protection of victims and witnesses from intimidation;
    c. Require restitution in all cases, unless the court provides specific reasons for failing to require it;
    d. Develop and implement guidelines for the fair treatment of crime victims and witnesses; and
    e. Prohibit a criminal from making any profit from the sale of the story of his crime. Any proceeds should be used to provide full restitution to his victims, pay the expenses of his prosecution, and finally, assist the crime victim compensation fund.

Legislation should be proposed and enacted to establish or expand employee assistance programs for victims of crime employed by government.

Legislation should be proposed and enacted to ensure that sexual assault victims are not required to assume the cost of physical examinations and materials used to obtain evidence.

In sum, these twelve recommendations enumerated the specific rights every victim of crime should be afforded when interacting with the criminal justice system, whether at the state or federal levels. At the heart of this set of recommendations is an aspiration that every victim will be treated with the fairness, dignity, and respect, that he or she deserves.

The Task Force also laid out additional recommendations that Congress enact legislation to fund specific types of programs and/or selected areas for further study. These recommendations include: to provide federal funding to assist state crime victim compensation programs; to provide federal funding to assist victim/ witness assistance agencies that provide comprehensive services (regardless of whether progam is publically or privately funded); to establish a federally based resource center for victim and witness assistance; to establish a task force to specifically study the intimate partner and family violence, as well as abuse of the elderly, and to review and evaluate the national, state, and local efforts to combat such violence; to commission a study to evaluate the juvenile justice system from the perspective of the victims; and to commission a study to address how to effectively hold state parole board officials accountable when releasing dangerous criminals back into the community.

A Constitutional Amendment

One of the most notable recommendations of the Task Force was the augmentation of the Sixth Amendment of the U.S. Constitution. The Sixth Amendment addresses the rights afforded to defendants in all criminal prosecutions. The Task Force recommended that the final line of the Amendment also address the rights of victims. The Amendment as proposed by the task force with the recommended augmentation in the last line (in bold) is provided in Figure 5.1.

Despite numerous efforts and multiple adjustments to the language, this Amendment was never adopted. The issue of a Constitutional provision sparked national debate. Proponents of the Amendment note that the current system is dismissive of the rights of crime victims. The Constitution only provides protection for criminals and denies protections for victims. Some advocates and legislators assert that a Federal Amendment would be symbolic; it would serve to officially recognize the plight and worth of crime victims. In addition, proponents have noted that many states have constitutional provisions; however, the provisions vary

© Getty Images, David Buresh

President's Task force on Victims of Crime Denver, Colorado, October 05, 1982

In all criminal prosecutions the accused shall enjoy the right to a speedy and public trial, by an impartial jury of the State and district wherein the crime shall have been committed, which district shall have been previously ascertained by law, and to be informed of the nature and cause of the accusation; to be confronted with the witnesses against him; to have compulsory process for obtaining witnesses in his favor and to have the Assistance of Counsel for his defense. **Likewise, the victim, in every criminal prosecution shall have the right to be present and to be heard at all critical stages of judicial proceedings.**

FIGURE 5.1 Sixth Amendment of the U.S. Constitution

in terms of intensity and protections for victims. A federal amendment would provide uniformity to victims' rights, ensuring that all victims would be entitled to the same set of rights.

Opponents of the inclusion of victims' rights in the Constitution note that the Framers of the Constitution purposefully created an imbalance between the rights of the accused and the rights of the victims, by favoring the rights of the accused (Stevens, 2000). They were aware that they needed to tip the power in favor of the defendant, at least procedurally, as all other power would be intrinsically with the State. For example, government interests represented by the prosecutor would be better positioned, given its access to more resources. Therefore, if rights are officially granted to the victims, who are represented by the State, then the State (the government) will have an even greater advantage. Furthermore, the American Civil Liberties Union has argued that due process protections under the Constitution do not exist to protect the guilty from punishment, but rather the innocent from arrest and imprisonment. Therefore, there is no need for a federal Amendment to promote the rights of victims, as they are not at risk for being officially denied their liberty.

While the adoption of a federal Victims' Right Amendment has not yet been achieved, the debate it generated gave rise to the creation and adoption of constitutional provisions for victims of crime at the state-level. These laws will be discussed later in the chapter.

Key Federal Victims' Rights Legislation

In the wake of the release of the Task Force's report and subsequent recommendations, numerous state and federal laws were passed to address the needs of crime victims, and to and improve official responses to victims of crime. Much of this legislation extends beyond what can be covered in this discussion. However, this section highlights the most significant federal legislation that addresses victims of crime. While the chart below presents a list of all of the major federal victim-focused initiatives that have been enacted over the past forty years, three of these laws will be discussed in greater detail.

Key Federal Victims' Rights Legislation	
1974	Child Abuse Prevention and Treatment Act
1980	Parental Kidnapping Prevention Act
1982	Victim and Witness Protection Act
1982	Missing Children's Act
1984	**Victims of Crime Act**
1984	Justice Assistance Act
1984	Missing Children's Assistance Act
1984	Family Violence Prevention and Services Act
1985	Children's Justice Act
1988	Drunk Driving Prevention Act
1990	Hate Crime Statistics Act

> **Key Federal Victims' Rights Legislation (Continued)**
>
> 1990 Victims of Child Abuse Act
> 1990 Victims' Rights and Restitution Act
> 1990 National Child Search Assistance Act
> 1992 Battered Women's Testimony Act
> 1994 Violent Crime Control and Law Enforcement Act
> 1994 Jacob Wetterling Crimes Against Children and Sexually Violent Offender Registration Act
> **1994 Violence Against Women Act**
> 1996 Community Notification Act ("Megan's Law")
> 1996 Antiterrorism and Effective Death Penalty Act
> 1996 Mandatory Victims' Restitution Act
> 1997 Victims' Rights Clarification Act
> 1998 Crime Victims with Disabilities Awareness Act
> 1998 Identity Theft and Deterrence Act
> 2000 Trafficking Victims Protection Act
> 2001 Air Transportation Safety and System Stabilization Act (established September 11th Victim Compensation Fund)
> 2002 National Association of VOCA Administrators
> 2003 PROTECT Act ("Amber Alert" law)
> 2003 Prison Rape Elimination Act
> 2003 Fair and Accurate Credit Transactions Act
> **2004 Justice For All Act,** including Title I *The Scott Campbell, Stephanie Roper, Wendy Preston, Louarna Gillis, and Nila Lynn Crime Victims' Rights Act*
> 2005 Matthew Shepard and James Byrd, Jr.. Hate Crimes Prevention Act
> 2006 Adam Walsh Child Protection and Safety Act
> 2008 Identity Theft and Restitution Act
> 2010 Tribal Law and Order Act
>
> For more information see: https://victimsofcrime.org/docs/ncvr-w2013/2013ncvrw_5_landmarks.pdf?sfvrsn=0

Victims of Crime Act (VOCA) of 1984

The Victims of Crime Act of 1984, originally sponsored by Rep. Peter W. Rodino Jr. (NJ-D) was established to help compensate victims of crime and to support victim services. The Act Establishes within the Treasury the Crime Victims Fund and requires that the Fund consist of: (1) most fines collected in Federal criminal cases; (2) penalty assessments on convicted persons; and (3) proceeds of all forfeitures (appearance bonds, bail bonds and collateral) in Federal criminal cases. These funds are then distributed to the States to support victims of crime. This can include financial aid for crime assistance programs, restitution, or support for other victim's services. In 1988, the Victims of Crime Act was amended to create the Office for Victims of Crime (OVC) within the Department of Justice. The mission of OVC is to provide aid and promote justice for victims. Given its charge, OVC was then made responsible for the management of the Crime Victims Fund.

States can apply each year for VOCA grants to assist with victim compensation. If awarded, the States can then distribute the funds to victims to reimburse them for medical expenses (including mental health counseling), loss of wages, and funeral expenses that were the direct result of the crime. However, in order to qualify for these funds, VOCA stipulates the victim must report the crime to law enforcement within a specific timeframe, and if other financial resources are available (e.g., private insurance), compensation is only paid to the extent that the collateral resources does not cover the losses. VOCA also stipulates that the distribution of funds can not cannot discriminate against nonresident citizens.

States can also apply each year for a VOCA grant for the financial support of crime assistance programs they offer. This includes, but is not limited to crisis intervention, counseling, emergency shelter, criminal justice advocacy, and emergency transportation. However, these funds may only be used for direct services to crime victims, therefore States are prohibited from using any of the funds for crime prevention initiatives.

VOCA also established the Children's Justice Act in 1985. Each year VOCA designates the first $10 million dollars of the fund to fund grants that support the investigation and prosecution of child abuse and neglect cases, as well to projects administered by nonprofit organizations that provide services to these victims.

Violence Against Women Act (VAWA) of 1994

In 1994, Senators Joe Biden Jr. (DE-D) and Orrin Hatch (UT-R) co-sponsored The Violence Against Women Act (VAWA) to address the severity of crimes being committed against women, and improve criminal justice and community-based responses to victims of domestic violence. The Act aimed to improve the investigation and prosecution of these crimes by equipping criminal justice agents with the resources and training, as well as support programs that offered assistance to these victims. The ACT has since been reauthorized three times—in 2000, 2005, and 2013 (Office on Violence against Women [OVW], 2016). These reauthorizations included revised language and provisions that enhanced services for victims of sexual assault, dating violence, and stalking. In addition, legal protections have been enhanced for all victims, but especially for victims who are presented with barriers to accessing services because of their race, ethnicity, immigration status, age, disability, sexual orientation, or gender identity (OVW, 2016).

In 1995, the Office on Violence against Women (OVW) was created within the Department of Justice, to administer financial and technical assistance to communities across the country that are developing programs, policies, and practices aimed at ending violence against women (OVW, 2016). According to OVW, funding is currently awarded to local, state, and tribal governments; courts; nonprofit organizations; community-based organizations; secondary schools; institutions of higher education; and state and tribal coalitions. Funds are used to develop responses to violence through direct services, crisis intervention, transitional housing, legal assistance to victims, court improvement, and training for law enforcement and courts. In addition to work with all victims, fund recipients are expected to work directly with special populations, such as the elderly, persons with disabilities, college students, teens, and culturally and linguistically specific populations. To date OVW has awarded more than $6 billion in grants and agreements to address violence against women.

Crime Victims' Right Act (CVRA) of 2004

The Crime Victims' Rights Act (CVRA) of 2004 was part of the Justice for All Act. The Justice for All Act was comprised for four sections related to crime victims and the criminal justice process. Some of the objectives of the Act were to protect crime victims' rights, eliminate the substantial backlog of DNA samples collected from crime scenes and convicted offenders, and improve and expand the DNA testing capacity of federal, state, and local crime laboratories (OVC, 2006).

The first section of the Act enumerated eight specific rights crime victims have in federal proceedings, and outlined the mechanisms to assert and enforce those rights. These rights include:

The right to be reasonably protected from the accused.

The right to reasonable, accurate, and timely notice of any public court proceeding or any parole proceeding involving the crime, or of any release or escape of the accused.

The right not to be excluded from any such public court proceeding, unless the court, after receiving clear and convincing evidence, determines that testimony by the victim would be materially altered if the victim heard other testimony at that proceeding.

The right to be reasonably heard at any public proceeding in the district court involving release, plea, sentencing, or any parole proceeding.

The reasonable right to confer with the attorney for the Government in the case.

The right to full and timely restitution as provided in law.

The right to proceedings free from unreasonable delay.

The right to be treated with fairness and with respect for the victim's dignity and privacy.

In addition to the establishment of these rights for victims of crime in federal proceedings, the Act also authorized funding for grants to state, tribal, and local criminal justice agencies, as well as qualified public and private organizations, to develop, establish, and maintain programs for the enforcement of crime victims' rights; as well as for technical assistance and training to state and tribal jurisdictions that seek to develop innovative crime victims' rights laws and compliance measures to enforce them (OVC, 2016). To date, Congress has not yet appropriated any of these funds.

Title IX

As part of the Education Act Amendments of 1972, Title IX was a response to growing concern about the problem of sex discrimination in educational programs. "Congress wanted both to avoid the use of federal resources to support discriminatory practices and to provide individual citizens effective protection against those practices (Ruth, 1996, p. 190). Title IX is a federal civil rights law passed in 1972 that prohibits discrimination on the basis of sex in education programs and activities. The law states: "No person in the United States shall, on the basis of sex, be excluded from participation in, be denied the benefits of, or be subjected to discrimination under any education program or activity receiving federal financial assistance." Title IX applies to gender equity provisions in the following areas: Access to Higher Education, Career Education, Education for Pregnant and Parenting Students, Employment, Learning Environment, Math and Science, Sexual Harassment, Standardized Testing, and Technology.

Title IX is most often discussed in terms of victimization because of its provisions on sexual harassment, which has come to include sexual violence. In the late 1990s two events changed how sexual harassment in educational settings was viewed and addressed (titleix.info). On March 13, 1997 (updated in 2001) the Office of Civil Rights (OVC) issued "Sexual Harassment Guidance: Harassment of Students by School Employees, Other Students, or Third Parties." The following year, in *Davis v. Monroe County Board of Education*, the Supreme Court held that students can sue for student-on-student sexual harassment under Title IX and schools are liable for money damages if: (1) the harassment is so severe, pervasive, and offensive that it interferes with the victim's educational environment; and (2) the school knows about the harassment and its response is clearly unreasonable under the circumstances.

As a result of the Supreme Court decision, evolving legislation, and research in the early 2000s that found that sexual harassment and assault was widespread in high schools and on college campuses (Robers, Zhang, Truman, & Snyder, 2010; Fischer, Cullen, & Turner, 2000), the federal government took further action. The Office for Civil Rights at the U.S. Department of Education issued a Dear Colleague

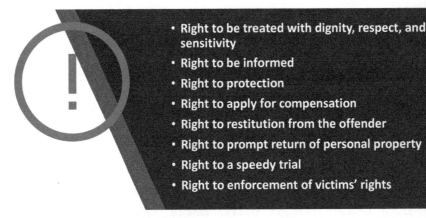

- Right to be treated with dignity, respect, and sensitivity
- Right to be informed
- Right to protection
- Right to apply for compensation
- Right to restitution from the offender
- Right to prompt return of personal property
- Right to a speedy trial
- Right to enforcement of victims' rights

FIGURE 5.2 Rights of Victims of Crime

Letter (DCL) on Sexual Violence, on April 4, 2011. The DCL was issued to "explain that the requirements of Title IX cover sexual violence and to remind schools of their responsibilities to take immediate and effective steps to respond to sexual violence" (Dear Colleague Letter Fact Sheet, 2011). A summary of the guidelines are outlined in the figure below.

Landmark cases

According to Reitler (2010) landmark cases include cases that establish new legal principles or change existing law and have impacted the evolution of the victims' rights movement (p. 515). These cases have changed the enforcement of laws that protect victims, and considered the participation of victims in the criminal process. Below are some of the most influential cases of the victims' rights movement.

Thurman v. Torrington

In 1982, after years of abuse, Charles Thurman, estranged husband to Tracey Thurman, was convicted of breach of the peace for breaking Tracey's windshield. He was given a suspended sentence that included a no-contact type of order. Despite the order, Charles continued to contact Tracey. During these encounters, he continued to be physically and verbally abusive, and he threatened her life and the life of their child. Tracey attempted numerous times to have Charles arrested for violating the terms of his conditional discharge. The Torrington Police Department either did not respond to Tracey's requests or told her to come to the police department at another time. On June 10, 1983, Charles showed up at the home in which Tracey was residing and demanded to see her. After about 15 minutes Tracey emerged, as she feared that Charles would take and/or harm their child. Althought she had called the police prior to going outside to speak with Charles, they did not arrive until approximately 25 minutes after Tracey's call to them. When Tracey emerged Charles began to stab and kick her multiple times. When a police officer finally arrived, Charles dropped the bloody knife and kicked Tracey, and then he went into the home to take their son. Charles dropped their child on his wounded mother, and kicked Tracey one last time in the head, while a Torrington Police Department officer stood by. Moreover, Charles was allowed to continue to walk around and threaten Tracey for a number of minutes, until other officers arrived and Charles was finally arrested.

Tracey sued the city and the police department for violating her equal protection rights. During the course of trial court documents also noted that Charles Thurman had worked from time to time at a local diner and served officers from the Torrington Police Department. In the course of his employment Charles Thurman told police officer patrons that he intended to kill his wife.

The court found that the police department was negligent and awarded Tracey $2.3 million. The result of the case would bring nationwide domestic violence reform, including the "Thurman Law," which ordered mandatory arrest for domestic violence. This case also opened the door to other victims who did not receive protections from law enforcement.

Victim Impact Statements

Three cases, related to the admission of a Victim Impact Statement (VIS) at trial, have shaped the use of VISs. These cases occurred within four years of one another. All of these cases involved murder convictions in which the victims were considered particularly vulnerable. And all three cases resulted in the defendant being sentenced to death.

Booth v. Maryland, 482 U.S. 496 (1987)

In *Booth v. Maryland* (1987), Booth was accused of murdering an elderly couple. At the time, Maryland law required that a victim impact statement be read during the pre-sentence report. Booth argued that the Maryland law violated his rights under the Eighth Amendment, asserting that the effect of the victim impact statement was unduly inflammatory and irrelevant. The state trial court denied Booth's motion to suppress the victim impact statement. Booth was convicted of murdering the elderly couple, and the jury sentenced Booth to death. United States Supreme Court agreed to hear Booth's case after the Court of Appeals affirmed the trial court's decision.

U.S. Supreme Court held that the Maryland law was invalid because "the introduction of a victim impact statement at the sentencing phase of a capital murder trial violates the Eighth Amendment . . . its admission creates a constitutionally unacceptable risk that the jury may impose the death penalty in an arbitrary and capricious manner." Furthermore, the Court held that the use of a victim impact statement during the sentencing phase of a capital trial was improper because it focused on the victim, rather than the actions of the offender. The court noted that there is no "justification for permitting such a decision [life or death] to turn on the perception that the victim was a sterling member of the community rather than someone of questionable character."

South Carolina v. Gathers 109 S. Ct. 2207, 104 L. Ed. 2d 876 (1989)

The second case made clear that VIS could be used but not at the sentencing phase. *South Carolina v. Gathers* (1989), Gathers was convicted of a murder in which the victim was tortured and then killed. Gathers was sentenced to death in a bifurcated trial (the trial to determine guilt or innocence was separate from the trial to determine the imposed sentence). During the end of the sentencing phase, the prosecutor read a religious tract that was found on the victim, and also noted that the victim was a registered voter. In a five to four decision the Supreme Court held that "a prosecutor's comments pertaining to personal characteristics of the victim made during the sentencing phase of a capital trial were irrelevant to the sentencing decision." The Court also concluded that, ". . . allowing the jury to rely on [this information] . . . could result in imposing the death sentence because of factors about which the defendant was unaware, and that were irrelevant to the decision to kill." As a result, Gather's conviction was upheld, but the case was granted a new sentencing hearing.

Payne v. Tennessee, 501 U.S. 808 (1991)

Finally, *Payne v. Tennessee* (1991) reversed the prior two case decisions by upholding the constitutionality of victim impact statements. Payne was tried for the murder of Charisse Christopher and her daughter Lacie. To avoid the death penalty, Payne provided witness testimonies to the jury about his good character. In response, the prosecution presented victim impact statements from Charisse's mother and surviving son; the survivors explained how the deaths impacted their lives. The jury convicted Payne and sentenced him to death. As a result, Payne argued that the prosecution could not use victim impact testimonies as it violated his Eighth Amendment rights. The Tennessee Supreme Court ruled against him.

The U.S. Supreme Court agreed to hear the case. They overruled *Booth v. Maryland* and *South Carolina v. Gathers*, concluding that,

> "... *virtually no limits are placed on the relevant mitigating evidence a capital defendant may introduce concerning his own circumstances ... assessment of the harm caused by the defendant has long been an important factor in determining the appropriate punishment, and victim impact evidence is simply another method of informing the sentencing authority about such harm.*"

The Court also acknowledged that their reversal, in a short period of time, is rare. They stated,

> "*although adherence to the doctrine of stare decisis is usually the best policy, the doctrine is not an inexorable command. This Court has never felt constrained to follow precedent when governing decisions are unworkable or badly reasoned ... Booth and Gathers were decided by the narrowest of margins, over spirited dissents challenging their basic underpinnings; have been questioned by Members of this Court in later decisions; have defied consistent application by the lower courts and, for the reasons heretofore stated, were wrongly decided.*"

Simon & Schuster, Inc. v. Members of N. Y. State Crime Victims Bd., 1991

In 1977, New York passed what is known as the "Son of Sam" law. This law "was enacted to prevent 'Son of Sam' David Berkowitz and other criminals from profiting from their crimes through the commercial exploitation of their stories. Under the law, any money that could potentially be earned by a criminal due to the commission of a crime would first be used to compensate the victim and others who have the right to sue under the law" (The New York State Senate). Instead, any profits made would be deposited into escrow accounts and made available to victims of crime.

Victim Impact Statements: A potential conflict?

Victim impact statements, especially in death penalty cases, present a conflict in which the rights of the defendant under the Eighth Amendment, as well as with the theory of legal relevance, are pit against victims' desire to be heard. In addition, a VIS may influence a jury to consider punishment based upon their perceptions of the value of the lives in question (victim and offender), rather than the crime. Finally, a VIS may appeal to emotions rather than rationality. For instance, Stevens (2000) considers that case of *Gather v. Tennessee*. He asks whether Gathers would be less culpable if the victim was an atheist or didn't vote, and whether the victims' character plays any part in Gather's' decision to kill. Furthermore, if the facts of the case were the same, but the victim was a convicted murderer, would the defendant not be as culpable or be less deserving of the death penalty?

Finally, one must consider the impact of the statement in relation to the victim delivering the statement. For instance, is the statement of a White, middle-class victim more impactful than that of a victim who is of color, and/or poor? Research has shown that these factors impact the sentences of defendants; could they also impact the weight of a VIS? Research has also shown that there are social myths about who is a good victim, versus a victim who is responsible for their victimization. Could this also impact how the VIS is received by the jury or judge? If so, are VISs predisposed to bias? Should some VISs matter more than others? What does this mean for the pursuit of justice?

In 1987, a former New York City mobster and associate of the Lucchese crime family, Henry Hill, was ordered to turn over the profits he made from a book deal with a publisher, Simon & Schuster, Inc. The publisher challenged the order, stating that the "Son of Sam" law violated the First Amendment. A District Court found the law to be consistent with the First Amendment.

In 1991, the case was brought to U.S. Supreme Court, and the Court ruled that the "Son of Sam" law violated the free speech clause of the First Amendment. The court recognized that the "State has a compelling interest in compensating victims from the fruits of crime. However, contrary to the Board's assertion, the State has little if any interest in limiting such compensation to the proceeds of the wrongdoer's speech about the crime." The Court concluded that "New York has singled out speech on a particular subject for financial burden that it places on no other speech and no other income"

In the years following the decision, New York State made alterations and amendments to the original "Son of Sam" law. In 2001, an additional provision was added that allowed victims of certain crimes to sue the perpetrators for as long as the perpetrator is under the supervision of the criminal justice system. This new provision permits recovery from any and all of a convicted person's assets (Yager, 2003).

Connecticut Department of Public Safety v. Doe

Connecticut Department of Public Safety v. Doe, 538 U.S. 1 (2003) involves a challenge to the use of the sex offender registry under the Fourteenth Amendment. A man identified as John Doe became subject to "Megan's Law" after being convicted of a sexual offense. The Department of Public Safety, under State mandate, posted sex offender data (such as demographic data: age, address, photographs) on public sex offender registries. John Doe challenged the law's requirement that the sex offender information be made public, as it was a violation of the Fourteenth Amendment Due Process Clause. A District Court ruled in favor of Doe. A Court of Appeals affirmed the District Court's decision stating that "... such disclosure violated the Due Process Clause because officials did not afford registrants a pre-deprivation hearing".

The case was then brought to U.S. Supreme Court, which ultimately reversed the Second Circuit Court's decision. The Supreme Court held that "... due process does not require the opportunity to prove a fact that is not material to the State's statutory scheme. Mere injury to reputation, even if defamatory, does not constitute the deprivation of a liberty interest" (*Connecticut Dept. of Public Safety v. Doe*, 2003). Reitler (2010) notes that this case signals the Court's "continued protection of victims" (p. 517). Furthermore, supporters' have argued that "... registration laws are not unfair, since convictions are already a matter of public record" (Maers, 2003).

Additional Remedies

In addition to landmark federal legislation and cases, additional remedies for victims of crime have resulted from state victims' rights amendments. For example, many states have subsequently enacted legislation and policies related to mandatory reporting laws and sex offender registries.

State victims' rights amendments

Although Congress has failed to amend the U.S. Constitution to guarantee equal protection for crime victims, many states have amended their state constitutions to provide for greater rights for victims of crime. As of today, 32 states have made amendments to their state constitutions to include victims' rights. Many of the state amendments clearly state who are considered victims of crime and the specific rights that they are afforded. For example, many states afford victims the right to confer with the prosecutor, to a timely disposition of the case, to be treated fairly, to be reasonably protected from the accused, to be informed of the accused's current state in court, to have the right to restitution, and the right to obtain information about the accused's case. Some states provide additional rights such as making statements during trial and being present during criminal proceedings.

According to the National Crime Victim Center (NCVC) (2012) there are eight specific rights that are afforded to victims by law in most jurisdictions. These rights vary, depending on federal, state, or tribal law. These rights are similar in wording to those put forth under the VOCA of 2004. These rights are outlined in Figure 5.3.

Some states have since adopted such language in their respective Constitutions, however, not all states have done so. The map below illustrates which states that have adopted a Victims' Rights Amendment, as of 2014. The map and other tools to explore victims' rights by state can be found at the Klaas Kids Foundation.

Provides guidance on the unique concerns that arise in sexual violence cases, such as the role of criminal investigations and a school's independent responsibility to investigate and address sexual violence.

Provides guidance and examples about key Title IX requirements and how they relate to sexual violence, such as the requirements to publish a policy against sex discrimination, designate a Title IX coordinator, and adopt and publish grievance procedures.

Discusses proactive efforts schools can take to prevent sexual violence.

Discusses the interplay between Title IX, FERPA, and the Clery Act as it relates to a complainant's right to know the outcome of his or her complaint, including relevant sanctions facing the perpetrator.

Provides examples of remedies and enforcement strategies that schools and the Office for Civil Rights (OCR) may use to respond to sexual violence.

FIGURE 5.3 Dear Colleague Letter Guidelines

© mirec/Shutterstock.com

Mandatory Reporting Laws

Today, every state and the District of Columbia have laws mandating the reporting of child maltreatment by designated professionals (Child Welfare Gateway,
2015). These designated professionals include, but are not limited to, persons such
as social workers, teachers, principals, other school personnel, physicians, nurses,
other health care workers, counselors, therapists, other mental health professionals,
child care providers, medical examiners/coroners, and law enforcement officers. In
addition, many states require commercial film or photograph processors, computer
technicians, substance abuse counselors, probation or parole officers, employees,
and volunteers at entities that provide organized activities for children, and domestic violence workers on the list of mandated reporters. In addition, 11 states now
require faculty, administrators, athletics staff, and other employees and volunteers
at institutions of higher learning, including public and private colleges and universities and vocational and technical schools, to serve as mandatory reporters; and 18
states mandate the reporting of any suspected child abuse, neglect, or maltreatment
by *any* person (Child Welfare Information Gateway, 2015).

Mandatory reporters are required to report suspected child maltreatment to
an appropriate agency, such as child protective services, a law enforcement agency,
or a state's toll-free child abuse reporting hotline. According to the Child Welfare
Information Gateway (2015) a report must be made when the reporter, in his or

her official capacity, *suspects* or *has reason to believe* that a child has been abused or neglected, or when the reporter has knowledge of, or observes a child being subjected to, conditions that would reasonably result in harm to the child. Mandatory reporters are required to report the facts and circumstances surrounding their suspicions, but they do not have the burden of providing proof that abuse or neglect has occurred. These provisions also apply to non-mandatory reporters who decide to make an official report.

Sex Offender Registration Laws

Sex offender registration laws have evolved over time. The first Act was the Jacob Wetterling Crimes Against Children and Sexual Violent Offender Registration Act of 1994. It provided states with financial incentives to establish and maintain registries for persons convicted of certain sexual crimes. In 1996, the Wetterling Act was amended via the Pam Lychner Sexual Offender Tracking and Identification Act. This Act established guidelines for reporting and registering convicted sex offenders. The Act notes that upon release, convicted sex offenders are notified of their lawful duty to register their sex offender status with appropriate authorities. They are required to notify authorities within 10 days upon moving to a new state or residence. Failure to notify authorities of moving to a new state or residence is a criminal act.

In 2006, the Adam Walsh Child Protection and Safety Act was enacted. This Act sought to close existing loopholes and to strengthen the existing legislation; and, established the Sex Offender Registration and Notification Act (SORNA). The changes this law mandated are outlined in the table below:

Extends the jurisdictions in which registration is required beyond the 50 states, the District of Columbia, and the principal U.S. territories, to include also federally recognized Indian tribes.
Incorporates a more comprehensive group of sex offenders and sex offenses for which registration is required.
Requires registered sex offenders to register and keep their registration current in each jurisdiction in which they reside, work, or go to school.
Requires sex offenders to provide more extensive registration information.
Requires sex offenders to make periodic in-person appearances to verify and update their registration information.
Expands the amount of information available to the public regarding registered sex offenders.
Makes changes in the required minimum duration of registration for sex offenders

As a result of these legal remedies, sex offender registries were created. Currently, every state has a sex offender registry; however these registries are not uniform in the information they collect, the manner in which they classify offenders, or the types of offenders they require to register. Although there is variation among states, all states must comply with federal Acts that establish guidelines. In return, states are eligible for financial assistance in the development and management of registries. According to the National Center for Missing & Exploited Children (NCMEC) by December of 2014, there were approximately 819,218 registered sex offenders in the United States (Sacco, 2015).

Conclusion

This chapter has presented many of the most influential legal remedies for victims of crime. Founding documents, including the Constitution and state laws, did not address the needs of victims. Therefore, much work was and is still needed to address the matter. That being said, the landmark legislation, laws, and remedies that were presented should provide the reader with a sense that legislators and criminal justice allied professionals are committed to priortizing the needs of victims of crimes. The next stage of this journey in ensuring the rights of victims by creating universal and consistent laws so that victims across jurisdictions are afforded the most progressive remedies. In addition, legal remedies must ensure the simultaneous protection of victims and the accused. Denying rights to victims is unjust; however, justice will not be served if the rights of victims supersede those of the accused. Finding the right balance and ensuring a just legal system is not an easy task, but the landmark legislation, cases, and other remedies presented in this chapter represent a solid beginning.

Discussion questions

1. What are the most significant provisions of the President's Task Force of 1982? Why?
2. Victims' advocates have proposed that the United States Constitution be amended to include language that addresses victims of crime. The Amendment has been proposed, but has never passed. Why? Describe the two positions (for and against) regarding the inclusion of such language. Which position do you support?
3. The use of Victim Impact Statements at trial has been widely debated. First, discuss the pros and cons of including VISs at trial. Next, discuss whether or not you support the use of VISs at trial.
4. The case of Tracey Thurman was instrumental in pushing law enforcement to protect victims of domestic violence. First, present at least three errors made by law enforcement when interacting with Tracey and Charles Thurman. Next, describe how this case changed law enforcement's response to victims of crime.

References

Child Welfare Information Gateway. (2015). *Mandatory reporters of child abuse and neglect*. U.S. Department of Health & Human Services. Retrieved from https://www.childwelfare.gov/pubPDFs/manda.pdf#page=1&view=Introduction

Fischer, B. S., Cullen, F. T., & Turner, M. G. (2010). *The sexual victimization of college women*. U.S. Department of Justice. Retrieved from https://www.ncjrs.gov/pdf-files1/nij/182369.pdf

H.R.6403—*Victims of Crime Act of 1984*. Retrieved from https://www.congress.gov/bill/98th-congress/house-bill/6403

Maers, B. (2003). *Supreme Court upholds sex offender registration laws*. CNN. Retrieved from http://www.cnn.com/2003/LAW/03/05/scotus.sex.offenders/

National Center for Victims of Crime. *Issues: Constitutional Amendments*. Retrieved from http://victimsofcrime.org/our-programs/public-policy/amendments

National Sex Offender Public Registry. *About*. National Sex Offender Public Registry. U.S. Department of Justice. Retrieved from https://www.nsopw.gov/en/Home/About

Office for Victims of Crime. (2016. April). *The Justice for All Act*. [OVC Fact Sheet]. Retrieved from: https://www.ovc.gov/publications/factshts/justforall/welcome.html

Office of Justice Programs. *About SMART*. Office of Sex Offender Sentencing, Monitoring, Apprehending, Registering, and Tracking. Retrieved from https://www.smart.gov/about.htm

Office of Justice Programs. *SORNA*. Office of Sex Offender Sentencing, Monitoring, Apprehending, Registering, and Tracking. Retrieved from https://www.smart.gov/sorna.htm

Office on Violece against Women. (2016). *Twenty Years of the Violence Against Women Act: Dispatches from the Field*. Department of Justice. Retrieved from: https://www.justice.gov/ovw/file/866576/download

Office on Violence against Women. (2017). *About the Office*. Department of Justice. Retrieved from: https://www.justice.gov/ovw/about-office

Pam Lychner Sexual Offender Tracking and Identification Act of 1996, S.1675. 104th Cong. (1996). Retrieved from: https://www.congress.gov/bill/104th-congress/senate-bill/1675

Reitler, A. K. (2010). Landmark victim-related court cases, Federal, United States. *Encyclopedia of Victimology and Crime Prevention*. Thousand Oaks, CA: SAGE Publishing.

Robers, S., Zhang, J., Truman, J., & Snyder T. D. *Indicators of school crime and safety: 2010.* U.S. Department of Education. Retrieved from http://nces.ed.gov/pubs2011/2011002.pdf.

Ruth, D. P. (1996) Title VII & Title IX: Is Title IX the exclusive remedy for employment discrimination in the educational sector. *Cornell Journal of Law and Public Policy, 5(2),* Article 4, 185-238. Retrieved from http://scholarship.law.cornell.edu/cjlpp/vol5/iss2/4

Sacco, L. N. (2015). *Federal Involvement in Sex Offender Registration and Notification: Overview and Issues for Congress, In Brief.* Congressional Research Service. Retrieved from https://fas.org/sgp/crs/misc/R43954.pdf

Simon & Schuster, Inc. v. Members of N. Y. State Crime Victims Bd., 502 U.S. 105 (1991)

Stevens, M. (2000). *Victim impact statements considered in sentencing:* Constitutional concerns. *California Criminal Law Review, 3,* 2.

The New York State Senate. (2017). *Senate passes bill to close loophole in "Son of Sam" law.* [Press Release]. Retrieved from: https://www.nysenate.gov/newsroom/press-releases/dean-g-skelos/senate-passes-bill-close-loophole-"son-sam"-law.

U.S. Department of Education. *Clery Act Reports.* Retrieved from https://studentaid.ed.gov/sa/about/data-center/school/clery-act-reports

U.S. Department of Education. (2011). *Dear Colleague Letter Fact Sheet.* Retrieved from https://obamawhitehouse.archives.gov/sites/default/files/fact_sheet_sexual_violence.pdf

U.S. Department of Justice. *Sex Offender Registration and Notification Act (SORNA).* Retrieved from https://www.justice.gov/criminal-ceos/sex-offender-registration-and-notification-act-sorna

Yager, J. (2003). Investigating New York's 2001 Son of Sam Law: Problems with the recent extension of tort liability for people convicted of crimes. *New York Law School Review, 48,* 433–488.

CHAPTER 6

Navigating Victims through the Justice System

Objectives

Upon completion of this chapter, you will be able to:
- understand the importance of the initial contact between law enforcement and the victims,
- understand and discuss the phases, stages, and options available to victims of crime as they navigate through the criminal justice system, and
- understand the similarities and differences among different victim compensation programs with restitution.

Introduction

This chapter examines the phases, stages, and options available to victims of crime as they navigate through the criminal justice system. The chapter is composed of three sections. The first section, *Initiating a Case*, primarily examines the contact experienced between victims and law enforcement. Activities such as making the initial report, the investigation, and the presentation of options are explored. The second section, *Prosecution and the Courts*, reviews the stages that constitute the prosecution of a criminal case. During this phase the victim may be involved with the prosecutor's office or other courthouse offices when the charges are filed or dismissed, when a plea bargain is entered, and at sentencing. Finally, the third section, *Protections, Redress, and Services*, discusses options offered to victims throughout the criminal justice system. Special attention is given to orders of protection, victim compensation, and civil remedies.

Initiating a Case

Generally, victims of crime enter the criminal justice system after initiating contact with a law enforcement agency or being questioned about their involvement in a criminal matter; this can occur at the local, state, or federal level. Once contact is made, a series of criminal justice system phases can follow, or the responding law enforcement agency or victim can drop the matter. The contact usually occurs in fixed stages, such as reporting, then interviews, and then evidence collection; however, the stages do not always progress in that order and the stages can be repeated or skipped depending on the details of the case. Law enforcement officers have more contact with victims than any other criminal justice system representative; therefore, these interactions set the tone for the victim's view of the system and participation in the investigation and prosecution of the case (National Association of Sheriffs in collaboration with the Office of Victims of Crime, 2008). The following discussion reviews the stages of official contact in the order in which they most often occur.

The Initial Report

Law enforcement officers are generally the first responders when a crime is reported. Reports can come from the victim, the perpetrator, witnesses, or third parties such as schools, work places, or neighbors. Once a law enforcement officer becomes aware of a crime the official criminal justice system process often begins. It is for this reason that the initial response is critical as it sets the tone for how the victim perceives the criminal justice system.

Officers will speak with victims at various points; however, the initial report includes general information about the victim, the accused perpetrator, and the nature of the victimization. The initial report often differs from more detailed discussions that occur at the investigation stage, if the case proceeds. Officers also assess the mental and physical wellbeing of the victim at this point. If the victim appears to need medical intervention, the initial report-taking ceases and the officer contacts medical professionals.

The initial report-taking process may differ depending on the nature of crime and type of victim. The National Sheriffs Association, in collaboration with the Office of Victims of Crime (OVC) (2008) developed a guidebook for initial responses to victims of crime; these responses suggest officers should consider the nature of the victimization and type of victim. For instance, elderly victims or victims who speak English as their second language may require more time to respond to questions or collect their thoughts. Additionally, child victims should have a parent or guardian present, unless they are the suspected perpetrator.

When discussing initial reports, it is important to consider the amount of crime not reported by victims to law enforcement. Truman and Morgan's (2016) review of the 2015 National Crime Victimization data reports that there was no significant change in the percentage of violent victimizations reported to police from 1993 (42%) to 2015 (47%). As for property offenses, the percentage of victimizations reported to police also did not show a significant increase from 1993 (32%) to 2015 (35%). Most disconcerting, this data shows that only about one-half of violent crimes and one-third of property crimes are reported to the police. Table 6.1 displays data from the National Crime Victimization Survey for 2014 and 2015 to illustrate the percentage of crimes that were reported to the police.

Table 6.1 Percent of victimizations reported to police, by type of crime, 2014 and 2015

Type of Crime	2014*	2015
Violent crime[a]	46.0%	46.5%
Rape/sexual assault[b]	33.6	32.5
Robbery	60.9	61.9
Assault	44.6	45.8
Aggravated assault	58.4	61.9
Simple assault	40.0	41.7
Domestic violence[c]	56.1	57.7
Intimate partner violence[d]	57.9	54.1
Stranger violence	48.8	42.1
Violent crime involving injury	54.9	57.0
Serious violent crime[e]	55.8%	54.9%
Serious domestic violence[c]	60.0	60.8
Serious intimate partner violence[d]	56.7	49.6
Serious stranger violence	65.4	54.3
Serious violent crime involving weapons	57.6	56.3
Serious violent crime involving injury	61.0	59.0
Property crime	37.0%	34.6%[†]
Burglary	60.0	50.8[†]
Motor vehicle theft	83.3	69.0[†]
Theft	29.0	28.6

Note: See appendix table 8 for standard errors.

*Comparison year.

[†]Significant difference from comparison year at 95% confidence level.

[a] Excludes homicide because the NCVS is based on the interviews with victims and therefore cannot measure murder

[b] BJS has initiated projects examining collection methods for self-report data on rape and sexual assault. See *NCVS measurement of rape and sexual assault* in Methodology for more information.

[c] Includes victimization committed by inititate partners and family members.

[d] Includes victimization committed by current or former spouses, boyfriends, or girlfriends.

[e] In the NCVS, serious violent crime includes rape or sexual assault, robbery, and aggravated assault.

Source: Bureau of Justice Statistics, National Crime Victimization Survey (NCVS), 2014 and 2015.

Investigations

If a case proceeds beyond the initial report, the law enforcement agency will begin the investigation. The investigation involves interviews with the victim, the accused perpetrator(s) when identified, and other witnesses. Investigators interact with victims to discover facts and collect evidence (Osterburg & Ward, 2010). Two primary forms of evidence used in cases with human victims are eyewitness reports and physical evidence. During the investigation phase, the victim is considered a witness. As a witness the victim is asked to recall information about the nature of their victimization, the perpetrator, and factors associated with the crime, such as bank records, weapons, vehicles, and/or audio or visual recordings.

Victim interviews are a crucial part of the investigation process. The investigator's style and tone can have an impact on the victim's decision to cooperate, as well as impact the victim's emotional state. Patterson (2011) found that detectives who respond to victims' emotional distress appear "to help victims endure the investigational  interview, contribute more information to the investigation, and subsequently build a stronger case for prosecution" (p. 1363); whereas victims whose cases did not proceed past the investigation process noted detectives "asked questions in a rapid, forceful manner and communicated disbelief of their stories, which made the participants feel uncomfortable" (p. 1363).

Physical evidence is also collected during the investigation. Physical evidence includes biological matter such as semen, blood, and saliva. Other forms of physical evidence include photographs of injuries, video or audio recordings of interactions, and documents. Evidence collection is highly dependent upon the nature of the victimization, and often requires victims to be part of the physical evidence collection process. For example, victims of sexual assault may be asked to undergo a sexual assault examination (also known as a rape kit), and victims of identity theft may be asked to surrender their electronic devices.

FIGURE 6.1

Focus on an issue: Rape Kits

Sexual assault evidence collection kits, also known as rape kits, have recently received national media attention after advocates and victims complained about the backlog of untested kits throughout the United States. As a result, research and policy efforts are currently underway to measure the extent of the problem and suggest reform to improve responses to victims and increase investigation effectiveness. Figure 6.1 is a product of End the Backlog, a nonprofit project focused on exposing the rape kit backlog problem. Students can visit the site and utilize the interactive map to learn how many backlogged kits exist per state, and whether or not the state is engaging in some level of reform.
Visit: http://www.endthebacklog.org

THE 21ST CENTURY TRANSFORMATION OF VICTIMOLOGY

The Presentation of Options

Increasingly, victims interact with officers beyond reporting a crime and participating in the investigation. There are additional options that officers may present to the victim, depending on the situation. The National Sheriffs Association, in collaboration with the Office of Victims of Crime (OVC) (2008) stress that after ensuring the safety of the victim, officers should also explain next steps. In particular, victims should be aware of their rights, how their case will proceed through the system, and what type of victims' services are availale to them.

One example of an available service is the Lethality Assessment Program (LAP). The LAP is comprised of a risk assessment screening and follow-up protocol to be used by first responders to Intimate Partner Violence (IPV) calls. It allows officers to assess the risk of the victim, inform victims of their risk, provide options and encourage the victim-survivor to seek services (Messing et al., 2017). Victims of IPV can also be given information about orders of protection. In most states, officers are required to inform victims of their right to order of protection. Additionally, in most states officers are required to enforce an order of protection unless it is fraudulent or expired (DeJong & Burgess-Proctor, 2006). Victims in some states may also be eligible for an emergency protection order against the person who is arrested. Officers can issue the EPO at the scene. The victim then has a short period of time to obtain a court-issued temporary or permanent order of protection.

Another service available to victims of sexual assault at the investigation phase is a sexual assault examination; in most states the examination involves a Sexual Assault Nurse Examiner (SANE) who administers a rape kit. SANE programs provide post-assault care to victims of sexual assault within hospitals or community-based clinics. Nurses trained in the SANE program are registered nurses with an advanced education in the forensic examination of sexual assault victims (Department of Justice, n.d.). As of 2013, the National Institute of Justice estimated that there were over 600 SANE programs operating in the U.S. and Canada (Pearsall, 2013).

Some police departments also partner with victim service providers or have in-house experts to enhance responses to victims of crime. For example, the New York State Police has a Crime Victim Specialist (CVS) assigned to each upstate department; the specialist provides information about safety planning, criminal court procedure information, and available victims services.[1] In California every law enforcement agency is required to present victims with a written card that contains information about their rights and a list of services available to victims of crime (National Crime Victim Law Institute, n.d.).

---

[1] See: New York State, Division of Criminal Justice Services. http://www.criminaljustice.ny.gov/pio/crimevictims.html

> **Victim Resources: Marsy's Card**
>
> Marsy's card is a project in the state of California that provides victims with a list of their rights under the state constitution and available community resources. The card is published in over twenty languages. Victims receive this information at point of contact with the criminal justice system. The card is a result of California's Victim's Bill of Rights Act of 2008, also known as Marsy's Law. The law and card are named after Marsalee (Marsy) Nicholas, a University of California Santa Barbara student, who was stalked and killed by her ex-boyfriend in 1983. Her family, and, in particular, her brother Henry Nicholas, worked with the State of California to adopt Marsy's Law.
> To learn more about Marsy's law and the card visit:
> https://oag.ca.gov/victimservices/marsy

Arrest

Law enforcement officers can either make arrest at the scene of the crime if there is immediate probable cause, after a further investigation, or when a judge signs an arrest warrant after there is a grand jury indictment (America Bar Association, 2017). The primary responsibility of an officer at the point of arrest is to safely secure the suspect and ensure the suspect is aware of his/her rights. There are currently very few arrest protocols that consider the impact of the arrest on the primary or secondary (e.g., children) victims at point of arrest.

Recently, attention has been given to arrests, particularly in cases of Intimate Partner Violence, in which children are present. A report sponsored by the Office of Justice Programs puts forth data and recommendations for police when making an arrest in front of children. The report estimated that between 1.2 and 5.2 million children witness parents being arrested each year, many of whom were involved in IPV (Office of OD & Thorou, 2015). The report also notes that by the time police arrive to the scene the child has already witnessed the violence, and that the arrest of a parent can compound the trauma already experienced by the child. Therefore, the report puts forth valuable recommendations for officers who must make an arrest when a child is present. One recommendation is that officers should have a dispatcher provide information about whether or not a child is present so that officers can contemplate their course of action before entering the home when a child is present. Other suggestions are that officers should allow parents to comfort their children, when possible, and if the parent is calm, officers should avoid handcuffing the parent in front of the child.

Prosecution and The Courts

When a case proceeds past the investigation phase, the case is handed to the office of the prosecutor or district attorney (different states use different titles) at the state level or a U.S. attorney at the federal level. After a prosecutor or U.S. attorney reviews a case and meets with involved parties, the case moves through a series of steps. The preliminary steps can include charging, initial hearings, discovery, and preliminary hearings. Not all steps occur in all cases. Following the preliminary steps there are generally three options. The case can be dropped, the prosecutor can offer the accused a plea bargain, or the case can proceed to trial. Very few cases actually proceed to trial.

Before reviewing the specific steps, it should be noted that the prosecutors are advised to consider a universal set of guidelines. Specially, prosecutors are advised, and in some states mandated under the Victims' Rights Amendments to State Constitutions, to ensure victims are notified of each stage in their case and afforded protections against intimidation. The American Bar Association (ABA) (2017) General Standards, notes the following:

(a) A prosecutor should not compensate a witness, other than an expert, for giving testimony, but it is not improper to reimburse an ordinary witness for the reasonable expenses of attendance upon court, attendance for depositions pursuant to statute or court rule, or attendance for pretrial interviews. Payments to a witness may be for transportation and loss of income, provided there is no attempt to conceal the fact of reimbursement.

(b) A prosecutor should advise a witness who is to be interviewed of his or her rights against self-incrimination and the right to counsel whenever the law so requires. It is also proper for a prosecutor to so advise a witness whenever the prosecutor knows or has reason to believe that the witness may be the subject of a criminal prosecution. However, a prosecutor should not so advise a witness for the purpose of influencing the witness in favor of or against testifying.

(c) The prosecutor should readily provide victims and witnesses who request it information about the status of cases in which they are interested.

(d) The prosecutor should seek to insure that victims and witnesses who may need protections against intimidation are advised of and afforded protections where feasible.

(e) The prosecutor should insure that victims and witnesses are given notice as soon as practicable of scheduling changes which will affect the victims' or witnesses' required attendance at judicial proceedings.

(f) The prosecutor should not require victims and witnesses to attend judicial proceedings unless their testimony is essential to the prosecution or is required by law. When their attendance is required, the prosecutor should seek to reduce to a minimum the time they must spend at the proceedings.

(g) The prosecutor should seek to insure that victims of serious crimes or their representatives are given timely notice of: (i) judicial proceedings relating to the victims' case; (ii) disposition of the case, including plea bargains, trial and sentencing; and (iii) any decision or action in the case which results in the accused's provisional or final release from custody.

(h) Where practical, the prosecutor should seek to insure that victims of serious crimes or their representatives are given an opportunity to consult with and to provide information to the prosecutor prior to the decision whether or not to prosecute, to pursue a disposition by plea, or to dismiss the charges.

Charging

The decision to file or dismiss charges has generally been the role of the public prosecutor. Although the prosecutor has always had the option to confer with the victim, it did not happen often until after the 1982 President's Task Force Recommendations. Tobolowsky, Beloof, Gaboury, Jackson, and Blackburn (2016) explain that state guidelines on the involvement of victims at the point of charging are varied. For example, twelve states include a provision that permits victims to confer with the prosecutor, including regarding charging decisions. In addition, approximately twenty states allow for or require victim input regarding case dismissals. Tobolowsky et al. also note that many states allow victims to hire a private attorney for the purpose of consulting with or assisting the prosecutor.

Regardless of formal guidelines that encourage or disregard the role of the victim, the prosecutor makes the final decision to proceed with or drop charges; this is known as prosecutorial discretion. Two of the most noted forms of prosecutorial discretion are (1) the decision not to prosecute although there is adequate evidence, and (2) the ability to afford concessions to a perpetrator if s/he accepts a plea (LaFave, 1970). Each of these forms of discretion can affect a victim at the charging stage.

Methods of Handling Cases

The National District Attorney's Association (NDAA) (2017) put forth a white paper outlining ways to handle cases of domestic violence. Although the paper focuses on domestic violence, case-handling methods can apply to other cases. First, they discuss vertical prosecutions. Vertical prosecutions involve one prosecutor handling a case from beginning to end. This allows for victims to interact and tell their story to only one person. In jurisdictions with large caseloads, vertical prosecutions are not always possible; therefore, the jurisdiction may utilize a horizontal method. Horizontal prosecutions involve multiple prosecutors, in which each prosecutor performs the same task for each case. In these cases, one prosecutor may file cases, while another handles plea bargains. The NDAA acknowledges that this can result in the victim needing to interact with more than one prosecutor; therefore, engagement with a singular victim advocate is important. The victim advocate can help to mimic a vertical prosecution, in that the advocate is a consistent, singular point of contact throughout the process.

Another noted form of prosecution is victimless prosecution (also known as evidence-based prosecution); it is a strategy used by prosecutors to build a case against an individual regardless of the victim's engagement in the case (NDAA, 2017). This is most often used in cases of domestic violence, in which victims may be unwilling or reluctant to cooperate with the prosecutor because of fear of the perpetrator, lack of faith in the system, or numerous other reasons. Victimless prosecutions allow for the prosecutor to rely on other forms of evidence (e.g., crime scene evidence, detailed police reports) to build the case, rather than relying on victim testimony. This type of prosecution has been criticized for not involving or sidestepping the wishes of the victim; however, it has been praised for removing the entire burden from the victim, and encouraging police to conduct more thorough investigations.

Pretrial Release

According to the American Bar Association (2017B), pretrial release decisions include "providing due process to those accused of crime, maintaining the integrity of the judicial process by securing defendants for trial, and protecting victims, witnesses and the community from threat, danger or interference." Decisions are made by a judge or judicial officer who decides whether to release a defendant, and under what conditions (e.g., own recognizance or unsecured appearance bond). Nearly all states have developed victim's rights in the pretrial release decision making process, through legislation or a constitutional amendment.

Keilitz (2015) notes two important rights afforded to victims at the pretrial decision-making phase: notice, and participation and input. Keilitz states that as of 2013, 24 states require that the victim be notified of the defendant's pretrial release hearing and 41 states provide victims the right to notice at the point of pretrial release. She also notes that victim input and participation at all pretrial stages, including release decisions, is critical to ensuring the safety of the victim, and for increasing victim participation in the process.

Plea Bargaining

In most cases, the prosecutor will determine whether a case will be the subject of a plea offer and whether to make a plea agreement. In fact, Devers (2001) notes that although there are no exact estimates on the percentage of cases that result in a plea agreement, estimates suggest that about 90 to 95 percent of both federal and state court cases are resolved through plea bargaining. Therefore, victims of crime are far more likely to have their case resolved through the plea process than at trial.

The American Bar Association's (2006) policy is that consideration should be given to the interests of victims, and that victims should have the opportunity to confer with the prosecutor prior to the submission of the plea agreement. However, these are only suggestions; the actual inclusion of victims' perspectives at the point of plea-bargaining varies by state.

The Office of Victims of Crime (OVS) (2002) notes that depending on the state, a victim may have the right to be engaged at this stage when: (1) conferring with the prosecutor during plea-bargaining and (2) when addressing the court before the entry of the plea. In some states the law requires that a prosecutor confer or consult with the victim about the bargaining or negotiated plea agreements; however, these states do not define "consult" or "confer." OVS also notes that in some states, "confer appears to be limited to notifying, informing, or advising victims of a plea bargain or agreement that has already been reached before presenting the proposed plea to the court." As such, *confer* does not mean that the victim has the final say or even that victim input is prioritized.

Trial

First, it should be understood that very few criminal cases proceed to trial; as previously noted, most cases end in a plea bargain. That being said, it is relevant to review how victims are engaged at trial. Prior to the President's Task Force in 1982, many states excluded the victim from participating in at least part of the criminal trial. The exclusion of victims was permissible under the "rule on witnesses." This rule was developed to limit the possibility that a witness might be influenced by hearing the testimony of other witnesses, and therefore adversely impact the rights of the accused. However, the Task Force concluded that victims deserved the right to attend trials, explaining that crime victims, like defendants have a "legitimate interest in the fair adjudication of the case" (Beloof & Cassell, 2005, p. 504). As a result of the recommendations and the 2004 Crime Victims' Rights Act, which strengthened victims' right to be present during trial, all 50 states and the federal government recognize a victim's right to be present at court proceedings in some way (Tobolowsky, et al., 2016).

There are numerous ways that victims may be engaged during a trial; Beloof and Cassell's (2005) review of the crime victim's rights to attend trial highlights some of the ways that victims can participate during a trial. First, they note that seventeen states provide victims with an unqualified right to attend trial; whereas, approximately twenty-five states have given victims a qualified right to attend. They classify these states into six groups, based on the qualifications:

1. the right to attend subject to exclusion for interference with the defendant's constitutional rights
2. the right to attend subject to exclusion if necessary to protect a defendant's fair trial rights
3. the right to attend unless testimony is affected
4. the right to attend if practicable
5. the right to attend subject to the discretion of the court
6. the right to attend after testifying (p. 506).

Beloof and Cassell (2005) also note that in addition to states' laws that give victim's rights to attend trial, federal law also guarantees that almost all victims can attend trials. Thus it appears that states and federal sentiment no longer assume a victim's right to participate in a trial adversely impacts the accused, in all instances.

Sentencing: Victim Impact Statements

Until recently, victims of crime had very little impact on the sentencing of an offender. However, with the inclusion of Victim Impact Statements (VIS) at point of sentencing, the sentiments and recommendations may at least be considered. Victim impact statements are written or oral testimonies from the victim about how the crime impacted the victim, physically, emotionally, financially, and in other ways. All 50 states allow these statements at some phase of the sentencing process, most often at the pre-sentencing report presented to the judge (National Center for Victims of Crime (NCVC), 2008). A judge may use the statement to guide the sentence, but this is not required under law. A VIS may be used to determine type of sentence, such as probation, jail or prison, or diversionary programs.

VIS should address the following:

- Physical damage caused by the crime.
- Emotional damage caused by the crime.
- Financial costs to the victim from the crime.
- Medical or psychological treatments required by the victim or his or her family.
- The need for restitution (court-ordered funds that the offender pays the victim for crime-related expenses).

- The victim's views on the crime or the offender (in some states).
- The victim's views on an appropriate sentence (in some states) (NCVC, 2008).

VIS not only provide victims with an opportunity to participate in the process, but they also do so without compromising the rights of the defendant. Cassell (2009) notes four advantages of VIS. He states that they provide information to the sentencing judge or jury about the resulting harm caused by the crime. Sec-

ond, they may be therapeutic for the victim. Third, VIS provide the defendant with a complete picture of the consequences of the crime, thereby creating a greater opportunity for rehabilitation. And finally, they create a perception of fairness, by ensuring that all relevant parties are heard (pp. 611 – 612).

Protections, Redress, and Services

Victims of crime can also engage with the criminal justice system and legal system to receive additional remedies. For instance, victims of crime have the right to an order of protection, to request victim compensation funds, and to seek out civil recourse, such as litigation, and third party lawsuits. This section will review these remedies and explain some differences, such as the difference between compensation and restitution.

Victims also may be engaged in court approved or ordered services such as mediation or other therapeutic models. This section briefly addresses these additional services, as these services are discussed in detail in other chapters.

Orders of Protection

In all 50 states and the District of Columbia victims have the right to a civil order of protection. The name of the order and the provisions of the order vary by state. Some names include civil order of protection, restraining order, and peace order. In general, civil orders of protection are court-issued mandates that prevent the named respondent from contacting or harassing the named victim. Orders can also temporarily mandate custody arrangement, when children are involved, and put forth visitation stipulations. Furthermore, orders can force respondents to leave the home, and establish economic provisions such as child support or restitution (Meyer, 2010). Civil orders of protection are valid in other jurisdictions, allowing the victim to move and/or travel. The Violence Against Women Act (VAWA) includes a Full Faith and Credit Clause, which ensures that civil orders issued in one jurisdiction are recognized and enforced in other jurisdictions.

Most orders of protection are issued in cases of IPV, but increasingly states have orders of protections available in cases of stalking. As of 2016, 24 states in the United States had provisions for orders of protection for victims of stalking (Stalking Resource Center). In addition, orders of protection can extend beyond the primary victim to cover family members and other persons involved with the victim. As of 2017, 32 states also have provisions for pets when issuing an order of protection (Animal Legal and Historical Center).

Victim Compensation

Victim compensation programs were one of the first forms of financial assistance provided to crime victims (Parent et al., 1992). Victim compensation legislation passed in Great Britain, New Zealand, and other nations influenced the development of victim compensation programs in the United States. In 1965, California passed legislation establishing the first state victims' compensation program (www.victims.ca.gov/board/, 2020). Today, every state in the country has some type of compensation program. Another form of financial assistance provided to crime victims is restitution. Restitution has always been a component of the common law in the United States; however, in 1982, a federal statute was passed authorizing restitution in addition to, or instead of, any other sentence in a criminal proceeding (OVC, 1998). Victim compensation programs were established under the Crime Victims Fund, which is supported by collecting fines, penalty assessments, and bond forfeitures from convicted federal offenders. The Office of Victims of Crime (OVC) explains that they distribute money deposited into the Fund to states to support state compensation and assistance services. These funds can be used for victims and survivors of numerous crimes, such as domestic violence, sexual assault, child abuse, drunk driving, and homicide.

Orders of protection: Are they victim-friendly?

The table below is from DeJong and Burgess-Proctor's (2006) analysis of each state's Personal Protection Order (PPO) statute. Their analysis measured how victim-friendly the statue was. Victim-friendliness was measured by assessing four factors: Compliance with the Violence Against Women Act (VAWA), the relationship between petitioner and respondent (Do statutes allow for a wide range of relationship types, such as same sex and dating?), ease of the PPO administrative process, and severity of punishment for violations. High scores indicate greater victim-friendliness.

Table 6.2 Score for Strength of PPO Statute by Slate

State	Number of States With Score	Score
Missouri	1	10.0
Massachusetts	1	9.0
Florida, Indiana, Kan,as, Michigan, New Hampshire, Washington, Wyoming	7	8.5
California, Illinois, Maine, Texas, Wisconsin	5	8.0
Nebraska, North Dakota, Oklahoma	3	7.5
Colorado, Louisiana, Minnesota, North Carolina	4	7.0
Alaska, Arizona, Iowa, Kentucky, Pennsylvania	5	6.5
Alabama, Maryland, Montana, Nevada, New Jersey Rhode Island, Tennessee, Utah, Vermont, W. Virginia	10	6.0
Arkansas, Connecticut, Hawaii, Idaho, New Mexico, Ohio, South Dakota, Virginia	8	5.5
Delaware, Mississippi	2	5.0
District of Columbia, Georgia, New York, Oregon	4	4.5
South Carolina	1	4.0

Note: PPO = personal protection nuke.

OVC also explains that funds can be used to reimburse victims for costs such as medical expenses, mental health counseling, funeral and burial costs, and lost wages or loss of support. Furthermore, compensation is paid when other financial resources are not available. In addition, expenses such as damaged property, property loss, and expenses related to terrorist acts are not covered by most compensation programs. Compensation programs do not require that the offender is convicted of the crime. Funds can be distributed so long as the victim complies with the outlined process. For example, in order for a victim to receive funds, they must comply with reasonable requests of law enforcement and submit a timely application to the compensation program.

The OVC (2017) reports that for the year 2015, nearly 250,000 persons applied for compensation funds. Of this number of persons who sought compensation, 196,057 were victims and the remaining 53,605 people included family members, witnesses, and survivors. OVC also reports that 162,906 applications were deemed to be eligible, and that over 344 million dollars were awarded to applicants nationwide.

Table 6.3, from the OVC (2017) shows nationwide victim compensation awards by crime type:

Table 6.3 Summary of Claims Paid by Crime Type

Crime Type	Claims Paid	Amount Paid
Arson	214	$281,311
Assault	82,276	$177,823,805
Burglary	2,342	$1,724,472
Child Physical Abuse/Neglect	9,022	$6,882,894
Child Pornography	92	$101,753
Child Sexual Abuse	44,891	$32,844,309
DUI/DWI	2,851	$11,631,972
Freud/Financial Crimes	197	$247,881
Homicide	18,191	$56,807,128
Human Trafficking	203	$230,624
Kidnapping	830	$817,594
Other Vehicular Crimes	3,960	$13,445,831
Robbery	12,211	$13,910,239
Sexual Assault	30,268	$25,648,289
Stalking	1,253	$1,327,557
Terrorism	803	$971,582
TOTAL	**209,604**	**$344,697,242**

Restitution

Restitution refers to payments made directly to a victim by an offender, as a result of the offender's wrongful actions. Restitution requires the offender to reimburse the victim for damages and losses due to the victimization. The 1982 President's Task Force recommended that legislation be proposed at the federal and state level requiring restitution in all cases, unless the court can provide a specific reason for not requiring it. Additionally, Congress passed the Mandatory Victims Restitution Act in 1996. This Act made restitution mandatory in almost all cases in which the victim suffered an identifiable monetary loss (Dickman, 2009). As a result, courts can order convicted offenders to pay restitution as part of their sentences.

According to the National Center for Victims of Crime (NCVC) (2012), approximately one-third of state courts are required to order restitution to victims in cases involving certain types of crimes, typically violent felony offenses, but sometimes other serious offenses as well. They note that restitution can cover any out-of-pocket losses directly relating to the crime, including medical expenses, therapy costs, prescription charges, counseling costs, lost wages, and crime-scene clean up, or any other expense that resulted directly from the crime.

Restitution differs from compensation. Compensation is a program sponsored and paid for from government funding. Whereas the philosophy behind compensation programs is that society should bear part of the burden when one member is harmed, restitution assumes the offender is responsible for the harms experienced by the victim. Additionally, for restitution to be ordered, an offender must be convicted; this is not the case with compensation programs.

Although restitution holds offenders personally financially accountable, it depends on the offender's willingness and ability to pay. It has been noted that approximately 45% of all restitution orders are paid (Kercher, Johnson, Yun, & Proctor, n.d.). When restitution is unpaid many states have provisions that allow for restitution orders to become civil judgments. As such, this allows for orders to stay in effect for many years, typically ten to twenty years (NCVC, 2012).

Litigation

Crime victims can file a civil lawsuit against the perpetrator, regardless of whether or not the perpetrator was convicted of a crime. The civil process does not seek to determine the guilt or innocence of the perpetrator, but rather whether the perpetrator is liable for the victim's injuries. Injuries can include physical injuries, such as in a drunk driver-involved car accident, or emotional injuries in the case of stalking, or economic injuries in the case of identity theft. In a civil case the offense is referred to as a tort. Examples of torts are wrongful death (in cases of vehicular homicide), false imprisonment (in cases of rape), intentional or reckless infliction of emotional distress (in cases of stalking), battery (in cases of attempted murder, rape, or molestation), and conversion (in cases of larceny and embezzlement) (National Crime Victim Bar Association).

Victims can initiate a lawsuit by filing what most states refer to as a complaint. There is a statute of limitations on filing a civil suit; these statutes vary by state. Once the lawsuit is filed the victim becomes the plaintiff and the perpetrator becomes the defendant, then a series of steps follow. The first step is discovery; this step is similar to the investigation phase in a criminal case. Discovery allows both sides to interview witnesses and relevant parties, and collect documents and information. If not settled at this stage, cases then move to trial. At trial, the plaintiff can win or lose the case. If the plaintiff wins, the judge or jury can award damages. If the plaintiff loses, the case generally ends, unless the plaintiff appeals. However, it should be noted that a win does not automatically result in a victim receiving the awarded damages. Defendants may be unable or unwilling to pay damages.

Third Party Lawsuits

In some cases, a third party is liable for the damages or harm experienced by the victim or survivors. Third parties are not the actual person that committed the crime in question, but rather parties who contributed to the outcome. Tobolowsky et al. (2016) note that victims generally bring third party actions "on theories of negligent conduct by third parties that permits that criminal conduct to occur" (p. 229). For example, colleges that do not provide adequate security, or employers who do not conduct background checks on persons who work with the public, especially children, the elderly, or persons who are disabled.

Often third party lawsuits receive media attention because of the egregious negligence exercised by the third party. The American Civil Liberties Union presents two examples of third party lawsuits in which victims received settlements. In 2007, the University of Georgia was held liable for recruiting, admitting, and neglecting to supervise a student athlete who later raped a fellow student. University administrators were aware that the athlete had been removed from other institutions for harassing women. The second case (Simpson v. University of Colorado Boulder) involved college football recruiting practices at the University of Colorado Boulder. The university paid $2.45 million to victims when the court found that the risk of rape during football recruiting visits was so obvious that the university violated Title IX by ignoring the risk.

Mediation Programs

Victim offender mediation is a process that can be offered to victims who want to meet directly with the offender for the purpose of obtaining closure, while holding the offender accountable. Umbreit and Lewis (2015) explains that most often mediation is offered in cases of property offenses or minor assaults, as the process can be in lieu of other punishment (e.g., incarceration). Mediation can be suggested at both the diversion and post-adjudication level, by officials involved in the juvenile justice system, although some programs also receive referrals from the adult criminal justice system.

Mediation programs are generally facilitated by a trained mediator who provides victims with the opportunity to meet with offenders. During mediation the goal is often to hold the offenders directly accountable while providing important assistance and/or compensation to victims (Umbreit & Lewis, 2015). In addition, victims can ask questions of the offender and make suggestions about how they should be compensated. In return, offenders can take responsibility for their actions, understand the impact of their actions on the victim, and assist in planning for how best to restore or compensate the victim.

The use of mediation is a relatively new approach for the criminal justice system. Umbreit's (1998) review of research on mediation suggests that in some instances mediation can reduce recidivism; that it can reduce fear and anxiety among juvenile victims; and most notably, that mediation has been shown to result in high levels of victim and offender satisfaction with the justice system. Other research has revealed some shortcomings with mediation. For example, mediation can marginalize the victim, as victims may not be prepared for the process, or that victims may be pressured by the mediators, or that victims can feel intimated by the offender and/or their families (Jin Choi, Gilbert, & Green, 2012). Given these findings, more research is needed to measure the benefits and shortcomings of mediation.

Parole Hearings

A parole hearing is a hearing that determines whether an offender is ready to be released back into the community. Victims in all states and at the federal level also have the right to be notified of hearings, and the right to be present during parole hearings. Victims in all states and at the federal level also have the right to submit a VIS at the hearing; the statement can be read orally or submitted in writing. Following the hearing victims have the right to be notified of the outcome; for example, if the offender is being released.

Research on victims' engagement with parole hearings indicates that victim influence is a predictive factor in the decision to grant or deny parole; the more letters of protest in an offender's file and the more persons who object to an offender being paroled at a hearing, the more likely that parole will be denied (Morgan & Smith, 2005). Although this research requires further explanation to determine if the rights of the offender and victim are balanced, it does suggest that victim sentiments are considered by parole boards.

Conclusion

This chapter examined the various phases and encounters victims experience while navigating through the criminal justice system. It should be obvious that the phases depend upon the nature of the crime, the severity of the crime, the amount of evidence, and the impact on the victim. In addition, the manner in which a victim interacts with the system varies by jurisdiction; each state and the federal system have different provisions and requirements when interacting with victims of crime. Also, victims may be involved with the criminal justice system for a few days, or years. Therefore, there is no one way that victims move through the system, and the level of victim involvement varies by state. This variation can create confusion, but it also allows for flexibility. As a result, the treatment of victims depends on the level of commitment to victims of crime afforded under state law and policy, and by the individuals working in the system.

Discussion questions

1. Why is the initial contact between law enforcement and the victim so important? What can law enforcement do to ensure that victims see the criminal justice system as a supportive option at the point of initial contact?
2. This chapter explored many phases in which the victim interacts with the criminal justice system. Should the victim be excluded from participation at any of the phases? Why or why not?
3. Some victims are reluctant to cooperate with the criminal justice system; therefore, methods such as victimless prosecutions were created. First, explain and describe this method. Next, explain whether or not victimless prosecutions are in the victim's best interest.
4. Compare and contrast victim compensation programs with restitution. Which is better at meeting the needs of victims?

References

American Bar Association. (2006). *The victim in the criminal justice system*. Retrieved from Apps.americanbar.org/dch/thedl.cfm?filename=/CR300000/.../victimsreport.pdf

American Bar Association. (2017). *How courts work*. Retrieved from https://www.americanbar.org/groups/public_education/resources/law_related_education_network/how_courts_work/arrestprocedure.html

American Bar Association. (2017a). *Prosecution function*. Retrieved from: https://www.americanbar.org/publications/criminal_justice_section_archive/crimjust_standards_pfunc_blkold.html

American Bar Association (2017b). *Pretrial release*. Retrieved from https://www.americanbar.org/publications/criminal_justice_section_archive/crimjust_standards_pretrialrelease_blk.html

American Civil Liberties Union. Retrieved from https://www.aclu.org/files/pdfs/womensrights/titleixandsexualassaultknowyourrightsandyourcollege%27sresponsibilities.pdf

Animal Legal and Historical Center. Michigan State University. Retrieved from https://www.animallaw.info/article/domestic-violence-and-pets-list-states-include-pets-protection-orders

California Victim Compensation Board (2020). Hisotry of the California Victim Compensation Board. Retrieved from www.victims.ca.gov/board/

Campbell, R. (2005). What really happened? A validation study of rape survivors' help-seeking experiences with the legal and medical systems. *Violence & Victims*, *20*(1), 55–68.

Campbell, R., Bybee, D., Kelley, K. D., Dworkin, E. R., & Patterson, D. (2012). The impact of sexual assault nurse examiner (Sane) program services of law enforcement investigational practices: A mediational analysis null. *Criminal Justice And Behavior*, *39*(2), 169-184.

Cassell, P. G. (2009). In defense of victim impact statements. *Ohio State Journal of Criminal Law*, *6*(2), 611-648.

Cassell, P. G., Mitchell, N. J., & Edwards, B. J. (2014). Crime victims' rights during criminal investigations: Applying the Crime Victims' Rights Act before criminal charges are filed. *Journal of Criminal Law & Criminology*, *104*(1), 59-104.

DeJong, C., & Burgess-Proctor, A. (2006). A summary of personal protection order statutes in the United States. *Violence Against Women*, *12*(1), 68–88.

Department of Justice. (n.d.). *Sexual assault nurse examiner: Development and operation guide*. Retrieved from https://www.ncjrs.gov/ovc_archives/reports/saneguide.pdf

Devers, L. (2011). *Plea and charge bargaining* [Research summary]. Bureau of justice Assistance. Retrieved from https://www.bja.gov/Publications/PleaBargainingResearchSummary.pdf

Dickman, M. (2009). Should crime pay? A critical assessment of the Mandatory Victims Restitution Act of 1996. *California Law Review*, *97*(6), 1687–1718.

International Association of Chiefs of Police. *Enhancing law enforcement response to victims: Training supplemental*. Retrieved from http://www.theiacp.org/Portals/0/pdfs/responsetovictims/pdf/pdf/Supplemental_pages_9_21C.pdf

Keilitz, S. (2015). *Addressing victims' rights in pretrial justice reform*. Retrieved from https://www.ncsc.org/~/media/Microsites/Files/PJCC/Pretrial%20victims%20issues%20brief%20Final.ashx

Kercher, G., Johnson, M., Yun, I., Proctor, A., & Center, C. J. (n.d.). *Restitution in Texas: A report to the legislature*. Retrieved from http://dev.cjcenter.org/_files/cvi/Restitution%20Report.pdf

Kynn, J., Steiner, J., Hoge, G. L., & Postmus, J. L. (2016). *Final report: Providing services to trafficking victims: Understanding practices across the globe*. Report prepared for Safe Horizon.

LaFave, W. R. (1970). The prosecutor's discretion in the United States. *American Journal of Comparative Law, 18*(3), 532-548.

Maryland Network Against Domestic Violence. *Lethality assessment*. Retrieved from http://mnadv.org/lethality/

Messing, J. T., Campbell, J., Sullivan Wilson, J., Brown, S., & Patchell, B. (2017). The lethality screen: The predictive validity of an intimate partner violence risk assessment for use by first responders. *Journal of Interpersonal Violence, 32*(2), 205-226.

Meyer, E. (2010). *Civil protection orders: A guide for improving practice*. Retrieved from http://www.ncjfcj.org/sites/default/files/cpo_guide.pdf

Morgan, K., & Smith, B. L. (2005). Victims, punishment, and parole: The effect of victim participation on parole hearings. *Criminology & Public Policy, 4*(2), 333–360.

Mothers Against Drunk Driving. (2019). *MADD: No more victims*. Retrieved from: https://www.madd.org

National Association of Sheriffs in Collaboration with the OVC. (2008). Retrieved from https://ojp.gov/ovc/publications/infores/pdftxt/FirstResponseGuidebook.pdf

National Center for Victims of Crime (2012). *Restitution*. Retrieved from http://victimsofcrime.org/help-for-crime-victims/get-help-bulletins-for-crime-victims/restitution

National Crime Victim Law Institute. (n.d.). Retrieved from https://law.lclark.edu/live/files/4920-california

National District Attorneys Association. (2017). *National domestic violence prosecution best practices guide*. Retrieved from http://www.ncdsv.org/NDAA_National-al-DV-Prosecution-Best-Practices-Guide_3-16-2017.pdf

Office of Victims of Crime. State Crime Victim Compensation and Assistance Grant Programs. https://www.ovc.gov/publications/factshts/compandassist/fs_000306.html

Office for Justice Programs Diagnostic Center & Thurau, L. H. (2015). *First, do no harm: Model practices for law enforcement agencies when arresting parents in the presence of children*. Retrieved from: https://strategiesforyouth.org/sfysite/wp-content/uploads/2012/09/First_Do_No_Harm_Report.pdf

Osterburg, J. W. & Ward, R. H. (2010). *Criminal investigation: A method for reconstructing the past*. New York: Routledge.

Office for Victims of Crime. (2017). *Victims of Crime Act Victim Compensation Formula Grant Program: Fiscal Year 2015 Data Analysis Report*. Retrieved from https://ojp.gov/ovc/grants/vocanpr_vc15.pdf

Patterson, D. (2011). The impact of detectives' manner of questioning on rape victims' disclosure. *Violence Against Women, 17*(11), 1349–1373.

Pearsall, B. (2013). *Evaluating sexual assault nurse examiner programs*. Retrieved from https://www.ncjrs.gov/ovc_archives/reports/saneguide.pdf

Renzetti, C. M., Bush, A., Castellanos, M., & Hunt, G. (2015) Does training make a difference? An evaluation of a specialized human trafficking training module for law enforcement officers. *Journal of Crime and Justice, 38*(3), 334–350, DOI: 10.1080/0735648X.2014.997913

Simpson v. University of Colorado Boulder, 500 F.3d 1170 (10th Cir. 2007).

Truman, J. L. & Morgan, R. E. (2016). Criminal *victimization, 2015*. [NCJ 250180]. Washington, DC: U.S. Department of Justice, Office of Jusice Programs, Bureau of Justice Statistics.

Umbreit, M.S., & Lewis, T. (2015). *Dialogue-driven victim offender mediation training manual: A composite collection of training resource materials*. Center for Restorative Justice & Peacemaking School of Social Work, University of Minnesota.

Wolitzky-Taylor, K. B., Resnick, H. S., McCauley, J. L., Amstadter, A. B., Kilpatrick, D. G., & Ruggiero, K. J. (2011). Is reporting of rape on the rise? A comparison of women with reported versus unreported rape experiences in the National Women's Study-Replication. *Journal of Interpersonal Violence, 26*(4), 807–832.

CHAPTER 7

Rethinking Victim Involvement in the Criminal Justice Process

Objectives

Upon completion of this chapter, you will be able to:

- understand the difference between the retributive and restorative justice approaches,
- understand and recognize the roles of victim, offender, and the community in restorative justice,
- recognize the differences between different models of restorative justice,
- explain how digital technology shapes public beliefs and attitudes toward a particular issue, and
- discuss how technology can be used to support and empower crime victims.

Introduction

As discussed in chapter two, crime statistics often serve as a measurement of the success and/or failure of the criminal justice system and its institutions. We often use crime rates and crime statistics to launch public policies and programs and to enact laws in order to control criminality and offenders, to protect victims and the public, and to restore public order. However, crime statistics are not necessarily an appropriate measure of what the criminal justice system does or should do about crime, offenders, or victims. As the crime rates change, so does the public opinion toward criminal justice institutions. The public mood often swings back and forth between calls for punishment, perpetrators' incapacitation, or pleas for their rehabilitation, treatment, and reintegration back into society.

In the past, despite the significant number of people being a victim of crime each year, the number of crime-related fatalities and injuries, and the burden of financial damage of crime on society, crime victims had relatively few rights and remedies available to them. However, as previously discussed, the victims' rights movement of the 1970s began to change the way victims of crime were viewed and treated by society, as well as the criminal justice system.

Since President Reagan's Task Force on Victims of Crime released their recommendations, crime victims have become recognized by the criminal justice system as citizens who have not only the responsibility, but also the right, to independently participate in the system in order to restore their lives that were harmed by the crime. The long history of frustration and dissatisfaction with the criminal justice institutions among crime victims, their family members, and victims' advocates led to the establishment of policies and laws that explicitly address crime victims' rights and remedies. Federal and state statutory provisions and laws granted some rights to the victims of crime, such as the right to participate and to be present in the criminal justice system's proceedings, the right to be informed and to be notified of key prosecutorial and correctional processes and outcomes, the right to protection, and the right to financial compensation/reparations for losses and harms suffered as a result of a crime. As a result, the offender-centered criminal justice process started slowly evolving into the victim-centered outcome (Tobolowsky, Beloof, Gaboury, Jackson & Blackburn, 2016).

The victim-centered outcome led to the expansion of victim-compensation orders, social services, crisis intervention, a variety of support programs, victim advocacy programs, victim-offender mediation and other restorative justice programs. The attention of the public and criminal justice system started to focus on victim awareness and wellbeing.

This chapter provides an overview of a new approach in the criminal justice system: the restorative justice model. The restorative justice approach is geared toward addressing the needs of crime victims; helping offenders become aware of the impact their crime had on victims, to take responsibility and to make amends for their harmful actions; and involving a community in the healing process and in the process of reintegration of the offenders back into society. The chapter also discusses the support services that were authorized for victims of crime throughout the criminal justice institutions such as the right to be informed, protected, apply for compensation, and the right to restitution from the offender. It also looks at how media enables victim advocates and others to challenge myths and stereotypes about victims of crime. Finally, the chapter concludes with a discussion on how technology is being used to support crime victims.

Restorative Justice

When a crime occurs, the victim is a party directly harmed by the offender's actions. However, the traditional "retributive" approach of criminal justice focused almost exclusively on the offender and the crime victim is largely relegated to the sideline. Additionally, under this paradigm, the criminal justice system is soley focused on punishing the offender but does not require the offender to address the harm they have caused to the victim or the community at large. Furthermore, this approach to justice fails to provide offenders with the opportunity to be reintegrated back into society by not addressing the real harm done to the victims, not promoting reconciliation, and by not supporting communities and their engagement in justice processes. In other words, the traditional criminal justice approach commonly left victims feeling silenced or stigmatized, and neglected the larger community affected. As a result, there has been growing interest in exploring alternative models of justice that can better address the real needs of victims and the community. One of the models that has been receiving an increasing amount of attention in the last three decades is restorative justice.

As shown in Table 7.1, the basic principles of restorative justice are significantly different from the retributive, offender-oriented approach that has long dominated the American criminal justice system where crime by its definition is a crime against the state (Lamely, & Russell, 2002). While there is no universal agreement among scholars and practitioners about the exact definition of restorative justice, many agree that a restorative justice model opposes punitive sanctions for the offender and opposes exclusion of the victims and the community from the justice process (Lamely, & Russell, 2002). Restorative justice takes a more inclusive, informal, and preventative approach to crime. A restorative justice model views crime as more than actions that break laws. It perceives crime as actions that cause harm to individuals and relationships, and thus weakens community ties and social capital (Centre for Justice and Reconciliation, 2020). Consequently, a restorative model views victims and communities as a central part of justice and it actively seeks input from both victims and the community in order to repair the harm done to victims, create new positive relationships, redevelop the community, as well as keep offenders accountable for their harmful actions. Thus, restorative justice involves the active participation of all three stakeholders (McCold & Wachtel, 2003).

Table 7.1 Comparison of Traditional Offender-Based Criminal Justice and Restorative Justice Models

Two Distinct Approaches to Justice	
Traditional Offender–Based Criminal Justice	*Restorative Justice*
Crime is a violation of the law and the state	Crime is a violation and harm is done to the victims
Violations create guilt	Violations create obligations
Justice requires the state to determine blame/guilt and impose pain/punishment	Justice involves victims, offenders and community members in an effort to restore the harm done and to put things right
Focus is on offenders and retribution	Focus is on victim needs, offender responsibility for repairing the harm, and on community responsibility and participation in members' welfare
Three Distinct Questions	
What laws have been broken?	Who has been hurt?
Who did it?	What are their needs?
What do they deserve?	Whose obligations are these?

Source: H. Zehr and A. Gohar (2002). The Little Book of Restorative Justice

There are a number of programs associated with the restorative justice philosophy, mostly because they were created and implemented with restorative justice features: addressing victims' harm and needs, holding offenders accountable, and involving victims, offenders, and communities in the process (Zehr & Gohar, 2002). Restorative justice programs are more informal responses to crime, and most programs with restorative justice pillars can be divided into three distinct models: victim-offender conferences, family group conferences, and the circle approach.

Another way to distinguish many existing programs of restorative justice is to separate their goals: diversionary and therapeutic (Miller, 2011). Diversionary restorative justice differs from the therapeutic post-conviction programs, as it focuses on first-time and non-violent offenders, low-level crime, and antisocial behavior without recourse to formal proceedings. Diversionary restorative justice programs divert offenders from the criminal justice process or sentencing, and the charges are ultimately dropped if the offender fulfills the settlement requirements. The therapeutic post-conviction approach focuses on more severe and violent crimes. It focuses more on healing victims, rather than to modify the outcomes for offenders, as offenders were already formally convicted and sentenced by the criminal justice system. Not all therapeutic programs require face-to-face dialogue between victim and the offenders as in the program Victims' Voices Heard. Instead, victim impact statements and a victims' panel are used for the offender rehabilitation and offenders' understanding of what harm they have done, and for taking responsibility for their actions.

Victim-Offender Conferences

Victim-offender conferences (VOC) also called victim-offender mediation or victim- offender dialogue, involve encounters between victims and offenders that are structured and facilitated by trained professionals/mediators. Victim-offender conferences provide victims with an opportunity to meet with their assailant face-to-face in a safe and structured setting. During this meeting, victims discuss the impact their victimization has had on their lives and they have the opportunity to ask their assailant questions to resolve any unanswered questions they may have about the actual event. In addition, victims are able to specify the type of restitution they feel is needed in order for the harm and trauma to be repaired. This method was recently profiled in a docu-series produced by CNN called *The Redemption Project*.

VOC programs are used either to resolve issues outside of formal court proceedings or are imposed as a condition of probation after the offender has formally admitted wrongdoing to the court. The majority of VOC programs are primarily referred as a diversion from prosecution involving predominantly juvenile offenders, and first-time offenders involved in non-violent offenses. For example, some schools are now utilizing this practice with students involved with bullying or fighting with other students at school rather than punish them via suspensions and expulsions (Davis, 2015). It is believed that the restorative approach restores relationships between students and teachers, improves school climate, creates a school environment of acceptance and tolerance, and increases academic achievement.

Even though most VOC programs are utilized primarily for nonviolent juvenile offenders, some programs have applied the VOC model to offenders who have been convicted of serious violent crimes such as rape and homicide. For example, Victims' Voices Heard (2020) is a program that brings survivors of severe violence face-to-face with their perpetrators in order to facilitate victims' healing and recovery, to receive personal insights and feel empowered. The program is a post-conviction program, which means that the offender was formally convicted by the criminal justice system and is often incarcerated or under community supervision. The offender does not receive any benefits such as a reduced sentence, or leniency for participating in the program, as the dialogue between offender and victim is for personal healing, and not legal purposes. However, the offenders are presented with the opportunity to express their remorse and empathy, make an apology, and acknowledge their role and responsibility in the crime(s) for which they have been convicted (Miller, 2011). The restorative justice philosophy stresses the idea that only offenders who face their past can face their future and be truly rehabilitated. Therefore, it is suggested that offenders appealing their convictions are not appropriate candidates for participating in VOC, as they can interfere with victims' healing (Presser & Lowenkamp, 1999).

Family Group Conferences

Family group conferences involve more stakeholders, including family members and community members, or individuals who are significant to the victims and/ or offenders, in order to make decisions that might otherwise be made by criminal justice professionals (Bozynski, 1999; McGarrell & Hipple, 2007). The family group conferences empower family members in a way that allows them to take the lead for the wellbeing of the family, to create a plan for the healing, and to find solutions that includes everyone affected. The family conference is predominantly used with juvenile non-violent offenders who would stay in the care of family, rather than be confined or placed into the state's custody and care (McGarrell & Hipple, 2007). The family group conferences are often coordinated by an independent and neutral third party who prepares all those affected to come together.

The family group conference is also often used by schools to prevent and address school-related behavioral problems such as truancy (Bozynski, 1999). Efforts to prevent and address truancy relies on a partnership and presence of students, school staff, families, communities, and social service agencies. The family group conference assists with the implementation of a restorative justice approach that includes prevention, intervention, and treatment services. Thus, the family group conference became a disciplinary diversionary alternative to suspension or expulsion.

Peacemaking Circles

Peacemaking circles, include a group of participants: victims, offenders, family members, sometimes justice officials, and community members (Zehr, 2002). These circles are often used in a variety of contexts. In neighborhoods, they provide support to those affected and harmed by crime, violence, and poverty. In schools, they create a positive educational environment to resolve disruptive behavioral problems. The purpose of the circles is to foster a safe space for open discussion about sensitive topics, and also to provide an encouraging environment for students to reach out for help when they have a problem or have academic or emotional needs. In the workplace, circles help address conflict by bringing all staff members together to share their emotions and understanding of the conflict situation and to identify ways to deal with the conflict in order to rebuild the damaged team relationships. The use of circles in the workplace replaces the traditional process of managing complaints, grievances, and work-policy violations by encouraging employees to actively participate in conflict resolution (Strang & Braithwaite, 2001).

Peacemaking circles are also often used in formal settings of the criminal justice system, such as sentencing circles, for more serious offenses such as drug offenses. Sentencing circles are sometimes used in drug courts as an alternative approach that can treat individuals suffering from drug addiction, and to rehabilitate offenders by believing that an offense is often a symptom of a larger problem.

Victim Impact Statement

The concept of victim impact statements was first introduced in 1976 by a chief probation officer in Fresno, California who believed victims had valuable information that they should be allowed to share with the court prior to sentencing (Hammond & Barton-Bellessa, 2014). Specifically, a victim impact statement provides crime victims with a unique opportunity to describe to the court (in writing or orally) the effect the criminal event has had on their lives, as well as on the lives of their loved ones (National Center for Victims of Crime [NCVC], 2011). In the statement, victims can describe the physical, psychological, and financial trauma they have experienced as a result of their victimization and provide input as to the type of punishment they feel their assailant should receive. This practice has proven to be particularly invaluable for victims who may have otherwise found it difficult to participate in the process, such as child victims, non-English speaking victims, and victims with disabilities (NCVC, 2011). Today, victim impact statements are used not only by the court at sentencing, but also by parole boards to help determine whether a particular offender should be released back into the community (NCVC, 2011).

Victim Impact Panel

Victim impact panels were introduced in the early 1980s by Mothers Against Drunk Driving (MADD, 2020). Today, the panels are predominantly used for victims of drunk driving but can be also used for other offenses such as intimate partner violence, child abuse, sexual abuse, and homicide (MADD, 2020). Panels can be held in the community, as well as in jails or prisons. The program provides a neutral forum for victims to tell a group of offenders how their victimization experience has affected their lives, and the lives of their family members (MADD, 2020). Victim impact panels differ from the victim impact statements, as the offenders attending the panel are not directly connected to the victims, but all of them have committed similar offenses. Most of the offenders are ordered by the court to attend the panel as a condition of probation or as part of a diversion agreement.

Panels are typically composed of three to four victims who were injured or had a loved one injured or killed. Unlike victim-offender mediation, the panel is not designed to encourage a dialogue between the victims and the offenders (MADD, 2020). Rather, the purpose of the program is to provide victims with the opportunity to speak out about their experiences, to support victims in their healing process and to educate offenders.

Empowering Victims of Crime

Victim empowerment is important because it is mutually beneficial for the victim and for professionals in the criminal justice system. Specifically, a victim empowerment approach is vital to reducing the likelihood of the victim experiencing secondary victimization throughout the criminal justice process, while increasing the likelihood of victim cooperation and promoting their full recovery (Cattaneo & Goodman, 2009; Pollack, 2017). In order for an approach to be considered empowering for the victim, professionals must take an empathetic approach when interacting with victims and ensure that appropriate services are rendered in a timely fashion in order to mitigate the consequences of victimization. In other words, victim empowerment is an approach that stresses the importance of the existence and availability of services and resources for people who suffered harm, trauma, or loss due to crime or disasters.

However, empowerment does not only involve service and resources for the victims. Empowerment also stresses the importance of building victims' own capacity to deal with the burden of trauma, violence, and crime; to make their own choices and take control over their lives and decisions. Not all victims need the same empowerment and support; thus, the approach for victim empowerment requires an integrated, multidisciplinary, and cooperative approach across the criminal justice system and other governmental agencies, nonprofit organizations, and civic society.

As previously mentioned, the restorative justice approach is a victim-centered approach that ensures that victims play a key role in criminal justice, and their input is considered throughout the entire process and proceedings. The restorative justice approach seeks to repair damages done to the victim. By ensuring victims' rights and allowing for victim participation, the restorative justice approach as a whole is a leading example of victim empowerment.

Services to to help mitigate the impact of victimization are offered by a variety of both governmental and non-governmental agencies. The National Center for Victims of Crime (OVC) is the largest government agency that focuses on assisting victims of crime, and works in conjunction with other government organizations at the federal, state, and local levels to address victim's needs and to design strategies that will enhance victims' efforts in their recovery. Sadly, however, fewer than 1 in 10 victims of violent crime receive any assistance (Langton, 2011). Langton notes some of this may be attributed to a victim's decision not to report the incident to authorities; however it may also be the result of their not knowing whom to contact for help. Moreover, Langton found that service providers similarly may be unaware of all of the resources available in their area to refer victims to, thus may end up duplicating each other's efforts and miss the opportunity to collaborate and share resources.

Therefore, OVC strives to create a multidisciplinary, collaborative, and coordinated responses to crime victims; one in which will help to educate victims of crime, offer culturally sensitive support, identify community resources, and provide counseling and trauma-informed services. Many of the programs OVC supports were created to promote victims' empowerment by helping them navigate the criminal justice system, as well as restore the harm caused and aid in their recovery. For example, every state has a crime victim compensation program to help victims to cover expenses related to the crime and to help them with their emotional, physical, and financial recovery. Other programs focus on providing them access to services, such as support groups and mental health counseling, and housing and transportation assistance. However, one of the most important parts of this strategy is victim advocates. Victims who have connected with an advocate are more likely to feel that the criminal justice system is fair and responsive to their needs. Thus, victim advocates play a crucial role in the victim's empowerment process. Victim advocacy services can be offered by any of the criminal justice agencies or by independent nonprofit organizations. However, both types offer important assistance and help to advance and direct the narrative surrounding victimization. Many advocates also dedicate time to lobby for legislation that expands rights and protections for victims; and some will also work with the media to help educate the public about crime trends, consequences of victimization, and highlight the importance of community support and the respectful treatment of crime victims.

Working with the Media and Crime Victims

As mentioned in chapter two, public perception of crime is often influenced by the media. Media not only has an impact on our perception of crime, but also influence our ideas about what constitutes a crime, as well as our ideas of who is or may become a victim of crime. Although not all victims receive equal attention by the media, and many believe that media portray opinion rather than facts, the power of the media cannot be underestimated. The mainstream media, such as newspaper, television, magazines, internet and social media, are often used by victim advocates and activists to challenge myths and stereotypes about certain criminal offenses, perpetrators, and their victims. The public's engagement with media is important to ensure that communities are enlightened about victimization and understand victims' needs. In addition, media often plays a significant role in how victims' stories are perceived and how much public attention they attract.

For many people involved in social media discussions, tweets and posting about politics or the economy, topics regarding marginalized populations may not be of particular interest or feature of their social context. However, we are constantly exposed to these topics through photos, videos, advertisements, etc. Thus, even though we may not be interested in a particular topic, we are still exposed to these online discussions, opinions, and ideas that can shape and reshape our view and facilitate our involvement in discussion, or motivate us to take some kind of action. Social media allows for mobile and quick communications with masses through posts of breaking news, scandals, crises and disasters, as the various digital communication tools do not recognize borders or physical distance. Consequently, politicians, lobbyists, for-profit companies, and others use online platforms to deliver their message to a large population, make their themes visible, and get people involved and inspire them to bring about radical changes. This intersection of globalization and advanced technology has transformed media into an everpresent part of people's lives, and how they communicate.

Media and Marginalized Groups

In today's world, the internet creates an additional space for marginalized groups such as lesbian, gay, bisexual, transgender, and queer (LGBTQ), undocumented immigrant victims of crime, or unaccompanied minors' refugees, to gain recognition and to be heard. The tweeting and retweeting, the number of likes, and crossover between different social media platforms has enabled people to mobilize around a specific issue, and to change the public discourse about the topic. Social media platforms are contemporary equivalents of newspapers, flyers, posters, and TV and radio broadcasts, but operate on a much larger scale. People share information on social media to support, to share, to build, to interact, and to participate. Consequently, social media has facilitated a kind of "digital activism" ; the likes of which keep growing as new issues are brought to light.. For example, th Pew Research Center (2018) noted #BlackLivesMatter has become of one of the most powerful of these movements. By May 1 of 2018, the hashtag of #BlackLivesMatter had been used nearly 30 million times on Twitter (PEW, 2018).

Activists in New York City march to protest police-involved shootings

Similarly, snapshots of children refugees stranded on the Mexican-American border generated an emotional reaction to the U.S. refugee crisis; and, the #MeToo social media movement has brought to light the prevalence and impact of sexual harassment and sexual assault among millions of people across the globe. For each of these three movements, social media enabled images and responses to spread quickly, and in turn, help advocates, survivors and their supporters to organize protests across the nation.

Another marginalized group that has mobilized through media is the LGBTQ community. Members of LGBTQ groups first gained significant attention in mainstream media after New York City police raided the Stonewall Inn, a gay club, in 1969, an event which led to six days of riots and violent clashes between community members and law enforcement (History Channel, 2019). The incident became known as the Stonewall Riots, and helped set the stage for the gay rights movement and the creation of organizations and other grassroots movements in the United States and around the globe. In 1997, the comedian and television star Ellen DeGeneres revealed that she is gay on her sitcom, and was subsequently profiled on the cover of *Time* magazine (History Channel, 2020). While highly controversial at the time, her decision opened the door for other notable public figures in entertainment and professional sports to begin to come out in the media.

In the years that have followed, social media has been embraced by the LGBTQ community as a tool to share information and identify issues that threaten their health and well-being (e.g., HIV awareness and prevention, mental health, victimization). For example, the *It Gets Better* project started in 2010 to address the issue of suicide in the LGBTQ community. Dan Savage and Terry Miller used social media and posted an encouraging video on YouTube to discuss their personal struggles with bullying and abuse in school because of their sexual orientation. They also touched on family issues that initially occurred as a result of "coming out" as gay. Their movement encouraged many others, including celebrities and President Barack Obama, to share their personal stories, or offer encouragement to the LGBTQ community.

Sadly, hate crimes against LGBTQ people are more common than we would like to believe. Even before the 2016 shooting at the Pulse nightclub, a well known gay establishement in Orlando, Florida, that left 49 people dead, research has shown LGBTQ people are victims of intolerance and hate more than any other minority groups (Office for Victims of Crime, n.d.). Therefore, to address victimization within the LGBTQ community, The Human Rights Campaign (HRC) was founded in 1980 in order to ensure basic rights for members of the LGBTQ community (HRC, 2020). Today, HRC commonly utilizes social media to increase awareness of hate crimes and hate speech and discriminatory treatment in the workplace, military, marriage, or adoption. Their most famous social media campaign was in March 2013, during which the HRC urged Facebook and Twitter users to change their profile pictures to show support for marriage equality, which was being argued in the U.S. Supreme Court at the time. Numerous celebrities showed their support on their social media pages, which helped the campaign go viral. Consequently, in 2014, Facebook added additional gender options for users in order to be more inclusive and provides the option to choose gender neutral pronouns (they/their) (Oremus, 2014).

The media has also helped to increase the awareness about the plight of undocumented immigrants, and the violence they often suffer. The Violence Against Women Act of 1994 was enacted in the United States as a remedy for abused and battered women, some of whom are faced with legal immigration status challenges. The following year, the United Nations met in Beijing for the Fourth World Conference on Women. During the conference, Hillary Clinton and Ambassador Madeleine Albright delivered speeches focusing on violence against women, women's rights, and the right to live free from abuse and exploitation. Following the conference, Clinton and Albright in 1997 developed the Vital Voices Democracy

Initiative (now Vital Voices Global Partnership), which helped women to advance their economic, political, and social status around the world by providing them with skills training, networking, and support.

The conference in Beijing and the initiative brought widespread attention to struggles that women around the world face, including trafficking. As the support surrounding women's rights continued to strengthen, the Violence Against Women Act was reauthorized in 2000, and it created two nonimmigrant visa categories (T-visa and U-visa) giving legal migration status to victims of crime such as sexual assault, intimate partner violence, and trafficking.

Media and Crimes against Children

The media commonly presents certain types of crimes and crime victims more frequently than others. For example, violent crime and children as victims of sexual crimes are often overrepresented in mainstream media. Apart from public interest in high profile crime, crime news also serves the purpose of changing public perception, to involve public in social change and pursue change in legislation and the criminal justice system. For example, the rape and murder of Megan Kanka at age 7 in 1994 by a convicted sex offender created a national outcry for change in legislation how offenders who were convicted of sex offenses must be handled by the criminal justice system (Megan Kanka Foundation, n.d.). The Kanka family stated that they would have taken proper precautions to prevent the crime had they known Jesse Timmendequas, a convicted sex offender, was living in their neighborhood. As a result, community members signed a petition urging legislators to pass a law to notify the public when a sex offender is a part of their community. The petition was widely covered by the media at the time, which further emphasized the urgency in creating such a legal provision. The media's extensive coverage, along with the support of the community, helped Megan's Law quickly move through legislation in less than three months after Megan's death (Megan Kanka Foundation, n.d.).

Similarly, the highly publicized case of Amber Hagerman, who was abducted and murdered in 1996 at age 9, led to a new law to help protect children (U.S. Department of Justice, Office of Justice Programs [OJP], n.d.). Amber's parents were interviewed by numerous media sources following the abduction, in hopes that an increase in coverage would result in a lead in the case. In doing so, Amber's story received national attention. This resulted in the development of the AMBER Alert System, which—while named after Amber Hagerman—stands for America's Missing: Broadcast Emergency Response (OJP, n.d.. As the name suggests, the initial goal of the AMBER Alert System was to quickly interrupt radio and TV broadcasts with information about a child abduction. Today, the AMBER alert is a national program and has broadened to highway signs and automatic

© Wonderfolio/Shutterstock.com

Cell phone AMBER alert

smartphone alerts. In addition to smartphones, social media provides a way to reach people with key details about missing persons throughout a wide-spread geographical location. For example, in 2015 Facebook started using AMBER alert features to involve their users in the viral efforts to spread the alert and crucial information (Vacher, 2015).

The murder of Polly Klaas is another case which received widespread attention after Polly Klaas, age 12, was kidnapped from her home in California in 1993 (Callahan, 2013). The case was followed by the media largely because of the offender, Richard Allen Davis. Davis' conduct in the courtroom resulted in national outrage, as he showed blatant disrespect toward court officials, and provoked the Klaas family throughout the trial. In addition to his behavior, Davis had an extensive criminal history including burglary, theft, robbery, and kidnapping. The year after Polly Klaas' murder, California politicians signed the state's Three Strikes law in order to modify sentencing guidelines for habitual offenders (California Courts, 2020).

The Penn State sex abuse case involving Jerry Sandusky also facilitated changes to federal laws, but not by changing criminal code but instead by expanding Title IX of the Education Amendments (U.S. Department of Justice [DOJ], 2015). First implemented in 1972, Title IX was designed to prohibit sexual discrimination from occurring during any educational program or activity that receives federal funding. The idea to extend the definition of sexual discrimination to sexual violence in schools came from the highly publicized sex abuse scandal at Penn State University, where Jerry Sandusky was a member of the coaching staff for its football program (Rammell, 2014). In 2011, Sandusky was accused of sexual abusing multiple boys, some of whom had been victimized while on campus. Two officials from the university were subsequently accused of perjury and failure to report abuse (Rammell, 2014). In 2012, Sandusky was convicted of 45 counts of sexual abuse, (Rammell, 2014). As a result, Penn State was criticized for failing to follow protocols mandated by Title IX.

While the case did not involve students of Penn State, the case received national attention in the media, and brought to light sexual violence occurring on college campuses and the failure of administrators to respond. In response, the Department of Education Office of Civil Rights (OCR) issued the Dear Colleague Letter (DCL) which elaborated and clarified specific mandates for the educational institutions how to respond to sexual violence that occurs on campus or during school sponsored activities (U,S. Department of Education [DOE], 2020). In effect, the DCL expanded the definition of sexual discrimination to include sexual violence, and therefore mandated that schools address and adequately respond to sexual violence in order to comply with the Title IX legislation (DOJ, 2015; DOE, 2020).

Technology used to Support Crime Victims

The media is not the only tool that has helped to change the way we interact with and respond to victims of crime. Other forms of technology have been developed to assist victims navigate the criminal justice process and to connect them to resources. Each of these iniatives have further helped to empower victims of crime and aid in their recovery. A summary of some of these tools are described below.

VINE: Victim Information and Notification Everyday

The Victim Information and Notification Everyday (VINE) system was developed in 1994 in response to the murder of 21-year-old Mary Byron, who was murdered by her ex-boyfriend after he was bailed out of jail. She did not know about his release, and was shot and killed by her ex-boyfriend while leaving work. Mary's parents advocated for the creation of a system that would prevent such incidents across the nation. Consequently, VINE was created one year after Mary's murder. Today, the VINE link is a free service that provides crime victims with real time access to the custody status of offenders in county jail, state prison, or under state parole supervision. It provides registered users with automated telephone, email and/or text message notifications of any change in an inmate's incarceration status, including release, transfer, or escape. In some states, VINE also offers protective order and court notifications. Victims may utilize the VINE mobile application, website, or phone number 24 hours a day. VINE is currently available in 48 states, and it is available in 195 languages via live operator support.

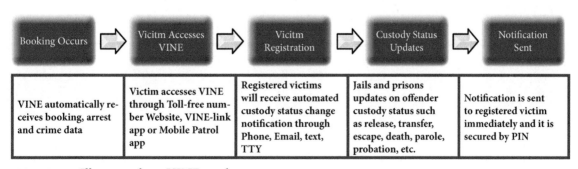

FIGURE 7.1 Illustrates how VINE works.

VINE empowers victims with safety, information, knowledge, and planning. However, it is also a valuable tool for criminal justice professionals and victims' service providers. Eleven states including Virginia, New York, Washington, and Nevada have an enhanced version of VINE; which includes a service provider directory, offender watch list, contact list, interactive voice response (IVR) technology, and a "quick escape" button. These new features were designed to promote empowering victims' safety, self-advocacy, access to the unified victims' services, and mobility. For example, the service provider directory was designed to close a gap between state-wide available professional services and victims by providing a central and comprehensive directory of services for all types of crime available for victims in a particular state.

ASK: Assault. Services. Knowledge

Another technology that has empowered victims by helping them to quickly identify and access resources when they need it is an mobile app and website called ASK (Assault. Services. Knowledge.) ASK provides assistance to victims of sexual assault, domestic violence, and intimate partner violence in real-time. First launched in 2012 in Washington, DC, the app allows victims to be immediately connected to advocates, medical professionals, and other local resources based on their location; and, includes editions in eight languages - Amharic, Chinese, English, French, Korean, Russian, Spanish, and Vietnamese. The ASK app also includes a panic button, which the victim can press at any time they do not feel safe, and they immediately be connected with emergency services; and, has an option to send a GPS location and message to specific individual(s) that the user has identified as emergency contacts. The ASK app has since been rolled out in three other states—Connecticut, North Dakota, and Arizona.

More recently, ASK has created a university-campus specific version of the mobile application for Washington DC, called U ASK DC, that brings together the resources at all eight university campuses in DC. Duke University has since created its own mobile app, U ASK Duke, for its campus community.

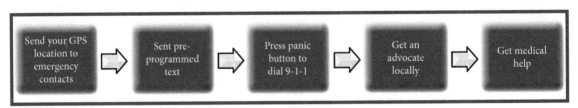

FIGURE 7.2 Summarizes the features of the ASK app.

Online Therapies and Directories for Services

As mentioned previously, empowering victims means providing victim-centered services and resources. However, there continue to be large gaps in the delivery of services to victims of crime. Many victims are living in isolated and remote areas where services are not readily available, and others are suffering from disabilities that prevent them from reaching out for help and support. The ability for providers to deliver the services to victims, regardless of distance, is particularly appealing for underserved victims living in rural America, in poverty, or with a disability.

Online therapies, including mental health counseling, are now available through the Internet. Online therapies are often known as e-counseling, distance or web therapy. The Internet allows the professionals and victims to use apps for texting, voice or audio messaging, and video conferencing that allows for a real time feedback and self-pacing therapy. Not only does this help to empower victims in their own recovery, but it also reduces the burden of providing outreach services to remote areas and underserved populations.

Online platform services can also be a convenient way for victims who are accustomed to interacting with people using technology. Due to the low-cost, convenient, and accessible nature of web-based and mobile applications, novel interventions utilizing technology are increasingly being developed and geared toward young people, as they are more likely to use digital tools to receive and share information.

Global Positioning System (GPS) Tracking

Another technological tool available to victims to help them stay informed, and maintain their safety and privacy is Global Positioning System Tracking (GPS). Today law enforcement agencies use GPS tracking devices as a way to monitor a variety of offenders (e.g., sex offenders, domestic violence offenders, violent offenders) by tracking their movements in real time. Commonly, if the offender violates any of the designated zones, the action will trigger a signal to a monitoring center, which in turn sends an alert to the victim and local law enforcement agencies.

GPS has also been used to help track autistic children, as well as elderly individuals suffering from dementia or Alzheimer's, that may wander away from their home and/or facility. It has also been used by parents

© aorpixza/Shutterstock.com

to monitor their child(ren)'s activity on cell phones, tablets, and computers to reduce their likelihood of becoming a victim of online predators and to help prevent cyberbullying. For example, the KidGuard app is popular service that provides parents with tools to digitally monitor their children's text messages, monitor GPS location, and track phone logs and chats.

Sexual Assault Kit Initiative (SAKI) and other DNA Databases

Another innovative use of technology to empower victims of sexual assault and rape allows them to track the status of their rape kit in a similar way they would track a package mailed through the U.S. mail system, UPS, or FedEx. Thus, the victim is able to track where their rape kit at at any givent time (e.g., medical facility, law enforcement agency, forensic laboratory, prosecuting attorneys). The ability to track their kit is an important step in victims' empowerment as it enables them to get information about what stage of the investigative process their case is at.

DNA databases such as the Combined DNA Index System (CODIS) are another important investigative resource. CODIS is administrated and maintained by the FBI and stores DNA profiles from federal, state and local DNA sample collections of convicted offenders, victims, and crime scenes. Today's advanced digital technology allows us to use DNA profiles from ancestry websites to match them with DNA from crime scenes. By using DNA profiles from ancestry websites that includes genetic information from relatives, law enforcement agencies expanded their DNA searches well beyond CODIS. For example, in early 2018, police were able to identify the suspected Golden State Killer, a serial killer active in California in the 1970s, by matching forensic evidence from the crime scene with DNA stored in one of the ancestry websites.

Conclusion

While crime victims rights have expanded to afford them increased access to the criminal justice proceedings and to resources, there are still notable gaps in how they are integrated into the criminal justice system, and how the public at-large views and treats victims of crime. One of the ways many communities are rethinking their approach to justice is to incorporate more restorative justice practices, both within the criminal justice system as well as a diversionary program. This alternate paradigm of justice continues to grow in popularity, not just here in the United States (see National Association of Commuity and Restorative Justice) but in many countries around the world (see International Institute for Restorative Practices). Regardless of the specific type of restorative justice practice that is used, the underlying goal remains to facilitate the healing and recovery of the victim and the community.

While these initiatives can be very empowering for many victims of crime, adovocates, survivors, and their supporters have looked for other ways to raise awareness and to mobilize the community to facilitate change in how the criminal justice system, as well as the public views and responds to victims of crime. One of the most powerful tools they have at their disposal is the media, particularly social media. Today, a single Tweet, Facebook Post, or Snapchat can reach thousands of followers in an instant. And if that post goes viral, it has the ability to reach millions of people around the globe, and may motivate people to take action. We have seen this with #BlackLivesMatter and the #MeToo movements in recent years. This collective action is a powerful force that can effect significant change to laws, policies, and practices.

Advancements in technology in recent years has also benefited victims of crime. Some of these tools have given victims greater access to resources (e.g., safety services, emotional support, professional services), while others have provided them with a mechanism that enables them to be more involved in the criminal justice process. All of these various technologies have helped to empower victims of crime and aid in their recovery.

As we move further into the 21st Centrury, it will be interesting to see if and how the criminal justice system evolves to include more restorative justice practices; how the power of social media continues to be harnassed to effect change in how the criminal justce system, as well as the public-at-large, respond to victims of crime; and, how continued advances in technology help to make the criminal justice processes more transparent and easier for victims of crime to navigate, as well as to link them to the resources and services that they need. As with any story—only time will tell,

Discussion Questions

1. What are the major differences between a restorative justice and traditional adversarial criminal justice model?
2. How has digital and other media helped to facilitate victims' empowerment? Explain and provide examples.
3. How have other types of advanced technology facilitate victims' empowerment? List at least three breakthroughs in technology that help victims of crime.

References

Bozynski, M. (1999). *Family group conferences* [inSummary]. Washington, DC: National Center for Juvenile Justice.

California Courts. (2020). California's Three Strikes sentencing law. Retrieved from: http://www.courts.ca.gov/20142.htm

Callahan, M. (2013). *Family, friends remember life, legacy of Polly Klaas.* [The Press Democrat] Retrieved from: https://www.pressdemocrat.com/news/2219178-181/family-friends-remember-life-legacy

Cattaneo, L.B. & Goodman, L.A. (2009). Through the lens of therapeutic jurisprudence: The relationship between empowerment in the court system and well-being for Intimate Partner Violence victims. *Journal of Interpersonal Violence, 25*(3), pp. 481–502.

Centre for Justice & Reconciliation. (2020). *About restorative justice.* Retrieved from: http://restorativejustice.org/#sthash.vzNS0s2Y.dpbs

Davis, M. (2015). *Restorative justice: Resource for schools.* Retrieved from: https://www.edutopia.org/blog/restorative-justice-resources-matt-davis

Guckenburg, S.; Hurley N., Persson, H., Fronius T. & Petrosino A. (2016). *Restorative justice in U.S. schools: Practitioners' perspectives.* WestEd, Justice & Prevention Research Center. Retrieved from: https://www.wested.org/wp-content/uploads/2016/11/1453742980resourcerestorativejusticeinusschoolspractitionersperspectives-3.pdf

Hammond, R.E. & Barton-Bellessa, S.M. (2014). Victim rights and restitution in sentencing. In B. Arrigo (Ed.) *Encyclopedia of Criminal Justice Ethics* (pp.979–983). Thousand Oaks, CA: SAGE Publishing.

History Channel. (2019). *Stonewall riots.* Retrieved from: https://www.history.com/topics/gay-rights/the-stonewall-riots

History Channel. (2020). *Controversial "coming out" episode of "Ellen" airs.* Retrieved from: https://www.history.com/this-day-in-history/coming-out-episode-of-ellen

Human Rights Campaign. (20200. *HRC Story*. Retreived from: https://www.hrc.org/hrc-story

It Gets Better Project. (2020). *About our global movement*. Retrieved from: https://itgetsbetter.org/about/

Lemley, R. & Russell, G. (2002). Implementing restorative Justice by "Groping Along": A case study in program evolutionary implementation. *The Justice System Journal, 23*(2), pp. 157–190.

Langton, L. (2011). *Use of victim service agencies by victims of serious violent crime, 1993–2009*. Washington, DC: U.S. Department of Justice, Office of Justice Programs, Bureau of Justice Statistics, NCJ 234212, August 2011. Retrieved from: http://www.bjs.gov/index.cfm?ty=pbdetail&iid=2432

McCold, P., & Wachtel, T. (2002). Restorative justice theory validation. In E. G. M. Weitekamp, & H. J. Kerner (Eds.), *Restorative justice: Theoretical foundations* (pp. 110–142). Devon, UK: Willan.

Megan Nicole Kanka Foundation. (n.d.). *Our mission*. Retrieved from: http://www.megannicolekankafoundation.org/mission.htm

Miller, S.L. (2011). *After the crime: The power of restorative justice dialogues between victims and violent offenders*. New York University Press.

Mothers Against Drunk Driving. (2020). *Victim impact panel program*. Retrieved from: https://maddvip.org/how-it-works/

National Center for Victims of Crime. (2011). *Victim impact statements*. Retrieved from: https://victimsofcrime.org/help-for-crime-victims/get-help-bulletins-for-crime-victims/victim-impact-statements

Office for Victims of Crime. (n.d.). *LGBTQ*. Retrieved from: https://ovc.ncjrs.gov/topic.aspx?topicid=109

Oremus, W. (2014, February 13). *Here are all the different genders you can be on Facebook*. [Slate]. Retrieved from: https://slate.com/technology/2014/02/facebook-custom-gender-options-here-are-all-56-custom-options.html

Pew Research Center (2018). *Activism in the social media age*. Retrieved from: http://www.pewinternet.org/2018/07/11/activism-in-the-social-media-age/

Pollack, J. M. (2016). Getting even: Empowering victims of revenge porn with a civil cause of action. *Albany Law Review., 80*(1), 353–380.

Presser, L. & Lowenkamp, Ch.T. (1999). Restorative justice and offender screening. *Journal of Criminal Justice, 27*(4), 333–343.

Rammell, N. (2014). Title IX and the Dear Colleague Letter: An ounce of prevention of worth a pound of cure. *Brigham Young University Education and Law Journal, Spring 3-1-2014,* 135-149.

Strang, H. & Braithwaite, J. (eds), (2001). *Restorative justice and civil society*. Cambridge University Press.

Tobolowsky, P.M; Beloof, D.E.; Gaboury, M.T.; Jackson, A.L. & Blackburn, A.G. (2016). *Crime victim rights and remedies* (3rd ed.). Durham, NC: Carolina Academic Press.

United States Department of Education. (2020). *Dear Colleague Letter*. Retrieved from: https://www2.ed.gov/about/offices/list/ocr/letters/colleague-201104.html

United States Department of Justice. (n.d.). *AMBER Alert*. Retrieved from: https://amberalert.ojp.gov/about/faqs

United States Department of Justice. (2015). *Title IX*. Retrieved from: https://www.justice.gov/crt/title-ix

Vacher, E. (2015). *Introducing AMBER Alerts on Facebook*. Retrieved from: https://about.fb.com/news/2015/01/introducing-amber-alerts-on-facebook/

Victims' Voices Heard. (2020). *Victim/offender dialogue*. Retrieved from: https://www.victimsvoicesheard.org

Zehr, H. & Gohar, A. (2002). *The little book of restorative justice.* Good Books.

SECTION III

THE TRANSFORMATION OF
THE FIELD OF VICTIMOLOGY INTO
THE 21ST CENTURY

Model Programs and Best Practices in Victim Services: Rethinking What Works

Objectives

Upon completion of this chapter, you will be able to:
- Define trauma and discuss the potential impact on crime victims
- Discuss the significance of Adverse Childhood Experiences (ACEs)
- Identify the principles that guide a trauma-informed approach to victim services
- Identify examples of best-practices of trauma-informed policies, practices, and programs designed to assist victims of crime

Introduction

The number of individuals impacted by trauma, directly or proximately, has increased in the United States as a result of abuse, neglect, discrimination, violence, and engagement in risky behavior. Growing research suggests that traumatic events can lead to short and long-term consequences affecting the individual's health and well-being, especially if the victim does not receive the appropriate services advocacy, and support. Research has found this is particularly true among children who experience trauma because it disrupts their developmental processes. Consequently, the need for the use of trauma-informed strategies and interventions has emerged, particularly for children and adults with a history of childhood trauma.

Today, best practices in victim services share a common goal to end violence and victimization and to help victims of crime to heal and to rebuild their lives. As such, over the past three decades, the field of victim services has significantly grown in size and evolved in level of expertise, drawing on the knowledge of those working in the field, as well as from research, to create a set of guidelines for trauma-informed victim services. To illustrate how the field has evolved, this chapter presents an overview of 1) the research on trauma, and how it effects individuals in the short and long-term; 2) the principles of trauma-informed care that should guide all victim services; and, 3) a selection of trauma-informed best-practices that are currently being used in programs, organizations, and communities across the United States.

The Impact of Trauma

According to the Substance Abuse Mental Health Services Administration (SAMHSA), trauma is defined as "an event, series of events, or set of circumstances that is experienced by an individual as physically or emotionally harmful or life threatening and that has lasting adverse effects on the individual's functioning and mental, physical, social, emotional, or spiritual well-being" (SAMHSA, 2014). A simpler way of conceptualizing trauma is that it refers to "anything that overwhelms a person's ability to cope." In order to understand how an individual may process trauma, one needs to be cognizant of three key elements - the **event**, the **experience**, and the **effects** (SAMHSA, 2014).

The *event* emphasizes the circumstances that caused the trauma. Focusing on the circumstances surrounding the event, rather than the individual, is important because it places the cause of the trauma in the environment, not on some defect of the individual. Thus, there is a marked shift from blaming the individual (e.g., "what's wrong with you?") to asking the individual "what happened to you?" Focusing on how the individual *experienced* the event highlights the fact that not every person will experience the same events as traumatic. How an individual may experience trauma may be profoundly affected by when, how, where, and how often it occurs. It can result from a single event (i.e., acute trauma) or from multiple traumatic events over time. Ultimately, how an individual processes the event is subjective; there is no 'right' or 'wrong' way an individual should react to trauma. In fact, the *effect* of trauma on an individual can be conceptualized as a normal response to an abnormal situation. Responses can vary widely; it can affect an individual's coping responses, psychological well-being, ability to engage in relationships, or interfere with cognitive functioning, or any combination thereof. Trauma can have both short- and long-term effects, and the impact may not be immediately recognized. It might manifest as increased levels of fear or anxiety, having difficulty concentrating, experiencing sleep disorders or nightmares, difficulty trusting others, being easily startled, feelings of numbness or detachment, difficulties with relationships with family, friends, and coworkers, loss of interest or motivation in life, and depression (NISVS, 2015; RAINN, 2020). None of these responses is always associated with trauma. How each individual responds to any given event is always going to be personal.

In addition to those responses, many victims also face adverse financial consequences as a result of their trauma. For example, IPV victims lose a total of 8.0 million days of paid work each year, and between 21-60% of IPV victims lose their jobs due to reasons stemming from their abuse (National Coalition Against Domestic Violence, n.d.). Others incur significant medical and mental health costs attributed to their victimization. For example, one national study estimated the average cost of being a victim of rape is $110,000, being a victim of drunk driving costs $36,000, and being a victim of robbery costs $16,000 (Restall, 2018). This added stressor can significantly compound the emotional, psychological, and mental strain they are already under.

For many victims, most of the adverse symptoms associated with the trauma will dissipate with time. However, for some victims, the incidence and severity of these symptoms can escalate. Research has found this to be particularly true for victims of rape and sexual assault. According to RAINN (2020), 70% of these victims reported moderate to severe levels of distress following their assault, which is significantly higher than what other victims of violent crime report. Ninety-four percent of women who are raped reported symptoms of post-traumatic stress disorder (PTSD) during the two weeks following the rape, and 30% reported symptoms of PTSD 9 months after their assault (RAINN, 2020). Sadly, 33% of these victims contemplated suicide, and 13% attempted suicide (RAINN, 2020).

Another group that is at higher risk for serious, long-term effects stemming from trauma are children. Given their developmental and neurophysiological immaturity, trauma has been found to have a greater adverse effect on children in both the short- and the long-term than what is observed among adults. Adverse childhood experiences (ACES) include all types of abuse and neglect as well as parental mental illness, substance abuse, divorce, incarceration, and domestic violence. Research has found that individuals who experience traumatic events prior to the age of 18 are at significantly higher risk for a variety of negative outcomes in adulthood, including poor physical and mental health, substance abuse, alcoholism, other risky behaviors (e.g. unplanned pregnancy, STDs, 10+ sexual partners), and revictimization (Felitti et al., 1998). As illustrated in Figure 8.1 (and discussed in chapter 2), a significant number of children in the United States have experienced at least one ACE. Moreover, nearly two-thirds of adults surveyed in the largest ongoing health risk study reported at least one ACE, and over 40% surveyed reported two or more ACEs (Felitti et al., 1998).

Despite all of the data available, there still remains a general lack of awareness and understanding about the prevalence and impact of trauma for many individuals living in in our community. Some of this is attributed to the fact that many victims remain silent about their experience because they may not fully understand what they experienced, or are struggling with feelings of shame, self-blame, or fear. Others worry if they do tell, they will be blamed or discounted, or their disclosure will cause too much distress for loved ones. Research has found that children, in particular, are less likely to disclose victimization, as are victims of intimate partner violence (American Civil Liberties Union, 2015; O'Grady & Matthews-Creech, 2019).

How others respond to a victim when he or she discloses a traumatic event has been found to be instrumental for their recovery. If they are believed, listened to, and not judged by others, they are more likely to recover. However, if they are blamed, ignored, or dismissed, they are more likely to be re-traumatized, and in turn, it will be more difficult for them to recover.

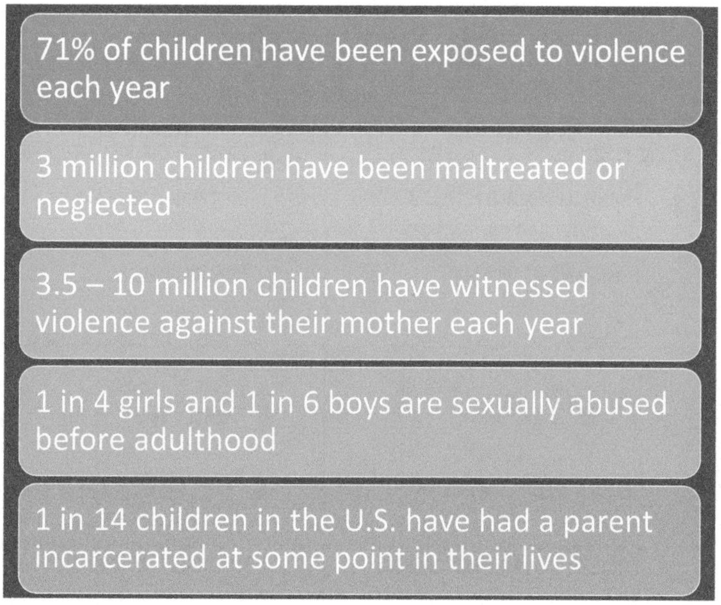

> 71% of children have been exposed to violence each year
>
> 3 million children have been maltreated or neglected
>
> 3.5 – 10 million children have witnessed violence against their mother each year
>
> 1 in 4 girls and 1 in 6 boys are sexually abused before adulthood
>
> 1 in 14 children in the U.S. have had a parent incarcerated at some point in their lives

FIGURE 8.1 Trauma Prevalence in Children

Unfortunately, sometimes members of the media and the community, as well as professionals working in systems designed to assist victims of crime, inadvertently re-traumatize victims because the policies and procedures currently in place are not trauma-informed. Some of these gaps are highlighted in Figure 2. Consequently, some victims choose to remain silent, refuse to participate in an investigation, or even to seek any assistance in order to avoid the risk being re-traumatized. For example, in a 2018 national survey only 10% of victims of a violent crime reported they had sought assistance from a victim-service agency (Morgan & Oudekerk, 2019). However, this problem can be mitigated if systems, organizations, and programs adapt their policies, processes, and practices to become trauma-informed.

Principles of Trauma-Informed Approach to Victim Services

Over the past three decades, the field of victim services has significantly grown and changed. Today, crime victim assistance and services are based on the best practices that were developed through collective experience and research. In 1992, the Office for Victims of Crime adapted a set of guiding principles from the American Psychological Association for victim services and advocacy to include

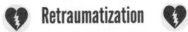

Retraumatization

WHAT HURTS?

SYSTEM (POLICIES, PROCEDURES, "THE WAY THINGS ARE DONE")	RELATIONSHIP (POWER, CONTROL, SUBVERSIVENESS)
HAVING TO CONTINUALLY RETELL THEIR STORY	NOT BEING SEEN / HEARD
BEING TREATED AS A NUMBER	VIOLATING TRUST
PROCEDURES THAT REQUIRE DISROBING	FAILURE TO ENSURE EMOTIONAL SAFETY
BEING SEEN AS THEIR LABEL (I.E ADDICT, SCHIZOPHRENIC)	NONCOLLABORATIVE
NO CHOICE IN SERVICE OR TREATMENT	DOES THINGS FOR RATHER THAN WITH
NO OPPORTUNITY TO GIVE FEEDBACK ABOUT THEIR EXPERIENCE WITH THE SERVICE DELIVERY	USE OF PUNITIVE TREATMENT, COERCIVE PRACTICES AND OPPRESSIVE LANGUAGE

FIGURE 8.2 Retraumatization: What Hurts?

a) respect for people's rights and dignity,
b) competence of high standards and capabilities,
c) promotion of integrity,
d) maintain professional responsibility,
e) contribute to the welfare of victims and survivors, and
f) being aware of professional, legal, and social responsibility to the community in which the service belongs (OVC, n.d.).

In order to evaluate existing practices in the field of victim services, the National Victim Assistance Consortium (NVASC) was established in 1999 by the Office for Victims of Crime (DeHart, 2003). The Consortium was comprised of professionals from different backgrounds who worked directly with victims and who had experience working in the field of criminal justice (e.g., law enforcement, attorneys, social workers, clinicians, healthcare professionals, advocates, researchers). The group was charged with evaluating existing standards within the field of victim services and to establish a set of standards for victim service professionals that would promote their competence, quality, and consistency within service delivery. The Consortium noted that in order to create a victim-centered, evidence-based practice, it must address the following ideals:

1. each victim has a different set of needs that require different services and approaches,

2. victims often need help navigating the criminal justice system and understanding their rights, and

3. many victims need assistance locating and obtaining services (DeHart, 2003).

As researchers began to better understand the prevalence and effects of trauma among victims of crime, the standards for best-practices in victim services evolved to embrace principles of trauma-informed care.

A trauma-informed approach reflects a fundamental shift in the culture of an entire system, organization, or program. However, to be trauma-informed it is not enough for an organization to simply know about trauma, rather it must recognize the many ways trauma may effect individuals, respond by integrating knowledge about trauma into each of its policies and processes, and be deliberate in all of its actions and decision-making to resist the risk of re-traumatizing the individuals it is charged with assisting (see Figure 3) (SAMHSA, 2014). To guide such changes, SAMHSA developed six principles each system, organization, and program should organize itself around, and use to develop a common language and framework to operate within, thereby provide a way to evaluate its effectiveness. These principles are safety, trustworthiness and transparency, peer support, collaboration and mutuality, empowerment, voice and choice, and cultural, historical, and gender issues (see Table 1) (SAMHSA, 2014).

FIGURE 8.3 The Four R's of a Trauma Informed Program, Organization, or System

Safety means that throughout the organization both staff and the people they serve feel physically and psychologically safe. This encapsulates not just the physical environment in which everyone operates, but also focuses on the nature of interpersonal interactions and prioritizes a sense of safety. It is important to recognize that safety may mean different things to different people. For example, for staff, safety may mean controlling the environment in order to minimize risk; however, for people who use the services of the organization safety may mean having control over their own lives. Therefore, a trauma-informed organization would adapt its policies and practices to attend to both parties' definitions.

Trustworthiness and Transparency refers to maximizing trustworthiness, making tasks clear, and maintaining appropriate boundaries. By making the organization's operations and decisions transparent, staff is in a better position to establish and maintain a sense of trust with the people they serve. One of the most effective ways of building trust is to give people full and accurate information. People do not like ambiguity or being excluded from decision-making, especially when it has a direct effect on their lives. Thus, it is critical to be clear about what policies and practices guide decisions that are made (e.g., explain why and how you must respond [or not] to a particular situation). and that staff is genuine and authentic in their interpersonal interactions with the people they serve.

Peer support refers to the mutual self-help that can be garnered from individuals who share lived experiences of trauma, and is focused on building mutual, healing relationships among equals. It is important to differentiate the concept of peer support from "peer counseling." While the former emphasizes shared knowledge and power among its members, the latter implies that one person knows more than the other, thus creates a power differential between parties. The goal of peer support is to empower all of its members. Thus, it relies on principles of self-determination, non-judgement, respect, reciprocity, and empathy.

Collaboration and Mutuality requires the leveling of power differences between staff and clients, and among organizational staff from direct care staff and administrators. It recognizes that healing happens in relationships that are authentic and prioritizes that everyone has a role to play in trauma-informed approaches rather than relying on a top-down approach.

Empowerment, Voice, and Choice embraces an individualized approach to service delivery. It recognizes that every person's experience is unique, and so too are their abilities to adapt to trauma. A trauma-informed model focuses on people's strengths, rather than "what's wrong with them" or focus on what they can't do. Thus, it requires staff to identify what people are doing right and build on their capacities to foster resilience.

Cultural, Historical, and Gender Issues emphasizes that trauma is context specific. Individuals from different backgrounds experience traumatic events differently, and the meaning individuals assign to an event is often heavily influenced by the culture they are a part of. Thus, a trauma-informed approach rejects the idea that there is a one-size-fits all interpretation of trauma, or how individuals respond to trauma, thus the services provided to a victim of crime must take into consideration the individual's culture, gender, and history.

As noted at the beginning of this section, developing a trauma-informed approach requires a fundamental shift in the culture of an organization. Thus, it requires change at multiple levels of that organization, from its governance and leadership, to how it drafts its standard operating procedures, to how it funds its activities, to how it evaluates its performance. To help organizations create a plan for implementing such changes, SAMHSA has identified ten domains within the organization that must be addressed. These ten domains are laid out in Appendix A.

To illustrate how some organizations have implemented these principles, the next section highlights various trauma-informed policies, practices, and programs found in communities, agencies, and systems across the United States. Each of these initiatives is considered a best-practice of a trauma-informed response.

Table 8.1 Samhsa's Six Key Principles of a Trauma-Informed Approach

Safety	Trustworthiness and Transparency	Peer Support	Collaboration and Mutuality	Empowerment, Voice, And Choice	Cultural, Historical, and Gender Issues
Throughout the organization, staff and the people they serve, whether children or adults, feel physically and psychologically safe	Organizational operations and decisions are conducted with transparency and the goal is to build and maintain trust among clients, family members, staff, and others involved with the organization	Peer support and mutual self-help are key vehicles for establishing safety and hope, building trust, enhancing collaboration, serving as models of recovery and healing, and maximizing a sense of empowerment	Partnering and leveling of power differences between staff and clients, and among organizational staff from direct care to administrators, demonstrates that healing happens in relationships, and in the meaningful sharing or power and decisionmaking	The organization fosters a belief in resilience. Individuals' strengths and experiences are recognized and built upon; the experience of having a voice and choice is validated and new skills are developed (e.g., self-advocacy, selfdevelopment).	The organization actively moves past cultural stereotypes and biases, offers gender-responsive services, leverages the healing value of traditional cultural connections, and recognizes and addresses historical trauma.

Trauma-Informed Policies, Practices, and Programs

To assess the state of the field and help researchers, policymakers, and service providers understand and prioritize what changes need to be made, the Office for Victims of Crime (2013) published a report, *Vision 21 – Transforming Victim Services*, which lays out a plan for how we may better respond to victims of crime. One of the most important pledges the plan makes is that "victims of crime will be served through a national commitment to support robust, ongoing research and program evaluation that informs the quality and practice of victim services through the Nation. Evidence-based, research-informed victim service programs will become the standard of excellence in providing assistance to support victims of all types of crime." (p. ix). One of the key provisions of this pledge is a commitment to utilize evidence-based practices in victim services, which requires the integration of the best research evidence with practitioner expertise and victim, survivor, and client values. It also requires transparency, to assure the community that the techniques and procedures utilized will provide the best possible outcomes. Moreover, this pledge requires that "all crime victims in the 21st century can readily access a seamless continuum of evidence-based services and support that will allow them to begin physical, emotional, and financial recovery" (p. 17). This statement acknowledges the multiple, complex challenges that prevent many victims from accessing the resources they need to assist with their recovery. Historically, certain types of victims (e.g., domestic violence, sexual assault, child abuse) have been more reluctant to seek assistance than others, but there are other barriers a victim may experience based on their age, race and ethnicity, socioeconomic status, or sexual orientation or gender identity that also may make it difficult for them to reach out or to access services (OVC, 2013). Thus, Vision 21 asserts that in order to meet the needs of *all* victims, the field must also assess and address historical, institutional, geographic, cultural, and other barriers that prevent victims from receiving services and support.

To achieve the goals laid out by OVC's Vision 21 report, the field of victim services must fully commit to adapting all policies, processes, and practices to become trauma-informed. While a number of agencies and organizations have adopted and implemented these principles decades ago, others are in the early stages of evaluating their policies and practices to identify the specific changes they need to make to achieve a similar standard. Thankfully, there is no need to reinvent the wheel. There are many examples of best practices that agencies and organizations can model from, as the next section illustrates. Some of these can be utilized when working with any crime victim, while others are best suited for a specific type of victim, or for individuals of a particular background (e.g., demographics).

Trauma-Informed Policies/Processes

One of the first points of contact victims of crime have with the criminal justice system is with law enforcement, and these interactions often shape how a victim perceives the justice system as a whole and influences their willingness to participate in the process. Unfortunately, for many victims, the investigative process can be highly traumatic since they are often asked to recount the details of their assault over and over again. Some may respond by stop participating. This not only reduces the likelihood that their specific case will be successfully prosecuted, but without a victim's willingness to engage in the process, the justice system's ability to function is seriously hindered. Thus, an increasing number of law enforcement agencies are training officers how to facilitate victim-centered interviews. One of these methods is the Forensic Experiential Trauma Interview.

The Forensic Experiential Trauma Interview (FETI) is a science-based and trauma-informed methodology for conducting interviews with victims and witnesses of crime that focuses on enhancing the quality and quantity of information obtained from victims who have undergone highly stressful or traumatic experiences (Strand, 2018). The practice was developed by Russell Strand, a former Army Special Agent and refined with experts on the neurobiology of trauma and memory, to create a way to interview victims without making them relive the event in a revictimizing manner (Buckley & Wood, 2014). To accomplish this, FETI teaches officers the neurobiology and science involved in trauma memory, and how to apply that knowledge during an interview. When a person experiences a major trauma, their brain records the memory differently than a non-traumatic event. The prefrontal cortex, which is responsible for executive functioning (e.g., reasoning, planning, impulse control, emotional regulation, etc.) often shuts down, leaving less advanced portions of the brain to record the event (Stetler, 2014). Typically, the information that is recorded during a traumatic event is centered around what the individual felt (e.g., sensory, emotions) rather than the objective facts associated with the event.

Traditional police interviews focus on the peripheral details associated with the event thus officers often pepper victims with questions about details that will give them information on who, what, where, and when things transpired, and expect victims to be able to recall that information in a clear, concise, and sequential manner (Stetler, 2014). During the interview, victims are often interrupted as they are answering questions with follow-up questions by the officer, thus disrupting their ability to recall information. Ultimately, this may cause inconsistencies in the victim's accounting of the event or lead them to edit their memory. This only ends up frustrating the officer, as well as the victim, and ultimately undermines the relationship between the two parties.

In contrast, FETI teaches officers a methodology that targets the more primitive areas of the brain by having them simplify the questions they ask victims (Strand, 2018). Examples of these questions may include, "what are you able to remember about (sight/smell/sound/taste/touch/body sensation)?" "what was the most difficult part of this for you?" "what, if anything, can't you forget?" By asking open-ended and non-leading questions such as these, it can help to cue or prompt a victim to share something about their experience that is meaningful to them, and allows them to decide where to begin and let their memory unfold naturally without interruption. Applying this strategy helps reduce a victim's anxiety during the interview process and helps to facilitate greater trust between the two parties.

Another difference between FETI and a traditional interview model is that with the former, officers must relinquish control of the interview process and allow the victim to control the pace and direction of the interview. Moreover, officers are taught to approach all interviews with victims as opportunities to simply hear what the person is able to share about their experience, rather than try to determine a conclusion or assess the credibility of the victim. To achieve this, officers must practice genuine empathy and learn to become good listeners. By practicing both of these skills, victims are more likely to feel safe, which in turn, may make them be more willing to share their story.

FETI Interviewing	Traditional Interviewing
Gathers psycho-psychological evidence	Uses who, what, where, when, why, and how questions
Same methodology for victims, witnesses, and suspects	Blurs the line between interviewing and interrogation
Uses brain-based cues	Requires sequencing
Empathic listening	Doesn't explore impact or context

* Adapted from CertifiedFeti.org

Research has found this interview technique significantly enhances the quality and quantity of information and evidence gathered from victims and significantly reduces victim recantations (Strand, 2014). It has also been found to increase victim cooperation and participation, and significantly improves chances for successful and prosecutions (Strand, 2014). Since 2009, more than 10,000 military and civilian investigators, prosecutors, victim advocates, health care professionals and over 150 national, international, state, and local agencies and organizations have been trained in the use of FETI (Buckley & Wood, 2014).

Another highly sensitive situation law enforcement must learn to navigate are **death notifications**. Learning of the death of a loved one often is the most traumatic event in a person's life, thus the moment of notification is one that most people remember vividly for the rest of their life – sometimes with pain and anger. Therefore, it is essential for officers to be trained in how to deliver such news in a trauma-informed manner. Research has established a set of best-practices for death notifications – when sharing this news with the deceased's next of kin, it should be completed in-person and by two people, completed in a timely manner, presented in plain language and with compassion, and an officer should conduct a follow-up visit with the family to provide them with any additional information they need (Coroner Talk, 2020). Table 8.2 explains each of these principles in greater detail and provides examples of how officers can implement these best-practices.

Table 8.2

Best Practices for Death Notification	
In Person	• Never take death information over the police radio, but instead collect the relevant information by telephone to prevent the information inadvertently being leaked out to the family through the media or private parties listening to police scanners. Learning of the death of a loved one from the media can be devastating. • Always make death notifications in person. It is critical the survivor has someone there during an extremely stressful time. Officers can help if the survivor has a dangerous shock reaction. • If surviving kin lives far away, contact the medical examiner or law enforcement department in the survivor's home area to deliver the notification in person.
In Time	• Provide notification as soon as possible, however, be absolutely sure that a positive identification has been made. • Prior to notification, gather as much information about the deceased and the circumstances surrounding their death as quickly as possible, as well as any health considerations concerning the survivors who must be notified and whether other people are likely to be present at the notification.
In Pairs	• Always try to have two people present during a notification. • Ideally, the parties would include a law enforcement officer, in uniform, and the medical examiner or other civilian (e.g., chaplain or clergy person, victim advocate, close friend of family). • The need for two notifiers is because survivors often experience severe emotional or physical reactions, and in some cases there may be several survivors present. Therefore, having two people onsite can provide the physical and emotional support needed for all parties involved. • Each notifier should arrive in a separate vehicle if possible, so if the need arises, one can accompany a survivor to the hospital to seek medical attention if necessary, while the other notifier can remain onsite to support the remaining survivors.

In Plain Language	• Notifiers should clearly identify themselves, present their credentials, and ask to come inside – do not make the notification on the doorstep. • Get the survivor seated in the privacy of their home, and confirm you are speaking to the correct person before sharing the news. If children are present, ask the adult survivor(s) to speak to them in private. Offer to speak with the children afterwards. • Relay the message directly and in plain language – avoid vague expressions such as "your daughter passed away." Instead use language such as "your daughter was in a car crash and she was killed." • Speak slowly and carefully give any details that are available, and always call the victim by name. • Patiently answer any and all questions the survivors may have about the cause of death, the current location of their loved one's body, whether an autopsy will be performed, and how and when their body will be released and transported to a funeral home. If you don't know an answer to any question, say so and offer to get back to the survivor when more information is available.
With Compassion	• Accept the survivor's emotions – never try to talk them out of their grief or to offer false hope. • Do not impose your own religious beliefs on them, instead simply and genuinely offer your condolences. • Plan to take time to provide information, support, and direction. These notifications are a lot to process for survivors, therefore, they often need some extra time and attention to help get through the initial shock. • Offer to call a friend or family member to come lend support, and stay until the support person arrives. • Offer to help contact others who must be notified (e.g., other family and friends) • Be available to transport the survivor or representative for the identification of the victim, if necessary. Explain the condition of the deceased's body and any restrictions on contact that may apply if there are forensic concerns. Providing this information empowers the survivor to choose whether to see their loved one immediately, or to wait until after he or she has been prepared by the funeral home.
Follow Up	• Always leave a name and phone number with survivors; if the death occurred in another county or state, leave the name and phone number of a contact person in that location. • Always follow-up with the next of kin the next day to check in on how they are doing, and to provide additional information or direction if requested.

** Adapted from Coroner Talk. (2020). Death notification – best practices.

Another victim-centered practice that is utilized in courtrooms are **closed-circuit televisions (CCTVs)**. CCTVs allows judges, witnesses, and others to participate in court cases when emotional distress, distance, travel limitations, or poor health would otherwise make participation difficult or cause significant harm to the victim. Courts often use CCTVs in cases involving victims who are minors, especially in sex crime cases (National Sexual Violence Resource Center [NSVRC, 2018]. Research has found that one of the reasons many victims of sexual assault fail to report their attack is because they fear having to testify in court (Kenniston, 2015). During court hearings, victims often come face to face with their offender and have to recount in explicit detail what happened to them, and answer pressing questions from defense counsel. Recalling these details within a stressful court-room environment can cause the victim significant physical and emotional distress. Thus, many victims may feel too intimidated to participate, and in turn, may choose to remain silent or refuse to cooperate. However, states have an interest in protecting victims from their assailant and in encouraging victims to seek justice through the legal system (Kenniston, 2015). Therefore, the use of video conferencing enables victims to participate in courtroom proceedings, give testimony and be cross examined, without being physically present (NSVRC, 2018).

While this practice is primarily used with child victims, the National Crime Victim Law Institute and trauma experts have argued in favor of using CCTV court cases involving adult sexual assault victims who wish to avoid the physical presence of their perpetrator (Kenniston, 2015; NSVRC, 2018). By not forcing adult rape victims to be physically present to give testimony and be cross-examined during trial, victims are still able to testify without subjecting them to extreme distress and the potential symptoms of PTSD that many adult victims suffer following rape. Ultimately, two-way video conferencing is an effective solution to minimize trauma suffered by adult rape victims and increase their access to justice (Kenniston, 2015).

Trauma-Informed Programs

In addition to the aforementioned policies and processes, there are a number of trauma-informed programs that have incorporated best-pratices in how they provide direct services to victims of crime. Table 8.3 presents a compilation of programs currently in operation around the United States. Some of these programs work with all victims of crime, while others focus on a specific type. Some of the programs have evolved into national organizations that now include networks that span across multiple jurisdictions, while others operate exclusively in one jurisdiction. Despite the variability in their size and scope of services, each one has been recognized for its dedication to providing trauma-informed services to victims of crime.

Table 8.3

PROGRAM PROGRAM	DESCRIPTION
Sanctuary Model www.sanctuaryweb.com	The Sanctuary Model was created in Philadelphia in 1980 by Dr. Sandra Bloom, Joseph Foderao (social worker), and Ruth Ann Ryan (nurse manager). The model is based on four pillars: knowledge about trauma, adversity and attachment; shared values of nonviolence, emotional intelligence, social learning, open communication, social responsibility, democracy and growth and change; shared language of S.E.L.F.; and shared practical skills that helps individuals and families to effectively deal with difficult situations. The language of S.E.L.F. refers to safety (attaining safety in self, relationships, and environment), emotional management (identifying levels of various emotions and modulating emotion to response to memories, persons, events), loss (feeling grief and dealing with personal losses and recognizing that all change involves loss), and future (trying out new rules, ways of relating, and behaving as a "survivor" to ensure the personal safety and help others). The model has since been duplicated for over 350 programs worldwide, and is currently used across a wide-range of settings including residential treatment, juvenile justice, schools and community-based programs and services.
Seeking Safety www.treatment-innovations.org/ss-description.html	Seeking Safety is a therapeutic program that was designed by Dr. Lisa Najavits, a licensed psychologist, for adults suffering from trauma, substance abuse, and/or posttraumatic stress disorder. The program focuses on a) prioritizing safety, b) integrating trauma and substance abuse, c) rebuilding a sense of hope for the future, d) building cognitive, behavioral, interpersonal, and case management skill sets, and e) refining clinician' attention to processes. The model is highly flexible, it can be conducted in group or individual format; for males, females and across all gender identities; all ages; any level of care (e.g., outpatient, inpatient, residential); and for any type of trauma. Clients do not have to meet formal criteria for PTSD or substance abuse, but has often been used as a general model to teach coping skills, The program has been successfully implemented over decades across vulnerable populations including homeless, criminal justice, domestic violence, severely mentally ill, veterans and military, and others. It is recognized as a best-practice by the Society of Addiction Psychology of the American Psychological Association.

Child Development-Community Policing New Haven, Connecticut www.medicine.yale.edu/childstudy/	CDCP was developed by the Child Study Center at Yale University School of Medicine as a model of secondary prevention that provides crisis intervention and follow-up community and clinic-based clinical and collaborative interventions for children exposed to violence. The program is a collaborative partnership between law enforcement and child mental health professionals to help parents support their children in the aftermath of crime and violence. After completing a ten-week intensive training curriculum on child development and trauma, officers are empowered to make referrals and obtain immediate clinical guidance for a child who witnessed a traumatic event. The CDCP has also expanded to include juvenile probation officers and other juvenile justice professionals who work with children and adolescents who may have experienced chronic exposure to violence and are becoming involved in delinquent activities. The CDCP program serves as a national model for police-mental health partnerships, and has since been replicated in several cities across the United States.
Courthouse Dogs www.courthousedogs.org	Created in 2003 by Senior Deputy Prosecuting Attorney Ellen O'Neill-Stephens of King County, Washington, Courthouse Dogs is a non-profit organization that promotes justice with compassion by helping legal professionals successfully use courthouse facility dog teams to help vulnerable people participate in stressful legal proceedings. Courthouse facility dogs are professionally trained to work in prosecutor's offices, child advocacy centers, and family courts. As legally neutral companions for witnesses during the investigation and prosecution of crimes, these dogs help the most vulnerable witnesses feel willing and able to describe the trauma they experienced, as well as provide emotional support to participants in family court proceedings and in specialty/treatment courts. Today, there are over 100 successful Courthouse Dog Programs across the United States.
Family Justice Center Alliance *Alliance for HOPE International* www.familyjusticecenter.org	The Family Justice Center Alliance is a program of Alliance for HOPE International, one of the leading domestic violence and sexual assault prevention and intervention organizations in the United States. The Family Justice Center model was first proposed in 1989 in San Diego. The vision was to create one place where victims could go to get all the necessary health, thereby reduce many of the obstacles and stress victims experience when trying to navigate the criminal justice system. Today, Family Justice Centers are

	multi-agency, multi-disciplinary co-located service centers that provide services to victims of inter-personal violence including, intimate partner violence, sexual assault, child abuse, elder or dependent adult abuse, and human trafficking. Both public and private partner agencies assign staff on a full-time or part-time basis to provide services from one location. Centers focus on reducing the number of times victims tell their story, the number of places victims must go for help, and look to increase access to services and support for victims and their children. In order to create standards for services within Centers, develop best practices, and establish a common language across the growing movement, Alliance for HOPE International has developed definitions that characterize Family Justice Centers. By 2018, there were 117 Family Justice Center models operating across the United States.
Safe Horizon www.safehorizon.org	Established in 1978, Safe Horizon is the nation's leading victim assistance organization, and strives to provide support, prevent violence, and promote justice for victims of crime and abuse, their families and communities. Direct services are provided to victims of domestic and sexual violence, child abuse victims, human trafficking, stalking, hate crimes and victims of other abuse. Today, the organization offers counseling programs, legal and court advocacy programs, crisis intervention, safe housing, and referrals to other services in 57 locations throughout the five boroughs of New York. The program relies on client-centered practices in which the clients are considered the experts in their own lives and staff collaborate with each client in addressing risks, needs, and concerns that are most important to that individual.
Futures Without Violence www.futureswithoutviolence.org	Futures Without Violence is a health and social justice non-profit organization established more than 30 years ago whose mission is to heal those who have been traumatized by violence and to create healthy families and communities. FUTURES has created programs, guided policy development, and developed public awareness campaigns on issues related to domestic violence, child abuse, sexual violence, human trafficking, and bullying. Today, the organization serves thousands of individuals who have experienced trauma across the United States, as well as globally.

CHILD VICTIMS	
Court Appointed Special Advocates Seattle, Washington www.nationalcasagal.org	Court Appointed Special Advocates (CASA) was established in 1977 by juvenile court judge Judge David W. Soukup to provide services and courtroom assistance to children who had experienced abuse and/or neglect by trained volunteers. CASA volunteers advocate on the child's behalf in the courtroom, address issues related to trauma, support early child development, assist in educational placement and securing service, help find a child a permanent home, and serve youth who have aged out of foster care. Today, CASA is a nationally recognized organization with a network of over 950 programs in 49 states and over 93,000 dedicated volunteers.
Kids' Court Seattle, Washington https://www.kingcounty.gov/depts/prosecutor/ victim-community-support/kids-court.aspx	Developed in 1989, Kids' Court is an experiential and activity-based program hosted at the King County Courthouse in Seattle or the Norm Maleng Regional Justice Center in Kent, Washington at least six times per year for children and their parents to help them become more familiar and comfortable with the courtroom setting. Using a standardized curriculum, children between the ages of 4-12 engage in discussions with a judge and a prosecutor, participate in role-plays and games, and engages in a question and answer session to help increase children's knowledge of courtroom personnel and procedures. Additional activities focus on increasing children's self-confidence with testifying, as well as help to reduce stress and anxiety when interacting with the legal system. While children attend Kids Court Program, parents and caretakers attend a concurrent program designed to address their needs and answer their questions about the justice system. The program has served thousands of child victim/witnesses of sexual abuse and other crimes and their families. It has been recognized as a "best practices" model program by the U.S. Department of Justice, Office for Victims of Crime for its innovation, development in partnerships, outreach methods and multidisciplinary approaches that address the needs of children.
The Childhood Violent Trauma Center New Haven, Connecticut www.medicine.yale.edu/childstudy	The Yale Childhood Violent Trauma Center is a part of Yale's Child Study Center which was founded in 1911. The CVTC is led by a multi-disciplinary team of child psychiatrists and clinicians, pediatric healthcare workers, researchers, and social service providers who are versed in trauma-informed treatments and services. The CVTC helped

found the National Child Traumatic Stress Initiative and partners with the Child Development-Community Policing program. The mission is to improve the mental health of children and their families. CVTC developed the Child and Family Traumatic Stress Intervention, which outlines early interventions and collaborative responses to childhood trauma. This model has been shared with clinicians around the country. In 1991, CVTC partnered with the City of New Haven and the New Haven Police Department to launch the Child Development-Community Policing Program (CD-CP), a collaborative partnership between mental health and law enforcement professionals to provide trauma-informed joint responses to children and families exposed to violence in their homes and neighborhoods. Today, CVTC offers a range of treatment interventions, research and training programs aimed at helping children, adolescents and families who are struggling with traumatic reactions and disorders, and for professionals working in the field, and has been designated as the National Center for Children Exposed to Violence by the White House and the U.S. Department of Justice, Office for Juvenile Justice and Delinquency Prevention.

The Child Witness to Violence Project Boston Medical Center www.childwitnesstoviolence.org	Introduced in 1992, The Child Witness to Violence Project (CWVP) is a counseling, advocacy, and outreach project that focuses on young children who have been exposed to domestic violence, community violence, or other trauma-related events. Referrals come from a variety of sources, including law enforcement, health and mental health providers, Head Start and other early childhood programs, schools, attorneys, shelters for IPV victims, court-sponsored victim programs, and self-referrals. CWVP is staffed by a multi-cultural staff of social workers, educational and clinical psychologists, early childhood specialists, and a consulting pediatrician. Staff use an evidence-based model of intervention for children and families called Child Parent Psychotherapy, and all services are free. Currently, the Project serves over 150 children and their families each year.
Handle with Care West Virginia www.handlewithcarewv.org	In 2013, the "Handle with Care" initiative was piloted at Mary C. Snow West Side Elementary School in Charleston, WV. The program is a partnership between local law enforcement and schools. When law enforcement responds to the scene of a traumatic event, they are trained to identify children at the scene, find out where they go to school

	or daycare, and then send the school/agency a confidential email or fax that simply says, "Handle X with care." No other details about the event are provided. The school implements individual, class and whole school trauma-sensitive curricula so that traumatized children are "handled with care." If a child needs more intervention, on-site trauma-focused mental healthcare is available at the school. The program has since been replicated in other school districts across the nation; and in 2018, a bipartisan bill was introduced in Congress, called the Handle with Care Act. to make this initiative a national model for replication and to boost coordination between law enforcement and school-level personnel to better support students affected by trauma-related events.
Cognitive Behavioral Intervention for Trauma in Schools (CBITS) Los Angeles, California	Developed in 1999 by researchers from RAND in collaboration with the Los Angeles Unified School District and the University of California, CBITS is designed to address trauma among the general school population. CBITS provides mental health screenings and standardized therapy sessions based on cognitive-behavioral therapy to students by school mental health clinicians, such as social workers, psychologists, and other clinicians. The curriculum can be adapted for special populations, including students in foster care and special education and children in racially, ethnically, and socioeconomically diverse groups. CBITS is recognized by the U.S. Department of Justice's Office of Juvenile Justice and Delinquency Prevention and the Substance Abuse and Mental Health Services Administration's National Registry of Evidence-Based Programs (NREPP) as a best-practice model.
DOMESTIC VIOLENCE VICTIMS	
Domestic Violence Units	Domestic Violence Units are specialized units within police departments to handle serious and chronic cases of domestic violence. When these units were first created in the early 1990s, the goal was simply to reduce the recidivism of serious domestic violence offenders. However, the subsequent evaluations of these units failed to find a significant deterrent effect for arrest alone in deterring domestic violence. Thus, many police departments realized additional steps were necessary and began to expand their units to include specialized services for the victims of these crimes to aid in their recovery, as well as assist them through the prosecution process. Today, DV Units today comprise of components – 1) intensive investigation, and

2) victim assistance. On the investigative side, each case is assigned a lead detective to conduct a thorough investigation, and aggressive measures are taken to ensure that the offender is prosecuted to the full extent of the law. For victim assistance, the DV unit partners with community organizations, as well as government and nonprofit organizations, to provide crisis intervention, help secure shelter, provide referrals to social services, help develop safety plans, and help guide victims through the specific criminal justice procedures, such as restraining orders and reminding them of upcoming court dates and accompany them to those hearings. Some DV units will have victim advocates or counselors embedded in the unit to help coordinate all of the aforementioned services.

House of Ruth
Washington, DC

www.houseofruth.org

The House of Ruth was opened in 1976 by Dr. Veronica Maz, a professor at Georgetown University, who wanted to provide safe housing and comprehensive services for battered women and their children. At the time, the District had only a few shelters for men, and none dedicated to serving women or their children. Over the next decade, the organization expanded the number of shelters it operated, added a 24-hour hotline, and created support groups for women in the community. In 1990, it launched Kidspace Child and Family Development Center for preschoolers. Today, the mission of the organization is to help women and children learn skills necessary to live independently, as well as help them heal from the trauma and abuse in their lives. Currently, the House of Ruth operates 14 shelters in Washington, DC that provide a mix of transitional, crisis, and permanent housing, as well as operates a child care center and therapy center. Each year, the House of Ruth helps more than 1,000 women and children.

DC SAFE
Washington, DC

www.dcsafe.org

Launched in 2006, DC SAFE provides comprehensive wraparound services to victims of domestic violence and their children. The program operates a Crisis Response team that operates a 24/7 bilingual Crisis Response Line, which is an action-oriented hotline for first responders. Victims in crisis are referred to the response line by police officers, hospital personnel and other community partners. Every victim who is referred is assessed for their level of risk for lethality, and those at the highest risk of re-assault or homicide are then triaged to receive expedited and enhanced services across city-wide systems. DC SAFE is also the only program to offer crisis housing 24/7 for immediate placements for survivors of domestic violence (SAFE Space Program). The program has leased fully furnished and equipped condominiums and apartments throughout the city which can accommodate large and diverse families for up to three weeks, and provides advocates on site seven days a week to assist clients with next steps in housing, healthcare, and the legal system. These advocates then work with members of the Domestic Violence Housing Continuum to find long-term placements. In addition, DC SAFE has embedded Supportive Advocacy teams in the city's courthouses to provide comprehensive court-based advocacy services.

Womankind, Inc. Support Systems for Battered Women Fairview Ridges Hospital
Minneapolis, Minnesota

WomanKind is the first program to provide case management services for domestic violence victims in a hospital setting. Launched in 1986 as a private nonprofit organization providing services for victims of domestic violence in small suburban hospital, the program soon expanded to two other hospitals and clinics within the Fairview Health System. The program adopted a three-phase case management model for working with victims of IPV – the first phase is crisis intervention, assessment, and evaluation which addresses the presenting domestic violence issues, immediate safety needs, and mental health concerns. The second phase is education and information, which provides support and short-term counseling and discusses the short and long-term effects of abuse on the victim and her family. The third phase is action and protection plans and resource referral, which involves the staff working with each client to explore options, identify resources, develop goals, create plans for the next 4-6 months. In 1992, WomanKind joined Fairview Health System and became a hospital department and is now an integral part of the health care system. Staff are included as members of the hospitals advisory boards, and regularly train the system's health care providers how to recognize signs of abuse and to intervene in a trauma-informed manner. As a result of this program's efforts, every patient who comes to one of the Fairview Hospitals is now automatically screened for domestic violence and abuse as a part of the standard admission form. Moreover, it was evaluated by the National Center for Injury and Prevention and Control (CDC), which found that its specialized staff development training, along with dedicated on-site client services, has a positive impact on the knowledge, attitudes, beliefs, and behaviors of health care providers interacting with IPV victims; and, is a best-practice for intervention with IPV victims within a health care setting.

Integrated Domestic Violence Court *Center for Court Innovation* New York, New York www.courtinnovation.org	The Center for Court Innovation helped develop the first specialized integrated court model for domestic violence in Brooklyn in 1996. The mission was to promote greater victim safety and improve court responses to intimate partner violence. An Integrated Domestic Violence courts (IDV) features a dedicated judge who hears both the criminal and the family law cases that relate to one family where the underlying issue is domestic violence, a fixed prosecutorial team, on-site victim advocacy, ongoing monitoring and judicial supervision, and coordinated response to domestic violence emphasizing collaboration among criminal justice agencies and community-based social services. All members of the team have been trained in best-practices of IPV and trauma, and use those principles guide their decision-making process. Evaluations of the IDV model have found cases assigned to the court are processed more efficiently and offender compliance increases. Today, there are more than 208 IDV courts across the United States.

SEXUAL ASSAULT VICTIMS

Sexual Assault Nurse Examiner Program www.sane-sart.com	The SANE program was established in 1977 by Dr. Linda Ledray at Hennepin County Medical Center in Minneapolis, Minnesota, who observed that services to victims of sexual assault were inadequate and were not equal to the high standards of care provided to other emergency department patients. Nurses led the effort to provide better, tailored services to victims seeking care after a sexual assault. The primary mission of a SANE program is to meet the needs of sexual assault victim by trained, professional nurse experts. Services include a comprehensive forensic exam of the victim, photo documentation of markings on the victim, a complete physical and emotional assessment of the victm, as well as providing emotional support and resources to the victim. It is now considered the standard of care for medical facilities for victims of rape and abuse. Today, there are over 800 SANE programs across the United States and Canada, and approximately one-half of the programs provide services for children, in addition to caring for adolescents and adults.
Sexual Assault Response/Resource Team www.sane-sart.com	SART programs, originally developed in California, were developed to support SANE practitioners. The program involves a coordinated response among law enforcement, prosecutors, victim advocates, medical personnel, nursing personnel, and crime lab personnel to prevent re-traumatization and repeat victimization, and to help victims navigate the health care and criminal justice systems.

Rape, Abuse & Incest National Network Washington, DC www.rainn.org	Founded in 1994, RAINN is the nation's largest anti-sexual violence organization in the United States; its mission is to educate the community on sexual violence and to develop and implement prevention programs. RAINN created and operates the National Sexual Assault Hotline, and partners with more than 1,000 local sexual assault service providers across the country. In addition, it operates the DoD Safe Helpline for the Department of Defense. The organization provides technical assistance and consulting services to work with clients across the public, private, and non-profit sectors to develop targeted, effective sexual violence education and response programs. Since its creation, the organization has helped over 3 million survivors and their families.
Grateful Garment Project San Jose, California www.gratefulgarment.org	The Grateful Garment Project was created by Founder and Executive Director, Lisa Blanchard, after completing an assignment for one of her college courses that focused on community outreach. After learning that many sexual assault victims leave hospitals with nothing more than a hospital gown, she reached out a local SART facility to find out how she could help. She soon began collecting new clothing and toiletry items to distribute to victims after their forensic exams. Soon afterwards, other SART facilities requested assistance. In 2011, Blanchard formalized the Grateful Garment Project to become a non-profit organization, and today it supports SART facilities throughout the state of California, and supports all victims of sexual violence, including Commercially Sexually Exploited Children and Human Sexual Trafficking victims. The Project has since been replicated in other states, and the overarching mission is to ensure that every victim of a sexual crime who crosses the threshold of a Sexual Assault Response Team facility or who seeks medical attention and/or law enforcement involvement is provided with whatever new clothing, toiletries, snacks, or other miscellaneous items they may require.
HOMICIDE SURVIVORS	
National Organization of Parents of Murdered Children Cincinnati, Ohio www.pomc.org	Parents of Murdered Children (POMC) was created by Robert and Charlotte Hullinger in 1978 following the murder of their 19-year old daughter, Lisa, by a former boyfriend. Wanting to connect with other parents who also lost a child to homicide, the Hullingers opened their home to a small group of parents to hold weekly support groups to assist one another through the bereavement process, as

	well as share information on resources. The group quickly grew in size and in 1981, the Hullingers formalized its status as a non-profit organization. Over the past three decades, POMC has expanded its membership to include local chapters all over the United States. Local chapters provide free bereavement support services for families of homicide victims, legal advocacy and court accompaniment services, and helps to coordinate various community outreach initiatives to raise awareness about the trauma associated with homicide. In addition to supporting the local chapters, the national office helps to organize a national conference and a Grief Retreat weekend each year, coordinates the National Day of Remembrance for homicide victims, and works with local, state, and federal lawmakers and community stakeholders to create more trauma-informed policies, practices, and programs to assist those who lose a loved one to homicide.
Tuesday's Children www.tuesdayschildren.org	Tuesday's Children was founded in 2008 to provide support and resources to families who have been impacted by terrorism, military conflict, or mass violence. The organization recognizes the importance of community and shared experiences as a mechanism for healing and positive growth, especially for young people. The organization offers an array of support services for children, adolescents and adults. In addition to crisis and grief counseling, and referrals to other support services, the organization manages mentoring and leadership programs for youth, as well as hosts an international retreat called Project COMMON BOND for teenagers from around the world who have lost a family member due to an act of terrorism, violent extremism, or war. The organization also coordinates a variety of adult and family programming to strengthen resilience by building a community among individuals and families who share similar experiences. To date, Tuesday's Children has served youth and their families from over 800 countries across the globe.
Restorative Retelling and Criminal Death Support Group	Restorative Retelling and Criminal Death Group is a comprehensive, wraparound intervention to screen homicide co-victims, offer trauma support, address psychological needs, and provide training on handling media and criminal justice agencies. Created in 1998 by Dr. Edward Rynearson, the program addresses unresolved trauma and separation distress due to the unexpected death of a family

	member or a friend through a combination of individual and group therapeutic sessions limited to 10 participants. The model is designed to help co-victims process the trauma associated with losing their loved one by restoring their resilience, retelling and commemorating the living memory of the deceased and self, participating in a number of creative exercises. It has been evaluated numerous times and identified as a best-practice by OVC.
Homicide Outreach Project Empowering Survivors *Wendt Center for Loss & Healing* Washington, DC www.wendtcenter.org	Based in the Wendt Center, HOPES provides comfort and support, information and practical assistance to families, individuals, and communities coping with homicide-related deaths. Services are provided by licensed clinicians, program staff, and trained volunteers with expertise in the areas of trauma, grief and loss, and child and family therapy. It also partners with their RECOVER program at the Office of the Chief Medical Examiner which enables clinicians to provide crisis response, emotional support, education and referral services to adults who must identify a deceased loved one, and then continues to check in with families several weeks following the homicide to see how they are doing. More recently, HOPES launched a new program, Project Change, in coordination with the Metropolitan Police Department and Medstar Hospital, to dispatch trauma-informed mental health counselors to provide crisis support on-site at the hospital and in the community in the aftermath of an attempted homicide to promote healing and facilitate violence de-escalation.
Roberta's House Baltimore, Maryland www.robertashouse.org	Created in 2007, Roberta's House is a non-profit community-based program where children, teens, and adults have the opportunity to share their grief over losing a loved one to homicide, and learn how to experience and express their feelings safely and in a healthy manner. Age appropriate programs are offered, and draws heavily on the principles of peer support, empowerment, and collaboration. Resources and referrals are provided to parents to other services in the community. The program was one of ten organizations selected for Black History Month Community Leaders Awards for its commitment and service to making a transformative impact in the community. In 2015, its Director and co-founder, Annette March-Grier was nominated as one of CNN's Heroes – she noted "we're giving families in this city a sense of hope, and helping to heal wounds and bring families back together."

Polaris Washington, DC www.polarisproject.org	Founded in 2002, Polaris has spent nearly two decades devoted to ending sex and labor trafficking in North America. Using data and the expertise of survivors, Polaris focuses on dismantling the underlying systems that facilitate trafficking by maintaining a dataset that law enforcement and service providers can use in real time to monitor trafficking activity. Since 2007, Polaris has operated the U.S. National Human Trafficking Hotline, which provides 24/7 support for survivors and link them to services through their partnerships with nearly 4,000 service providers and trusted law enforcement agencies. The hotline can communicate via phone in more than 200 languages through a translation service. In 2006, the organization opened its first transitional housing centers and launched a 24-hour Crisis Response Team to assist victims and survivors of trafficking.
Covenant House New York City, New York www.covenanthouse.org	Founded in 1972, Covenant House has helped transform and save the lives of more than a million homeless, run-away, and trafficked youth. The organization operates an outreach program to engage youth on the street, provides both short and long-term housing, and offers individualized case management that includes educational programming, job training and placement, medical services, mental health and substance abuse counseling, and legal aid. Today, the program offers housing and support services to more than 74,000 youth each year, in over 31 cities across six countries.
HOPE Court *FAIR Girls* Washington, DC www.fairgirls.org	HOPE Court is an innovative multi-disciplinary program that was launched in 2018 for youth victims of exploitation under the direction of the D.C. Superior Court, and assisted by FAIR girls, a non-profit organization that provides intervention and holistic care to survivors of human trafficking who identify as girls or young women. The program was created in response to the 2014 Sex Trafficking of Minors Prevention Act, which ensured youth victims of commercial sexual exploitation were protected from arrest for charges related to their exploitation, as well as ensuring at-risk children were identified and referred by law enforcement to child protective services. Youth who are brought to HOPE court are partnered with an anti-trafficking service provider from FAIR Girls, who provides them with personalized short- and long-term comprehensive mentoring, case management assistance, court advocacy, crisis counseling, psycho-education, medical and mental health referrals, safety planning, and transportation assistance.

GEMS
New York City, New York

www.gems-girls.org

In 1998, Rachel Lloyd, a survivor of trafficking, founded GEMS to give girls and young women of New York City who been commercially sexually exploited a place for support and a place to where they could formulate a plan to build a better life. GEMS' mission is to empower girls and young women, ages 12-24, who have experienced commercial sexual exploitation and domestic trafficking, to exit the commercial sex industry and develop to their full potential. In addition to direct intervention and crisis care, the organization provides comprehensive case management for survivors that includes educational support services, therapeutic groups, transitional and support housing, leadership development, and court advocacy. Today, GEMS is one of the largest providers of services to commercially sexually exploited youth in the United States, and provides training and technical assistance to agencies and institutions across the U.S. that work with at-risk youth, victims and survivors of domestic trafficking and commercial sexual exploitation.

CULTURALLY DIVERSE VICTIM POPULATIONS

The Multilingual Access Model
Asian Women's Shelter
San Francisco, California

www.sfaws.org

In 1988, the Asian Women's Shelter (AWS) was opened to provide culturally competent services for Asian battered women and their children. Prior to its opening, many women in the Asian community within San Francisco could not access existing shelter programs because of language and cultural barriers, and had similar difficulties when trying to attain legal assistance. Faced with the challenge of over 100 different Asian languages spoken in San Francisco, the AWS developed a multilingual access model to respond to the needs of non-English speaking battered women and their children. AWS recruited bilingual women from the different Asian communities as language advocates, and trained them on issues related to domestic violence and how the legal system operates. Within a short time, MLAM had over 30 language advocates providing services in 24 languages and dialects. The project later provided technical assistance with six other domestic violence shelters and service providers in the San Francisco area to create a coordinated citywide access plan.

UJIMA: The National Center on Violence Against Women in the Black Community
Washington, DC

www.ujimacommunity.org

UJIMA serves as a national, culturally-specific services issue resource center to provide support to and be a voice for the Black Community in response to domestic, sexual, and community violence. UJIMA coordinates community outreach and provides technical assistance to address the shortage of targeted, culturally-specific services for Black

	survivors of domestic and sexual violence. Ujima identifies and provides culturally-specific regional trainings across to the country to develop a learning community and offer opportunities to build peer-mentoring relationships in local communities.
Ayuda Washington, DC www.ayuda.com	Founded in 1973, Ayuda is now one of the largest non-profit organizations that provides critical legal and social services to immigrants and asylum seekers. In addition to immigration law, attorneys also provide domestic violence and family law legal services to victims and survivors of domestic violence, sexual assault, and stalking. Ayuda provides legal services to more than 3,000 women, men, and children each year.
Tahirih Justice Center Washington, DC www.tahirih.org	Founded in 1997, the Tahirih Justice Center is the only national, multi-city organization that provides a broad range of direct legal services, policy advocacy, and training and education to protect immigrant women and girls fleeing gender-based violence. Clients receive free immigration, family, and civil legal services, as well as referrals to a broad range of social services and other vital resources in their communities and in their native languages. In addition to addressing clients' immediate physical needs, the Center also provides mental health services to ensure their emotional well-being. Since opening, the Center has served over 25,000 clients across in 5 cities across the United States.
Casa de Esperanza St. Paul, Minnesota www.casadeesperanza.org	Founded in 1982 to provide emergency shelter for Latinas and other women and children experiencing domestic violence, Casa de Esperanza has grown to become the largest Latin@ organization in the country focused on domestic violence. It operates both locally and nationally to support families and work to end domestic violence. It provides innovative services and support, ranging from family advocacy and shelter services, to leadership development and community engagement opportunities for Latin@ youth, women, and men. It also serves as a resource to organizations and communities in the areas of sexual assault and trafficking. The organization has been recognized for its leadership in the field by the U.S. Department of Health and Human Services, and the U.S. Department of Justice.
Family Wellness Warrior Initiative Anchorage, Alaska www.southcentralfoundation.com	Established in 1982 under the Cook Inlet Region, Inc. tribal authority, Southcentral Foundation is an Alaska Native health care organization established to improve the health, well-being, and social conditions of Alaska Native

	People. In 1999, it launched the Family Wellness Warriors Initiative (FWWI) to apply a holistic approach to addressing domestic violence, abuse, and neglect by building on the strengths of the Alaska Native traditional values. It equips organizations and individuals to effectively address the spiritual, emotional, mental, and physical effects of violence. The key to the program's success is its formal implementation steps, which includes a targeted effort in relationship building with the tribal and community leadership before implementing any services; it also relies on the use of previously trained regional tribal leaders to train new leaders to continue strengthening partnerships. As of 2018, FWWI has been implemented across Alaska, and has served nearly 3,500 clients.
Wellbriety Movement Colorado Springs, Colorado www.wellbriety.com	Founded in 1994, by White Bison, Inc. Wellbriety Movement is dedicated to supporting healing from alcohol, substance abuse, co-occurring disorders, and intergenerational trauma by drawing on the teachings of the Medicine Wheel, the Cycle of Life, and the Four Laws of Change. Wellbriety means to be both sober and well, and is word translated into English from the language of the Passamaquoddy nation. It means going beyond "clean and sober" by entering a journey of healing and balance, which encapsulates physical, mental, emotional and spiritual well-being. For many Native Americans, it also means recovering culturally by incorporating the best attributes of traditional Native cultures, while standing firmly on the ground of contemporary life.
LGBTQ VICTIMS	
FORGE Milwaukee, Wisconsin www.forge.org	Started in 1994 as a small grass-roots organization to provide peer support to the transgender community living in the Midwest, FORGE was officially launched in 2000 after it merged with the Transgender Aging Network. The mission of FORGE is to support, educate, and advocate for the rights and lives of transgender individuals and SOF-FAs (significant others, friends, family, and allies). After discovering significantly high rates of childhood sexual abuse or adult sexual assault among its clients, it has since devoted the majority of its work to find effective ways to better serve these survivors and loved ones. In addition to provide direct services for members of the transgender community and SOFFAs, FORGE provides technical assistance and training nationwide to victim service agencies focusing on survivors of domestic violence, sexual assault, stalking, and dating violence violence survivors to increase the cultural competency of providers who serve these survivors and loved ones.

Violence Recovery Program *Fenway Institute* Boston, Massachusetts www.fenwayhealth.org	In 2001, Fenway Health launched the Fenway Institute, a national interdisciplinary center dedicated to ensuring cultural competence in health care for the LGBTQ community. As part of the Institute, Fenway's Violence Recovery Program (VRP) has been providing free counseling, support groups, advocacy and referrals to LGBTQ survivors of domestic violence, sexual violence, hate violence, and police misconduct for over 30 years. VRP also partners with TOD@S, an inter-agency collaboration designed to improve and increase access to intervention and prevention services for LGBTQ/T Black and Latin@ people affected by partner abuse in the greater Boston area.
The Network/La Red Boston, Massachusetts www.tnlr.org	The Network/La Red was formed in 1989 by a group of formerly battered lesbians who wanted to address domestic violence among lesbian and bisexual women. The group incorporated in 1991. In 2000, the organization was renamed The Network/LaRed and expanded its mission to assist survivors of IPV in the lesbian, bisexual women's and transgender communities, and in 2010 amended its mission again to include all members of the LGBTQ community. Today, the Network/La Red is a survivor-led, social justice organization that works to end abuse in the lesbian, gay, bisexual, transgender, S/M, polyamorous and queer communities. It provides direct services, including individual and peer support groups, a 24-hour hotline, and the Housing Pathways Program. Housing Pathways provides immediate housing for victims for up to 30 days in a confidential location (Safehome) somewhere within the state, and then transitional housing for up to two years that best meets their needs (e.g., sober living programs, sublets, apartments). The organization serves as a national resource and model for domestic violence service providers and batterer intervention programs who serve victims from the LGBTQ community.
Northwest Network of Bi, Trans, Lesbian and Gay Survivors of Abuse Seattle, Washington www.nwnetwork.org	Founded in 1987 by lesbian survivors of battering, the NW Network works to end abuse within the LBBTQ community. The network offers free emergency and ongoing advocacy-based counseling centered on survivors' choices and self-determination, support groups, safety and support planning, legal advocacy, and resources and referrals to other services the client may need.

ELDER ABUSE VICTIMS	
New York City Elder Abuse Center Enhanced Multidisciplinary Teams New York City, NY www.nyceac.org	Multidisciplinary teams for elder abuse bring professionals together from across disciplines and systems to solve complex cases associated with this vulnerable and often underserved population. The team carefully considers each older victim's situation and individual strengths, needs, and preferences when creating a response. The New York City Elder Abuse Center's Enhanced Multidisciplinary Teams (EMDTs) include a team of specialists from medicine, law, mental health, social work, protective services, law enforcement, geriatricians, and a forensic accountant, a specialist in applying accounting concepts and practices to financial exploitation cases. Each team has a coordinator who synchronizes the assessment and interventions of team members, and schedule follow-up team reviews. EDMTs are located in all five boroughs, and has been recognized as a best-practice for its ability to improve the efficiency and effectiveness of response to cases of elder abuse.
DOVES Program Phoenix, Arizona www.aaaphx.org	Established in 1996 by the Area Agency on Aging, the DOVES Program helps victims of late-life (ages 50+) domestic violence overcome the unique challenges that older victims face when they attempt to protect themselves and leave their abusers. The program provides a comprehensive set of services that include: crisis intervention, safety planning and case management, legal and financial assistance, emergency and transitional housing, peer support groups, and transportation. In addition, the program engages in community outreach and education to raise awareness about domestic violence within the elderly population. DOVES was recognized by the Office for Victims of Crime as a best-practice program for its innovative and comprehensive approach to reaching this underserved population.

Today, communities across the nation are exploring how they may adopt trauma-informed principles to create a more collaborative and holistic approach to responding to trauma. The first community to implement such a model was Tarpon Springs, Florida, which launched its Peace4Tarpon Trauma Informed Community initiative in 2010 (www.peace4tarpon.org). The program was created by Robin Saeger, Vice Mayor of Tarpon Springs, who sought to create a more peaceful and thriving community in which all of its residents are safe, healthy, educated, respected, and valued. To achieve this goal, Saeger educated community stakeholders and residents to use a "trauma-informed lens" to help identify the root causes of the town's most challenging issues (e.g., domestic violence, homelessness, drug addiction, bullying, etc.) rather than only addressing the symptoms, and then work collaboratively to assist individuals who have experienced trauma in order to promote resilience and facilitate their recovery. To create a holistic model, Saeger successfully recruited representatives from across disciplines, including law enforcement, schools, social services, healthcare, faith-based organizations, local businesses, and residents. In 2015, Peace4Tarpon was one of 14 sites across the United States to receive a large grant to support and expand its efforts in addressing childhood adversity and to become a member of a collaborative project called Mobilizing Action for Resilient Communities (MARC). A list of the participants is provided in Table 8.4. MARC program brings together a mix of cities, counties, regions, and states to help build a culture of health by translating the science of Adverse Childhood Experiences (ACEs) into practices and policies that foster resilience. Each of these communities have established multi-disciplinary networks, and have worked collaboratively to raise awareness via social media, the creation of online resource repositories, and hosting conferences and trainings. Today, they share best practices, develop new approaches, and serve as models for other communities to emulate. The program is coordinated by the Health Federation of Philadelphia with support from the Robert Wood Johnson Foundation and the California Endowment (www.marc.healthfoundation.org)

Table 8.4

Site	Description
ALASKA *Alaska Resilience Initiative*	The Alaska Resilience Initiative has worked to create a sustainable statewide network to educate all Alaskans on brain development, ACEs and resilience-building, and to support organizational, policy, and practice change to address trauma. In order to address the specific cultural and historical needs of the Alaskan native population, which comprises nearly one-fifth of the state's population, in 2016 ARI partnered with First Alaskan Institute and Chickaloon Village Traditional Council to put Native perspectives, culture, history, and hopes at the center of the initiative.
ALBANY, NY *The HEARTS Initiative for ACE Response*	Dr. Heather Larkin, an Associate Professor of Social Welfare at the University of Albany helped launch ACE Think Tank Action Team meetings to bring together local and state agencies with members of the community. In 2011, the group created a prototype website called HEARTS (Healthy Environments and Relationships That Support) Initiative for ACE Response to share the growing science of ACEs and resilience. This initiative originally started with just five member agencies, but today it comprises of the university, two state agencies, one health insurance company, and fifteen local agencies serving children, teens, adults, and seniors.

BOSTON, MA *Vital Village Community Engagement Network*	In 2010, Dr. Renee Boynton-Jarrett, an Associate Professor of Pediatrics at Boston Medical Center, led a multidisciplinary group of practitioners interested in health inequities and early childhood adversities. That group then gathered community residents and organizations in a series of conversations about child health and well-being, which ultimately led to the creation of the Vital Village Community Engagement Network. Vital Village is rooted in the principle of neighbors helping neighbors, and aims to facilitate a sustainable approach to system-level interventions that will improve the well-being and prevent child maltreatment by transforming neighborhood processes. The collaborative includes medical professionals, community residents, legal advocates, clinicians, and social service providers. Today, the initiative has over 75 agency partners and 200 active participants, and targets the three poorest neighborhoods in Boston (e.g., Dorchester, Roxbury, Mattapan).
BUNCOMBE COUNTY, NC *Buncombe County ACE & Resiliency Collaborative*	In 2012, Jan Shepard, the Director of Public Health Division of Buncombe County Health and Human Services, formed the Buncombe ACE Collaborative to educate the medical and mental health communities about ACE assessment. The group grew into a learning collaborative comprised of mental health and human service professionals, educators, and parents, who reviewed the literature on ACEs and created a handbook listing trauma and resilience resources and began piloting the ideas presented in the research. In 2014, the Collaborative developed a strategic results framework that outlined stakeholders roles and responsibilities, and actions and goals, and grew in membership to over 80 participants. The Collaborative now manages a website and resource guide for medical providers and school administrators, hosted a three-day ACEs Summit for practitioners and community members to learn how to build resilience, interdisciplinary teams, and support communities and families, and most recently, has begun collaborating with the County's Craggy Correctional Center.
COLUMBIA RIVER GORGE REGION, OR *Resilience Network of the Gorge*	In 2008, Trudy Townsend created a consortium of community stakeholders including the chief of police, the superintendent of schools, the regional manager of the Department of Human Services, and the director of Juvenile Justice to hold regular meetings to discuss what was wrong in their community, and to brainstorm how they might address the problems. The group learned of the Sanctuary Model and completed the training together. They then reached out to representatives from nonprofit organizations, the faith community, early childhood education, domestic violence prevention, drug and alcohol prevention, and the business sector to invite them to join the consortium. All of the partners agreed to work collaborative to apply the Sanctuary Model to the entire Columbia Gorge Region. To date, 20 organizations have joined the consortium, and the network now includes the Columbia Gorge Health Council.
GREATER KANSAS CITY, MO/KS	In 2011, six organizations came together, calling themselves Trauma Matters Kansas City (TMKC) to address the trauma and toxic stress experienced by children in the Kansas City metro area. TMKC quickly expanded into a multi-system, bi-state (Missouri and Kansas) organization that included 40 organiza

Trauma Matters KC & **Resilient KC**	tions representing human services, health, criminal justice, law enforcement, education, government, and community members, which hosted four regional summits on trauma-informed care. Soon afterwards, the Independence (Missouri) School District adopted trauma-informed practices in its classrooms, one of the courts received a federal grant to create a trauma-informed courtroom, and in 2014, the Kansas City Chamber of Commerce unveiled its "Healthy KC" initiative that placed special emphasis on trauma and has trained ambassadors who can bring ACEs message to colleagues, clients, and community members in business, the armed services, education, justice and health care. More recently, Resilient KC has been working with community partners to evaluate physical spaces (e.g., reception areas, exam rooms, hallways, etc.) through a trauma-informed lens to look at the impact environment has on people's sense of safety, of belonging, and of feeling supported.
ILLINOIS **Illinois ACEs Response Collaborative**	In 2011, the ACE Collaborative formed when statewide stakeholders saw increasing evidence that early adversity had long-term consequences in people's health, behavior, and financial stability. The group soon expanded to 34 members across a variety of disciplines. The group successfully petitioned the Illinois Department of Public Health to include ACE questions in the state's Behavioral Risk Factor Surveillance System. In 2015, the Collaborative hosted the Midwest Regional Summit on ACEs which was attended by stakeholders from more than a dozen states to learn about childhood stress and urban poverty, fostering community health and resilience, and translating ACE science into advocacy. In 2017, the Collaborative aided Dr. Audrey Stillerman, the Associate Director of Medical Affairs for the University of Illinois, Office of Community Engagement and Neighborhood Health Initiative, to create the Healthy Chicago 2.0 Trauma-Informed Hospital Collaborative, a workgroup comprised of stakeholders from 16 hospitals that aims to bring trauma-informed care to hospitals and medical systems across the metropolitan area.
MONTANA **Elevate Montana**	In 2013, Todd Garrison, the Executive Director of the ChildWise Institute, a non-profit that focuses on child well-being created Elevate Montana, an ACE-informed statewide initiative to boost the well-being and future of Montana's children. To educate statewide stakeholders, ChildWise has hosted a series of annual Summits and trained thousands of parents, teachers, and probation officers in early brain growth and development. In 2016, the network trained school staff from the Assiniboine and Sioux tribes to educate them about ACEs and help them develop trauma-informed practices that could be incorporated into classrooms; and, partnered with United Way of Flathead, Lake, Lincoln, Glacier & Sanders Counties to expand trauma-informed services in their communities. Today, the Elevate Montana network includes foundations, non-profit agencies, hospitals, Blue Cross Blue Shield insurance company, and the Montana Supreme Court.

PHILADELPHIA, PA *Philadelphia ACE Task Force*	The Philadelphia ACE Task Force (PATF) began as a group of pediatricians who wanted to put ACEs research into practice. In 2012, the workgroup expanded to include leaders and practitioners from pediatrics, primary care, juvenile justice, early childhood intervention, and anti-violence advocates. The group identified its mission to educate the wider community about ACEs and their impact, to develop a better understanding of trauma-informed programs and agencies in the city and to learn what kinds of interventions work best, and to collaborate with local universities to develop trauma-informed curriculum that could be embedded in programs in medicine and nursing, social work and counseling, education and law. In 2014, PATF was formally launched and soon grew to comprise of 175 members. In 2016, the TaskForce launched a new website (PhiladelphiaACES.org) to disseminate information about trauma-informed research and initiatives across the city and region. Since then it has partnered with the Children's Crisis Treatment Center, Philadelphia University, the Philadelphia School District, and the United Way of Greater Philadelphia and Southern New Jersey.
SAN DIEGO COUNTY, CA *San Diego Trauma-Informed Guide Team*	In 2008, Rosa Ana Lozada, the Chief Executive Officer of Harmonium, Inc., a non-profit that provides education, intervention, and prevention services to improve the well-being of children, youth and their parents/caregivers, launched the San Diego Trauma Informed Guide Team (SG-TIGT) to improve client care in a range of systems (e.g., social service, juvenile justice, education, behavioral health) by raising awareness about trauma, establishing a tool kit agencies could use to help implement trauma-informed practices, and providing regular trainings. In 2014, SD-TIGT partnered with the San Diego Unified School District to help implement wellness and restorative hubs throughout district schools, and assisted the City's Health & Human Service Agency to transition to a trauma-informed system. In 2017, SD-TIGT's leadership team partnered with San Diego's Urban Collaborative Project to work with town councils, neighborhood groups, and other stakeholders in Southeast San Diego to expand K-12 school support, healthy food access, improve community infrastructure, and support resident leadership training and advocacy.
SONOMA COUNTY, CA *Sonoma County ACEs Connection*	The Sonoma County ACEs Connection (SCAC) was founded by Karen Clemmer, Coordinator of Maternal, Child, and Adolescent Health for Sonoma County's Department of Health Services. Building on partnerships already established by DHS, Clemmer recruited 38 members representing 24 different organizations. The goal of the workgroup was to inform the community about ACEs, promote evidence-based strategies and programs to reduce the impact of ACEs, build resilience and change system to more effectively serve residents of Sonoma County who had been impacted by trauma. Given the semi-rural nature and culturally diverse background of many of its residents, SCAC launched a website to make information and resources more easily available, as well as conducted trainings with school administrators, family practice residents, and nursing students from across the county. It has since partnered with Roseland Pediatrics, a community health center, and the Santa Rosa Violence Prevention Partnership to help plan its annual Gang Prevention Seminar to include a focus on trauma.

TARPON SPRINGS, FL *Peace4Tarpon, Trauma Informed Community*	In 2011, Vice Mayor of Tarpon Springs, Robin Saenger launched Peace4Tarpon after she read the ACEs study and realized that so many of the problems her community faced – homelessness, violence, unemployment – were the result of untreated trauma. She initially started with a small workgroup to explore the prevalence of trauma within the community and to how to implement trauma-informed practices that would foster resilience. The network soon grew to over 90 members from government agencies, faith-based groups, mental health and human service providers, the school system, the business sector, and members of the community. Each member was required to sign a MOU to attend monthly meetings, serve on at least one work group or committee, complete ACE and resilience assessments, sign on to ACEs Connection, and practice trauma-sensitivity among family, friends, and co-workers. These efforts led to Tarpon Springs being the first trauma-informed community in the United States, and has since been replicated in Gainesville, FL (Peace4Gainesville) and Crawford County, PA (Peace4Crawford).
WASHINGTON *ACEs/Resilience Team & Children's Resilience Initiative*	Teri Barila, Coordinator of the Walla Walla Community Network and Director of the Children's Resilience Initiative (CRI), and Geoffrey Morgan, former Executive Director of the Whatcom Family & Community Network (WFCN), collaborated for over a decade to help disseminate information on ACEs and resilience in their communities, provided technical assistance to each other, and shared resources. Both networks include advisory groups comprised of parents, professionals, educators, business owners, and community members; and have led community conversations and facilitated formal trainings for child welfare, early childhood education, substance abuse prevention, mental health, juvenile justice, and human services. In 2014, CRI assisted Lincoln High School, an alternative high school in Walla Walla to become trauma-informed and adapt its disciplinary practices. The school was subsequently the focus of an award-winning documentary, *Paper Tigers*, that chronicles a year in the life for six of its students.
WISCONSIN *Children's Mental Health Collective Impact*	In 2007, Wisconsin's Department of Health Services convened a trauma summit that led to the hiring of a trauma-informed care consultant, the first such state-sponsored position in the nation. Soon afterwards, a trauma-informed care advisory committee representing state agencies, human services, and mental health consumers (CMHCI). The group has since partnered with the Center for Investigating Healthy Minds at the University of Wisconsin to share research on brain development, self-regulation and emotional styles; SaintA, a human services organization, to provide master trainers on ACEs to coach parents and do workforce training on ACEs throughout the state; and with Branch2, a technology firm to develop a mobile app to bring mindfulness and as well as provide content that focuses on ACEs and brain science, that can be used in the workforce as well as by people in the broader community.

THE 21ST CENTURY TRANSFORMATION OF VICTIMOLOGY

Conclusion

Over the past three decades, the field of victim services has undergone a significant expansion in the number of programs and types of services created to meet the needs of victims to help them heal and to rebuild their lives. To achieve such a goal, the field has drawn on the knowledge of practitioners and researchers to create a set of best-practices for victim services, some of which have been highlighted in this chapter. While great strides have been made in designing and implementing a variety of trauma-informed initiatives across different organizations and systems that victims of crime must navigate, there is still a great deal of work to be done. The diversity of victims' backgrounds has illustrated the need for coordination between advocates, service providers, researchers, and policymakers to address meaningful partnerships, and to strengthen providers' knowledge and skills through cross-training and sharing of information. Therefore, in the coming years and decades, every system, organization, and jurisdiction must continue to work diligently to identify and dismantle barriers that impede a victim's ability to access services, and utilize a "trauma-informed" lens to evaluate every policy and practice to ensure that it promotes safety, transparency, empowerment, and choice. Only then will we achieve the vision laid out by OVC of a system that is accessible, inclusive, and culturally relevant for all victims of crime.

Discussion Questions

1. What are some potential long-term effects of trauma for a victim of crime?
2. Why is trauma more likely to have an adverse effect on children than adults?
3. What are the key principles to trauma-informed services?
4. Provide an example of a trauma-informed practice currently used by law enforcement, and another by the courts.
5. Provide an example of a trauma-informed program for each of the following types of victims – children, domestic violence, sexual assault, human trafficking.
6. How do trauma-informed practices help to better reach underserved victims of crime?
7. What do communities need to do in order to become a trauma-informed community?

References

American Civil Liberties Union. (2015, October). *Responses from the field. Sexual assault, domestic violence, and policing.* Retrieved from https://www.aclu.org/responsesfromthefield

Buckley, M. K., & Wood, L. (2014, August 4). *Army civilian develops interview method to help unlock memories, reduce revictimization.* United States Army. Retrieved from https://www.army.mil/article/130936/army_civilian_develops_interview_methodtto_help_unlock_memories_reduce_revictimization

Coroner Talk. (2020, January 6). *Death notification – Best practices* [Podcast]. Retrieved from https://coronertalk.com/death-notification-best-practices

DeHart, D. (2003, May). *National Victim Assistance Standards Consortium : Standards for victim assistance programs and providers.* Columbia, SC: Center for Child and Family Studies, University of South Carolina.

Felitti, V. J., Anda, R. F., Nordenberg, D., Edwards, V., Koss, M. P., & Marks, J. S. (1998). Relationship of childhood abuse and household dysfunction to many of the leading causes of death in adults. The Adverse Childhood Experiences (ACE) study. *American Journal of Preventative Medicine, 14*(4), 245-258.

Finkelhor, D., Turner, H. A., Shattuck, A.., & Hamby, S. L. (2013). Violence, crime, and abuse exposure in a national sample of children and youth: An update. *Journal of American Medical Association Pediatrics, 167*(7), 614-621.

Kenniston, C. W. (2015). You may now "call" your next witness: Allowing adult rape victims to testify via two-way video conferencing systems. *Journal of High Technology Law, 16*(1), 96-126.

Morgan, R. E., & Oudekerk, B. A. (2019, September). *Criminal victimization, 2018.* Washington, DC: U.S. Department of Justice, Bureau of Justice Statistics.

National Coalition Against Domestic Violence. (n.d.). *National statistics.* Retrieved from https://ncadv.org/statistics

National Intimate Partner and Sexual Violence Survey. (2017). *The impact of intimate partner violence – A 2015 NISVS Research in Brief.* Retrieved from www.cdc.gov/violenceprevention/nisvs/

National Sexual Violence Resource Center. (2018). *Sexual assault response team toolkit: Closed circuit television.* Retrieved from https://www.nsvrc.org/sarts/toolkit/5-10

O'Grady, R. L., & Matthews-Creech, N. (2019). *Why children don't tell* [Lacasa Center].
Retrieved from https://lacasacenter.org/why-child-abuse-victims-dont-tell/

Office for Victims of Crime. (2013). Vision 21 – *Transforming victim services. Final Report.* Washington, DC: U.S. Department of Justice, Office for Victims of Crime.

Office for Victims of Crime. (n.d.). Guiding values for serving victims and survivors of crime. Retrieved from https://www.ovc.gov/model-standards/guiding_values.html

RAINN. (2020). *Victims of sexual assault. Statistics.* Retrieved from https://www.rainn.org/statistics/victims-sexual-violence

Restall, I. (2018). The cost of crime victimization [DC Student Defense]. Retrieved from https://dcstudentdefense.com/the-cost-of-crime-victimization/

Rosenberg, H. J., Vance, J. E., Rosenberg, S. D., Wolford, G. L., Ashley, S. W., & Howard, M. L. (2014). Trauma exposure, psychiatric disorders, and resiliency in juvenile-justice-involved youth. *Psychological Trauma: Theory, Research, Practice, and Policy, 6*(4), 430-437.

Rynearson, E. K. (2001). *Retelling violent death.* Philadelphia, PA: Brunner/Routledge.

Stetler, L. (2018, May 21). *How police investigators can conduct effective trauma victim interviews.* Retrieved from https://www.policeone.com/investigations/articles/how-police-investigators-can-conduct-effective-trauma-victim-interviews-wP6qbakb3SsD3A90/

Strand, R. W. (2018). *The Forensic Experiential Trauma Interview* (FETI). Retrieved from https://www.mncasa.org/wp-content/uploads/2018/07/FETI-Public-Description.pdf

Substance Abuse Mental Health Service Administration. (2014). *SAMHSA's concept of trauma and guidance for a trauma-informed approach.* Washington, DC: Author.

Wilz, T. (2016). *Having a parent behind bars costs children, states* [Stateline Article].

Pew Trust Research Center. Retrieved from https://www.pewtrusts.org/en/research-and-analysis/blogs/stateline/2016/05/24/having-a-parent-behind-bars-costs-children-states

Implementation Domains for a Trauma-Informed Approach

10 IMPLEMENTATION DOMAINS

Governance and Leadership	• How does agency leadership communicate its support and guidance for implementing a trauma-informed approach? • How do the agency's mission statement and/or written policies and procedures include a commitment to providing trauma-informed services and supports? • How do leadership and governance structures demonstrate support ofr the voice and participation of people using their services who have trauma histories?
Policy	• How do the agency's written policies and procedures include a focuse on trauma and issues of safety and confidentiality? • How do the agency's written policies and procedures recognize the pervasiveness of trauma in the lives of people using services, and express a commitment to reducing re-traumatization and promoting well-being and recovery? • How do the agency's staffing policies demonstrate a commitment to staff training on providing services and supports that are culturally relevant and trauma-informed as part of staff orientation and in-service training? • How do human resources policies attend to the impact of working with people who have experienced trauma? • What policies and procedures are in place for including trauma survivors/people receiving services and peer supports in meaningful and significant roles in agency planning, governance, policy-making, services, and evaluation?

Physical Environment	• How does he physical environment promote a sense of safety, calming, and de-esclation for clients and staff? • In what ways do staff members recognize and address aspects of the physical environment that may be re-traumatizing, and work with people on developing strategies? • How has the agency provided space that both staff and people receiving services can use to practice self-care? • How has the agency developed mechanisms to address gender-related physical and emotional safety concerns (e.g., egender-specific spaces and activities)
Engagement and Involvement	• How do people with lived experience have the opportunity to provide feedback to the organization on quality improvement processes for better engagement and services? • How do staff members keep people fully informed of rules, procedures, activities, and schedules, while being mindful that people who are frightened or overwhelmed may have a difficulty processing information? • How is transparency and trust among staff and clients promoted? • What strategies are used to reduce the sense of power differentials among staff and clients? • How do staff members help people to identify strategies that contribute to feeling comforted and empowered?
Cross Sector Collaboration	• Is there a system of communication in place with other partner agencies workting with the individual receiving services for making trauma-informed decisions? • Are collaborative partners' trauma-informed? • How does the organization identify community providers and referral agencies that have experience delivering evidence-based trauma services?

	• What mechanisms are in place to promote cross-sector training on trauma and trauma-informed approaches?
Screening, Assessment, Treatment Services	• Is an individual's own definition of emotional safety included in treatment plans? • Is timely trauma-informed screening and assessment available and accessible to individulas receiving services? • Does the organization have the capacity to provide trauma-specific treatment or refer to appropriate trauma-specific services? • How are peer supports integrated into the service delivery approach? • How does the agency address gender-based needs in the context of trauma screening, assessment, and treatment? For instance, are gender-specific trauma services and supports available for both men and women? • Do staff members talk with people about a range of trauma recations and work to minimize feelings of fear or shame and to increase self-understanding? • How are these trauma-specific practices incorporated into the organization's ongoing operations?
Training and Workforce Development	• How does the agency address the emotional stress that can arise when working with indivdiuals who have had traumatic experiences? • How does the agency support training and workforce development for staff to understand and increase their traum knowledge and interventions? • How does the organization ensure that all staff (diret care, supervisors, front desk and reception, support staff, housekeeping and maintenance) receive basic training on trauma, its impact, and strategies for trauma-informed approaches across the agency and across personnel functions?

	- How does workforce development/staff training address the ways identity, culture, community, and oppression can affect a person's experience of trauma, access to supports and resources, and opportunities for safety?
	- How does on-going workforce development/staff training provide staff supports in developing the knowledge and skills to work sensitively and effectively with trauma survivors.
	- What types of training and resources are provided to staff and supervisors on incorporating trauma-infomred practice and supervision in their work?
	- What workforce development strategies are in place to assist staff in working with peer supports and recognizing the value of peer support as integral to the organization's workforce?
Progress Monitoring and Quality Assurance	- Is there a system in place that monitors the agency's progress in being trauma-informed?
	- Does the agency solicit feedback from both staff and individuals receiving services?
	- What strategies and processes ddoes the agency use to evaluate whether staff members feel safe and valued at the agency?
	- How does the agency incorporate attention to culture and trauma in agency operations and quality improvement processes?
	- What mechanisms are in place for information collected to be incorporated into the agency's quality assurance processes and how well do those mechanisms addres creating accessible, culturally relevant, trauma-informed services and supports?

Financing	• How does the agency's budget include funding support for ongoing training on trauma and trauma-informed approaches for leadership and staff development? • What funding exists for cross-sector training on trauma and trauma-informed approaches? • What funding exists for peer specialists? • How does the budget support provision of a safe physical environment?
Evaluation	• How does the agency conduct a trauma-infomed organizational assessment or have measures or indicators that show their level of trauma-informed approach? • How does the perspective of people who have experienced trauma inform the agency performance beyond consumer satsifcation survey? • What processes are in place to solicit feedback from people who use services and ensure anonymity and confidentiality? • What measures or indicators are used to asses the organizational progress in becoming trauma-informed?

Adapted from Substance Abuse and Mental Health Service Administration (2014) *Concept of Trauma and Guidance for a Trauma-Informed Approach.*

Vicarious Traumatization—
Helping the Helpers

Objectives

Upon completion of this chapter, you will be able to:

- define secondary trauma and describe its relationship to working with victims of crime,
- differentiate the terms *secondary traumatic stress*, *compassion fatigue*, and *burnout*,
- identify signs of secondary traumatic stress, compassion fatigue, and burnout, and
- formulate a set of techniques to help monitor and manage one's stress level to promote resilience.

Introduction

Working with victims of crime as a victim service provider can be one of the most rewarding and challenging careers. It is rewarding because one has the opportunity to help others when they are most vulnerable. However, it can also be very

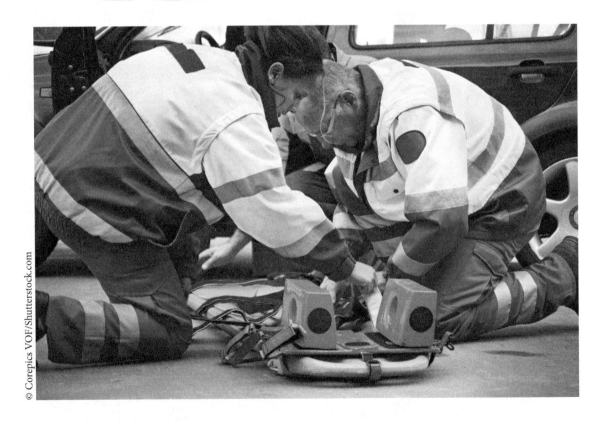

© Corepics VOF/Shutterstock.com

challenging, because one will be exposed to other people's pain and suffering on a regular basis.

Over time, such exposure can take a significant physical, emotional, and psychological toll on an individual. The question, therefore, is how can one process all of the trauma one is going to be exposed to, but not allow it to disrupt one's personal and professional life? This chapter will provide an overview of how to monitor the emotional stress, and possible physical and behavioral health conditions, that many victim service providers may experience as the result of exposure to secondary and vicarious trauma, and will detail a variety of resources and strategies providers can use to assist in managing their stress and to facilitate resilience.

Sergeant A. J. DeAndrea of Arvada, Colorado still recalls the overwhelming scene of carnage he witnessed upon entering Columbine High School after the mass shooting committed by Dylan Klebold and Eric Harris that took the lives of 13 students and teachers, and left 21 others injured. In an interview immediately following the mass shooting in San Bernadino in December 2015, Sergeant DeAndrea was asked to describe what it's like to be a police officer responding to a mass shooting. He stated, "When you walked out of the building, it was like 'Holy shit. What did we just experience?' It was surreal. People didn't know what to say … you felt like you were on an island." Although the incident at Columbine had occurred over fifteen years ago, Sergeant DeAndrea admitted he still struggles with intrusive images of the victims he found inside the high school that day. Anything can trigger another unpleasant memory, including hearing about another mass shooting, such as the one that occurred in San Bernadino. Sergeant DeAndrea noted that time has helped to temper the how often the memories of that fateful day crop up, but he stated, "these things stay with you." (Thompson, 2015, p.1)

The "Cost of Caring": Secondary Traumatic Stress, Compassion Fatigue, and Burnout

Becoming a victim service provider is one of the most noble and rewarding careers. In this role, one has the opportunity to help people who are suffering and provide them support during some of the darkest moments of their lives. But it is those very experiences that make this one of the most difficult and stressful jobs. For example,

> *"When I was a boy and I would see scary things in the news, my mother would say to me, "Look for the helpers. You will always find people who are helping."*
>
> **~ Fred "Mister" Rogers**

some may be asked to accompany police officers to a scene where they may witness firsthand the aftermath of violent crimes, such as shootings, incidents of domestic and child abuse, sexual assaults, and homicides. Others may be asked to accompany a victim to court where they must listen to testimony given by victims and witnesses that recounts in graphic detail a traumatic event and look at photographs and forensic evidence taken from the scene. In fact, many victim service providers will spend countless hours listening to numerous accounts of other people's suffering as the result of some form of trauma. In each of the aforementioned scenarios, the victim service provider has been exposed to "secondary trauma."

Secondary trauma occurs when an individual is exposed to another person's trauma by interacting and engaging with them (Figley, 1995). As a victim service provider, one will inevitably be exposed either directly or indirectly to people who are suffering physical, emotional, and/or psychological distress as a result of some type of trauma (SAMHSA, 2018). Sometimes that trauma is the result of a single event (e.g., a shooting), while other times it is the result of a recurring event (e.g., domestic violence), or a combination of events. Unfortunately, most of the time you will not know the exact nature and extent of a person's trauma history that you have been asked to help. Regardless of the source of the trauma, witnessing another person's suffering can elicit a strong emotional reaction within ourselves. When we see others in emotional distress, we may begin to feel similarly distressed. This can be attributed to *empathy*. Empathy is defined as the ability to understand and share the feelings of another (Webster's Dictionary). For example, a victim service provider who must help to inform parents that their child has been murdered may begin to experience the same feelings of sorrow, despair, and anger that the parents display immediately following that notification. Moreover, those same emotions may resurface again whenever that victim service provider recalls that scene in his or her mind or has to work on another child fatality case. This can be described as a *secondary traumatic stress response*.

> "The expectation that we can be immersed in suffering and loss daily and not be touched by it is unrealistic as expecting to be able to walk through water without getting wet."
>
> ~ Remen, 1996, p.1

Secondary traumatic stress (STS) refers to the natural subsequent behaviors and emotions that result from *knowing* about a traumatizing event experienced by another person, and the corresponding stress we feel from helping or wanting to help relieve the suffering of the other person (Figley, 1995). Many of these behaviors and emotions mirror those that are experienced by the individual who was directly affected by the traumatic event. Some of these symptoms may include flashbacks, sleep disorders, avoidance of reminders and cues, hyperarousal, difficulty regulating moods, loss of interest in things/activities, and withdrawal from others (see Figure 9.1). When these symptoms result in significant distress or impairment of the individual's ability to function, a diagnosis of *Secondary Traumatic Stress Disorder* (STSD) may be warranted (Figley, 1995). STSD is similar to Posttraumatic Stress Disorder (PTSD); however, it differs from PTSD in that it is the result of one's *exposure to the knowledge* of other people's trauma, rather than from one's direct experience of the traumatic event itself (Figley 1995).

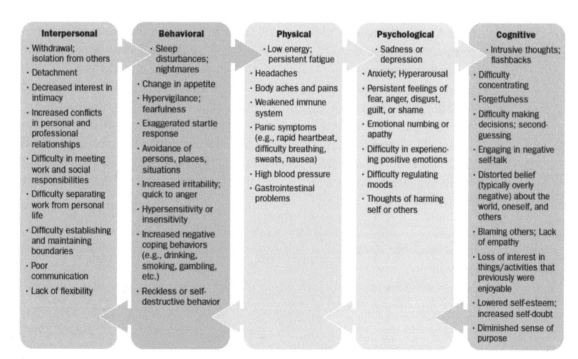

FIGURE 9.1 5 Domains for symptoms of STSD/VT.

Another challenge for victim service providers is that the longer one works in the field, the more likely one may experience *vicarious trauma* (Benedek, Fullerton, & Ursano, 2007; Figley, 1995; Mathieu, 2012; SAMHSA, 2018). Vicarious trauma, in contrast to secondary trauma, refers to the *cumulative* exposure to other people's pain over the long term, and can have a more serious negative effect on one's own physical, emotional, and psychological wellbeing (Figley, 1995). It is estimated between 40%–85% of "helping professionals" develop vicarious trauma and display high rates of traumatic stress symptoms (Mathieu, 2012). And 34% of victim service providers meet PTSD diagnostic criteria from secondary exposure to trauma (Bride, Radey, & Figley, 2007). This can be attributed to a number of factors. Victim service providers are often required to work long hours, and are often not given enough time to recover from traumatic events (Bentley et al., 2013). This can ultimately lead to *compassion fatigue.*

Compassion fatigue is what Figley (1995) refers to as "the cost for caring for others." Over the course of a career, victim service providers are witness to countless others' fear, pain, and suffering. Over time, this continual exposure to other people's tragedies can take a serious toll and leave the individual feeling physically and mentally exhausted. Signs of compassion fatigue may include increases in mood swings (e.g., irritability, anger, depression), sleep disturbances, chronic somatic health problems (e.g., headaches, gastrointestinal issues, compromised immune system), and decreases in cognitive functioning (e.g., memory, ability to focus) (The American Institute of Stress [ASI], n.d.). One of the notable consequences of compassion fatigue is that the sufferer may start to become desensitized to other's feelings, thereby making it more difficult to connect with others (Mathieu, 2012). Researchers have found that many individuals who have compassion fatigue begin to doubt their own self-worth and question their ability to effect positive change in other people's lives or their own, and thus experience a diminished sense of hope (ASI, n.d.). Others may also experience a significant shift in their worldview, resulting in the adoption of a more pessimistic and cynical attitude about others and the world in general, thus causing them to become less trusting of others and isolating themselves further (ASI, n.d.).

> *"Basically, it's a low level, chronic clouding of caring and concern for others in your life—whether you work in or outside the home. Over time, your ability to feel and care for others comes eroded through overuse of your skills of compassion. You also might experience emotional blunting—whereby you react to situations differently than one would normally expect."*
>
> **Dr. Frank Ochberg (Boaz, 1998)**

A similar, but unique, problem that many victim service providers experience as a result of chronic exposure to secondary trauma is *burnout*. Burnout is similar to compassion fatigue in that it also refers to a process rather than a fixed condition (Figley, 1993; 1995). It also begins gradually, and its symptoms progressively worsen over time, kind of like a slow leak in your tire, until one day you discover that tire is flat. However, the root cause of burnout differs from compassion fatigue in that it is most often associated with increased workload and institutional stress, rather than one's exposure to trauma itself (ASI, n.d.). Specifically, it is a combination of occupation-related factors (see Table 1) that cause more stress in the workplace that contribute to an individual's risk of burnout (Scott, 2018).

© CC7/Shutterstock.com

Table 9.1 Occupational stress associated with burnout (Scott, 2018)

Condition	Example
Unclear requirements	• Lack of specificity of job duties • Lack of direction for specific tasks • Continuously changing requirements/parameters of job duties
Unrealistic expectations	• Insufficient time and/or resources provided to complete job responsibilities effectively
Lack of down-time	• Insufficient time to decompress and recover fram high stress event(s) • Persistent pressure to work overtime and/or to give up personal leave
High-stakes environment	• Significant pressure associated with serious nature of the potential cosequences that may result from any mistake (e.g., loss of life, lawsuit, etc.)
Lack of personal control	• Micro-management of day to day operations • Lack of flexibility for individual decision-making
Lack of recongnition/ appreciation	• Little (or no) public and/or private acknowledgement for efforts made
Poor communication	• Lack of opportunity to talk through problems and concerns with leadership • Culture of silence (e.g., figure it out yourself)
Insufficient compensation	• Demands of the job do not align with level of compensation

When the symptoms associated with either compassion fatigue or burnout are allowed to accumulate and intensify, they can seriously compromise one's ability to function at work, at home, or both. Ultimately, if the situation is not addressed properly, it can cause irreparable harm in not just one's personal life, but it may even end one's career prematurely (Scott, 2018). Fortunately, neither of those scenarios ever has to happen. Both compassion fatigue and burnout manifest *over time*. You don't wake up one morning and suddenly "have compassion fatigue" or "have burnout." Our brain, as well as our body, will provide us with warning signals when we are starting to reach that critical level of stress that places us in that "danger zone" for compassion fatigue and/or burnout. Therefore, if you know what signs to look for, you can then begin to take appropriate steps to change course. The next section outlines some strategies and resources you can use to help monitor your own individual level of stress and help you manage the negative symptoms associated with such stress so you can continue to function at an optimal level.

Monitoring and Managing Stress

Although it is not possible to completely eliminate all of the stress that you will encounter as a victim service provider, there are a variety of strategies you can adopt to help manage your individual stress level. According to mental health experts, the first step in preventing stress from disrupting or jeopardizing your personal and professional life is to regularly monitor your stress level (ASI, n.d.). This requires you to a) identify your own personal threshold for tolerating stress, b) monitor your current stressors, and c) understand how you respond to stress. To help you with the first task, ask yourself how much stress you are comfortable with. Purves (n.d.) states that people don't always appreciate how much stress they are under, so they continue to just absorb more and more until they eventually break. Obviously, this is not a healthy way to live, therefore Dr. Purves recommends you explicitly define how much stress you are able to tolerate. To do this, he recommends you use a scale of 1–10 to identify the specific level of stress at which point you no longer feel you can cope effectively. This number may be low for some individuals, but higher for others. The level may also vary depending on the *type* of stress one is dealing with (e.g., personal v. professional). Dr. Purves recommends that throughout the day, you take a moment to

© Stuart Miles/Shutterstock.com

pause and take your "stress temperature" (e.g., on a scale of 1–10, with 1 being the lowest and 10 being the highest, how stressed am I right now?), and then ask yourself how you are feeling emotionally, physically, and mentally. Do you feel like you have things under control? When you find yourself beginning to feel like you cannot cope effectively (aka, entering your "danger zone"), you can then take steps to address the source of the stress, as well as your response to it, quickly rather than allow it to continue to build. Other tools to help monitor your current stress level are provided in Appendix A.

A second strategy to help monitor and manage one's stress is to take an inventory of what is currently on your plate so you can begin to identify the source of your stress (Mathieu, 2007; Mayo Clinic, 2016.; U.S. Department of Veterans Affairs, 2014). Stress can come from both internal and external factors (American Psychological Association [APA], 2016; Mayo Clinic, 2016). Internal stressors come from within and center around your own attitudes, thoughts, and feelings (e.g., desire for perfection, fear of the unknown, negative self-talk, etc.), whereas external stressors come from events or situations that happen to you (e.g., physical environment, work duties, major life events, relationships with others, etc.). There are also acute stressors versus chronic stressors (APA, 2016; Mayo Clinic, 2016). Acute stress, the most common type of stress, comes from either something that happened in the recent past or that we anticipate will happen in the future. Chronic stress, in contrast, comes from persistent and unrelenting demands and pressures that have been allowed to accumulate over long periods of time. One specific strategy that you can use to help monitor your stress level is to write a list of all the stressors you are currently dealing with, both personally and professionally. Once you have identified your current stressors, ask yourself two questions for each one: *Is this important to me? And, is this under my control?* (U.S. Department of Veterans Affairs, 2014). In regard to stressors that you do not feel are especially important, or are beyond your control, make a conscious decision to let them go. A good exercise to help you do this is to literally tear off the portion of your list that includes those stressors that are not a real priority or ones you cannot control, then crumple that piece of paper up and throw it away. Now, you can direct your energy to addressing only those items on the list that you feel are important *and* you have some degree of control (U.S. Department of Veterans Affairs, 2014). This is an important and invaluable exercise because energy is a finite resource. You need to conserve your energy for only those things on which you actually have the ability to effect positive change.

The final strategy to monitoring and managing one's stress level is to become aware of how you respond to stress. There are four different ways humans react to stress: physical (i.e., how our body works), behavioral (i.e., how we act), cognitive (i.e, how we think), and emotional (i.e., how we feel) (see Figure 9.2)

PHYSICAL	BEHAVIORAL	COGNITIVE	EMOTIONAL
• Rapid heartbeat • Chest pain • Breathlessness • Dizziness • Muscle tension or weakness • Heartburn • Constipation or Diarrhea • Headaches • Backaches • Insomnia • Weight gain or loss • Skin rashes • Compromised immune system	• Grinding teeth • Nervous habits (e.g., nail biting) • Initiating arguments • Poor hygiene • Poor diet • Self-medicating • Sleeping too much/little • Overreacting to things • Procrastinating or neglecting responsibilities • Overdoing things (e.g., shopping) • Avoidance	• Negative self-talk (e.g., I'm useless, there must be something wrong with me, etc.) • Difficulty focusing • Forgetfulness • Indecisiveness • Anxious or racing thoughts • Loss of objectivity • Pessimistic outlook • Constant worrying	• Sad • Irritated • Impatient • Restless • Lonely • Angry • Frustrated • Anxious • Apathetic • Overwhelmed • Hopeless

FIGURE 9.2 Common stress responses.

(HelpGuide, 2007). Some of these responses are involuntary (e.g., physiological changes, such as rapid heartbeat), while others are within our control (e.g., negative self-talk, negative emotions) (Ross, 2009). Moreover, different stressors may produce different responses. For example, you might develop a headache and become increasingly anxious when managing multiple deadlines for work, but when confronted with a personal conflict with a loved one, your stomach knots up and you become increasingly agitated. Thus, different circumstances and events may elicit very different responses.

Moreover, research has found that stress responses are often intertwined (Life-Link, 2010; Tugade, Frederickson, & Barrett, 2004). What we think can influence how we behave, and what we feel emotionally can influence how we feel physically (Karren, Smith, Gordon, & Frandsen, 2013; Tugade et al., 2004). This is often referred to as the "Mind/Body" connection (Karren et al., 2013). Research has also found that these stress responses can become cyclical in nature if they are not addressed properly (LifeLink, 2010). For example, the more negative physical symptoms we experience as a result of repeated exposure to stress, the more negative our mood becomes. The more negative our mood, our body reacts accordingly,

THE 21ST CENTURY TRANSFORMATION OF VICTIMOLOGY

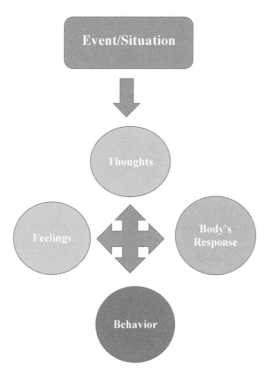

FIGURE 9.3 Cyclical stress response.

and we begin to experience more negative physical symptoms. Hence, we can get trapped in a kind of negative feedback loop that makes it more difficult for us to function. See Figure 9.3.

Therefore, in order to manage stress effectively you need to identify *how* you respond to stress and under different types of circumstances. What kind of physical symptoms do you experience when you get stressed? What kind of emotions do you typically feel? How does stress affect your ability to think clearly and carry out your job duties? One strategy Ross (2009) suggests is to use the following four-point checklist throughout the day to help assess your cognitive, emotional, and physical responses to your environment:

Pay attention to your attention	Am I able to focus? Am I losing interest in what I'm working on?
Check in with your mood	Is my frustration/anxiety/anger level rising? Am I falling into negative thought patterns (e.g., I can't deal with this, there's no use in trying, etc.)?
Assess your energy	Do I feel like I'm running out of steam?
What's your body telling you	Am I experiencing any negative physical symptoms (e.g., headache, stomachache, tight muscles, racing heart, etc.)?

Another strategy is to create a stress journal (see Appendix A) to document the different symptoms you experience when exposed to specific circumstances or events, in order to help you identify what your specific "stress triggers" are, and how you typically react.

Although there has been a great deal of research on the negative effects of stress, stress, in and of itself, is not bad. In fact, research has found moderate doses of stress help to promote resilience (Ross, 2009; Seery, Holman, & Silver, 2010). Under those conditions, productivity and creativity is often boosted and people become more adaptable, thereby helping them learn how to overcome challenges (Greenberg, n.d.; Ross, 2009; Seery et al, 2010). This, in turn, helps to increase self-confidence and decrease fear of the unfamiliar or the need for change, thus promoting personal growth (Greenberg, n.d.; Seery et al., 2010). However, it is when stress is persistent or increases in intensity that those benefits begin to diminish, and the individual is more likely to suffer from significant physical, cognitive, and emotional impairments (Ross, 2009). Therefore, it is important that you monitor your stress level on a regular basis, and track how it is affecting you so you can then begin to identify ways to manage it. One of the most effective strategies you can use to help manage your stress is to develop a self-care plan.

© litabit/Shutterstock.com

> *"In dealing with those who are undergoing great suffering, if you feel 'burnout' setting in, if you feel demoralized and exhausted, it is best, for the sake of everyone, to withdraw and restore yourself. The point is to have a long-term perspective."*
>
> **The Dalai Lama**

Developing Your Self-Care Plan

Unfortunately, regular self-care is often an afterthought for busy helping professionals. However, just as a flight attendant will instruct passengers to first put on their own oxygen mask before they try to help somebody else, first responders must be similarly diligent about incorporating self-care in their daily lives if they want to be effective in their job. The objective of self-care is to find ways you can enhance

FIGURE 9.4 Six domains of wellness.

your own wellbeing, thereby create a healthy balance to your life. There are multiple domains of wellness that you can focus on, including: physical, emotional, social, intellectual, occupational, and spiritual (see Figure 9.4).

The physical aspect of wellness focuses on how one can improve one's physical health. The emotional aspect of wellness focuses on how one can expand the awareness of one's feelings and how one can better manage those emotions. The social aspect of wellness focuses on how one can build connections with others to help create a stronger network of support. The intellectual aspect of wellness focuses on how one can expand knowledge and/or skills in order to strengthen competency and promote personal development. The occupational aspect of wellness focuses on how one can develop and establish a set of practices in one's job that can help to promote job satisfaction. The spiritual aspect of wellness focuses on how one can create and foster a sense of "belonging" in the world, or sense of purpose.

When developing a personal self-care plan, your goal should be to identify a mixture of strategies. None of the strategies needs to be difficult or to take a lot of planning. Rather, the key is to identify a set of activities that you enjoy and are easy to incorporate into your life. Additionally, your plan should include some strategies that you can complete quickly (e.g., that take less than 5 minutes) to help calm your mind and body when you begin to feel overwhelmed. Some examples might include breathing exercises, meditating for a few minutes, listening to a favorite song, taking a quick walk around your office, making a mug of tea, or reading a favorite motivational quote (see Figure 9.5). To promote long-term wellness, your plan should also include activities that require a greater level of time and attention but afford you the opportunity to really give your mind, body, and spirit time to rest and recharge. Some examples might include taking an exercise class, cooking a healthy dinner, going out with friends, taking a day off, or going on vacation (see Figure 9.5). Ultimately, you want to develop a self-care plan that includes a range of activities that can engage your senses, bring you pleasure, challenge your brain in a new way, strengthen your connections with others, reconnect you to your core values, help you reconnect with your own emotions, and boost energy (Markway, 2014). Fortunately, there are a significant number of online resources available to help you develop a plan for self-care (see Appendix A), as well as tools that are available on smart phones and tablets that can help you practice self-care on a daily basis (see Appendix B).

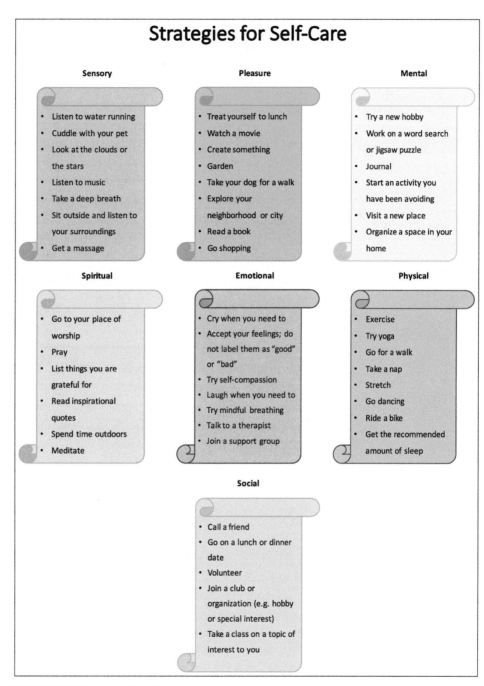

Strategies for Self-Care

Sensory
- Listen to water running
- Cuddle with your pet
- Look at the clouds or the stars
- Listen to music
- Take a deep breath
- Sit outside and listen to your surroundings
- Get a massage

Pleasure
- Treat yourself to lunch
- Watch a movie
- Create something
- Garden
- Take your dog for a walk
- Explore your neighborhood or city
- Read a book
- Go shopping

Mental
- Try a new hobby
- Work on a word search or jigsaw puzzle
- Journal
- Start an activity you have been avoiding
- Visit a new place
- Organize a space in your home

Spiritual
- Go to your place of worship
- Pray
- List things you are grateful for
- Read inspirational quotes
- Spend time outdoors
- Meditate

Emotional
- Cry when you need to
- Accept your feelings; do not label them as "good" or "bad"
- Try self-compassion
- Laugh when you need to
- Try mindful breathing
- Talk to a therapist
- Join a support group

Physical
- Exercise
- Try yoga
- Go for a walk
- Take a nap
- Stretch
- Go dancing
- Ride a bike
- Get the recommended amount of sleep

Social
- Call a friend
- Go on a lunch or dinner date
- Volunteer
- Join a club or organization (e.g. hobby or special interest)
- Take a class on a topic of interest to you

FIGURE 9.5 Strategies for self-care

Conclusion

Stress is a natural and inevitable part of life, and in moderate amounts can help to promote resilience and personal growth (Greenburg, n.d.; Ross, 2009; Seery, Holman, & Silver, 2010). As a first-responder, however, it is very likely that you will experience much higher rates of stress than the average individual because of the amount of secondary trauma you will be exposed to on a daily basis. Therefore, in order to manage the negative responses to stress that can potentially disrupt your life and increase your risk for compassion fatigue or burnout, it is critical that you practice self-care on a regular basis. Just as no two people will respond to stress similarly, you must find out which self-care strategies work best for you. If you incorporate a number of those strategies in your daily routine, you will be in a better position to perform your job effectively. As an old cliché goes, "take care of yourself first, or you will have nothing left to give others."

Discussion questions

1. Why do you think so many first-responders are reluctant to talk about the physical and emotional toll of their jobs?
2. What are some realistic strategies organizations can incorporate to promote the physical and mental wellbeing of their employees?
3. What are some barriers you currently have to practicing self-care? What are five strategies you can use to incorporate self-care into your daily life now that take a limited amount of time and resources?

References

Abbott, C., Barber, E., Burke, B., Harvey, J., Newland, C., Rose, M., & Young, A. (2015). *What's killing our medics?* Retrieved from: http://www.revivingresponders.com/originalpaper/pt5lehsknczsaofld89leijbmehz3c

American Counseling Association. (n.d.). *Vicarious trauma—Fact sheet 9.* Retrieved from: https://www.counseling.org/docs/trauma-disaster/fact-sheet-9—vicarious-trauma.pdf?sfvrsn=2

American Psychological Association. (2016). *Stress: The different kinds of stress.* Retrieved from: https://www.apa.org/helpcenter/stress-kinds.aspx

Benedek, D. M., Fullerton, C., & Ursano, R. J. (2007). First responders: Mental health consequences of natural and human-made disasters for public health and public safety workers. *Annual Review of Public Health, 28,* 55–66.

Best Start Resource Centre. (2012). *When compassion hurts: Burnout, vicarious trauma and secondary trauma in prenatal and early childhood service providers.* Retrieved from: http://www.beststart.org/resources/howto/pdf/Compassion_14MY01_Final.pdf

Bride, B. E., Radey, M., & Figley, C. R. (2007). Measuring compassion fatigue. *Clinical Social Work Journal, 35*(3), 155–163.

Boaz, J. (1998). *When helping hurts: Sustaining trauma workers* (DVD). Retrieved from: http://www.giftfromwithin.org/html/When-Helping-Hurts-Sustaining-Trauma-Workers.html#4

Figley, C. R. (1993, June). *Compassion fatigue and social work practice: Distinguishing burnout from secondary traumatic stress.* Newsletter of the NASW Florida Chapter, 1–2.

Figley, C. R. (Ed.) (1995). *Compassion fatigue: Secondary traumatic stress disorders from treating the traumatized.* New York: Brunner/Mazel.

Greenberg, M., (n.d.). *Why some stress is good for you.* Retrieved from: https://www.psychologytoday.com/us/blog/the-mindful-self-express/201612/why-some-stress-is-good-you

HelpGuide. (2007). *Understanding stress: Signs, symptoms, causes and effects.* Retrieved from http://www.helpguide.org/mental/stress_signs.htm

Karren, K. J., Smith, L., Gordon, K. J., & Frandsen, K. J. (2013). *Mind/body health: The effects of attitudes, emotions, and relationships* (5th ed.). London: Pearson.

Markway, B. (2014, March 16). *Seven types of self-care activities for coping with stress.* Retrieved from: https://www.psychologytoday.com/blog/shyness-is-nice/201403/seven-types-self-care-activities-coping-stress

Mathieu, F. (2012). Compassion fatigue. In C. R. Figley (Ed.), *Encyclopedia of trauma.* Thousand Oaks, CA: SAGE Publishing.

Mayo Clinic. (2016, April 28). *Stress management. Know your triggers.* Retrieved from: https://www.mayoclinic.org/healthy-lifestyle/stress-management/in-depth/stress-management/art-20044151

McCann, I. L., & Pearlman, L. A. (1990). Vicarious traumatization: A framework for understanding the psychological effects of working with victims. *Journal of Traumatic Stress, 3*(1), 131–149.

Pearlman, L. A., & McKay, L. (2008). *Vicarious trauma.* Retrieved from: http://www.headingtoninstitute.org/files/vtmoduletemplate2_ready_v2_85791.pdf

Pearlman, L. A., & Saakvitne, K. W. (1995). *Trauma and the therapist: Countertransference and vicarious traumatization in psychotherapy with incest survivors.* New York: W. W. Norton & Company.

Pearlman, L. A., & Saakvitne, K. S. (1996). *Transforming the pain: A workbook on vicarious traumatization.* New York: W.W. Norton & Company.

Purves, D. (n.d.). *Thoughts on stress-free living: The stress level test*—Free monitoring diary. Retrieved from: http://drpurves.com/stress-monitoring-diary/

Ross, J. (2009). How to manage your stress level. *Harvard Business Review*. Retrieved from: https://hbr.org/2009/03/monitor-and-manage-your-stress

Scheidegger, J. (2015, May 1). *Burnout, compassion fatigue, and depression—what's the difference?* Retrieved from: http://veterinarynews.dvm360.com/burnout-compassion-fatigue-depression-what-s-difference

Seery, M. D., Holman, E. A., & Silver, R. C. (2010). Whatever does not kill us: Cumulative lifetime adversity, vulnerability, and resilience. *Journal of Personality & Social Psychology, 99*(6), 1025–1041.

Substance Abuse and Mental Health Services Administration. (2018, May). *First responders: Behavioral health concerns, emergency response, and trauma.* [Disaster Technical Assistance Center Supplemental Research Bulletin].

Retrieved from: https://www.samhsa.gov/sites/default/files/dtac/supplementalresearchbulletin-firstresponders-may2018.pdf

Substance Abuse and Mental Health Services Administration. (2018). The effects of trauma on first responders. *The Dialogue, 14*(1). Retrieved from: https://www.samhsa.gov/sites/default/files/dtac/dialogue-vol14-is1_final_051718.pdf

Tend. (2016). *What is compassion fatigue.* Retrieved from: https://www.tendacademy.ca/what-is-compassion-fatigue/

The American Institute of Stress (n.d.). *Transforming stress through awareness, education, and collaboration.* Retrieved from: https://www.stress.org/military/forpractitionersleaders/compassion-fatigue/

The National Child Traumatic Stress Network. (2011). *Secondary traumatic stress. A fact sheet for child-serving professionals.* Retrieved from: http://www.nctsn.org/sites/default/files/assets/pdfs/secondary_traumatic_tress.pdf

Thompson, C. (2015, December 15). *What it's like to be a cop responding to a mass shooting.* Retrieved from: http://mashable.com/2015/12/06/police-officers-mass-shooting/#uW8Ow_T2iPqt

Tugade, M. M., Frederickson, B. L., & Barrett, L. F. (2004). Psychological resilience and positive emotions on coping and health. *Journal of Personality, 72*(6), 1161–1190.

United States Department of Veteran Affairs. (2014, June). *Manage stress workbook.* Retrieved from: https://www.prevention.va.gov/mpt/2013/docs/managestress-workbook_dec2013.pdf

Wendt Center for Loss and Healing. (2016). *For professionals—vicarious trauma.* Retrieved from: http://www.wendtcenter.org/resources/for-professionals/

APPENDIX A:

ASSESSMENT TOOLS	
Professional Quality of Life Elements Theory and Measurement (ProQOL) http://www.proqol.org/ProQol_Test.html	ProQOL is the most commonly used measure of the negative and positive affects of helping others who experience suffering and trauma, and is free for anyone's use. The assessment includes sub-scales for compassion satisfaction, compassion fatigue, and burnout, and is available in 25 languages.
Are You Stressed? http://socialwork.buffalo.edu/content/dam/socialwork/home/self-care-kit/are-you-stressed.pdf	This non-clinical assessment involves twenty yes/no questions to help you monitor your current stress level
WORKBOOKS/GUIDES	
Understanding & Addressing Vicarious Trauma http://www.headington-institute.org/files/vtmoduletemplate2_ready_v2_85791.pdf	Dr. Laurie Pearlman and Lisa McKay, of the Headington Institute, created a three-part training module to help users understand what vicarious trauma is, what are its symptoms and causes, and how to develop coping skills to offset its negative effects. The guide provides users with a mock action plan, as well as an extensive list of resources on the topic.
Manage Stress Workbook https://www.prevention.va.gov/mpt/2013/docs/managestressworkbook_dec2013.pdf	This workbook, designed by the National Center for Health Promotion and Disease Prevention for the U.S. Department of Veterans Affairs, includes tools to help identify and track stress, as well as provides strategies to incorporate into daily routines to help reduce stress.
What About You? A Workbook For Those Who Work With Others http://508.center4si.com/SelfCareforCare-Givers.pdf	Produced by The National Center of Family Homelessness, this online workbook provides tools to help monitor and control stressors. It provides multiple exercises to track one's stress level and how it is effecting one's physical and emotional well-being (e.g., "Taking Your Stress Temperature"), a self-care assessment tool to measure current efforts at addressing one's own needs and identify where one could improve, and strategies that can be readily incorporated into one's daily routine to offset the negative effects of stress.

6 Dimensions of Vicarious Trauma-Free Life: Your Own Personal Care and Wellness Starter Kit http://www.olgaphoenix.com/wp-content/themes/olg/pdf/vt%20Starter%20Kit.pdf	Olga Phoenix, a recognized expert on vicarious trauma and other trauma related disorders, has compiled an online workbook that explains what vicarious trauma is and how it can negatively affect one's life. On page 5 of the workbook, Ms. Phoenix has created a "Self-Care Wheel" which readers can then use to develop an action plan using her six dimensions. The workbook is available in English and Spanish.
What is Stress? Stress Management Workbook 1 https://safespot.org.uk/wp-content/uploads/2016/05/workbook1.compressed.pdf	Published by LifeLink, this workbook provides an overview of how stress can affects one's physical, emotional, and mental well-being; and provides a series of self-reflection exercises to help one identify one's own stressors, measure one's current level of stress, identify how one responds to stress, and a variety of steps one can take to begin to reduce and control stress responses.
Stress Monitoring Diary http://drpurves.com/wp-content/uploads/2012/02/Stress-Monitoring-Diary.pdf http://drpurves.com/stress-monitoring-diary/	Dr. David Purves' "Stress Monitoring Diary" is a daily stress-management tool to help document one's stress level at various time segments during the day (e.g., morning versus afternoon) in order to help identify patterns for when one is the most and least stressed. This worksheet also allows users to write down specific Do's and Don'ts to help create a mini action plan to help manage daily stressors. Dr. Purves demonstrates how to use the Daily Stress Diary on his website.
University of Buffalo School of Social Work – "Introduction to Self-Care" https://socialwork.buffalo.edu/resources/self-care-starter-kit/introduction-to-self-care.html	The University of Buffalo's School of Social Work provides information and tips on self-care for both students and professionals in this virtual *Self-Care Starter Kit.* The *Developing Your Self-Care Plan* link supplies users with details on how to begin and maintain a self-care action plan. The *Self-Care Assessments, Exercises, and Activities* link allows users a chance to learn more about vicarious trauma and burnout, while providing tips on self-care and exercises in mindfulness and relaxation. Additional resources, such as websites and articles on self-care, can be found under the *Additional Self-Care Resources* link.
21 Ways to Reduce Stress During the Workday http://socialwork.buffalo.edu/content/dam/socialwork/home/self-care-kit/exercises/21-ways-to-reduce-stress.pdf	Practicing mindfulness is one of the most effective strategies to help manage negative stress responses. This checklist provides 21 simple, but effective strategies to incorporate mindfulness into one's daily routine.

My Maintenance Self-Care Plan Worksheet http://socialwork.buffalo.edu/content/dam/socialwork/home/self-care-kit/my-mainte-nance-self-care-worksheet.pdf	This worksheet can be used to develop a personalized self-care plan that addresses each of the core areas of wellness, and requires the user to proactively identify possible barriers to self-care and then trouble-shoot how they may overcome such obstacles.
Emergency Self-Care Worksheet https://socialwork.buffalo.edu/content/dam/socialwork/home/self-care-kit/Emergency%20Self-Care%20Worksheet%20NEW-2.6.15.pdf	Too often when an individual becomes overwhelmed by a stressful event or set circumstances, (s)he may not know how to respond. This worksheet provides the user the opportunity to think proactively what steps (s) he can take when faced with an immediate, significant stressor to help avoid becoming overwhelmed. After completing the worksheet, the user is instructed to write it his or her specific plan on a 3x5 index card that can be carried with them at all times.

VIDEOS

What is Vicarious Trauma? https://www.youtube.com/watch?v=wVDSd-ta0mbM&feature=youtu.be	Dr. Laurie Pearlman, senior psychological consultant at the Headington Institute, provides a brief explanation of VT, its effects, and the "A B C's" on how to prevent it.
Drowning in Empathy: The Cost of Vicarious Trauma https://www.youtube.com/watch?v=-ZsaorjIo1Yc	In this Ted Talk, Amy Cunningham, the creator of the Compassion Fatigue training program for the Center for Health Care Services, discusses why so many caregivers and emergency responders suffer from compassion Fatigue, its most common symptoms, and how to treat it.
The Importance of Self-Care (A Playlist of Top Ted Talks) https://www.ted.com/playlists/299/the_impor-tance_of_self_care	This compilation of nine videos on the significance of self-care, produced by Ted Talks, addresses topics on mindfulness, emotional first aid, practicing gratitude, connecting with others, and slowing down. Each video ranges in length from 3 – 20 minutes.
How stress affects your brain https://www.youtube.com/watch?v=-bchj8uF8j2k	This video produced by TED-Education explains how chronic stress can affect brain size, its structure, and how it functions on a genetic level
Long term effects of stress on your body https://www.youtube.com/watch?v=-1B0PGFnYnv4	This short video explains the effects of chronic stress on one's body and how it can lead to serious long term diseases (e.g., heart disease, diabetes, infertility, etc.)

APPENDIX B:

Apps for Stress

Breathe2Relax	Headspace	Gratitude Journal	Balanced	The Worry Box	Personal Zen
iPhone and Android	iPhone and Android	iPhone	iPhone	Android	iPhone
Free	Free 10-day trial; $12.99 a month	$1.99	Free	Free	Free
Based on the concept of mindful breathing, *B2R* provides several diaphragmatic breathing exercises. Its goal is to reduce the "fight, flight or freeze" response we experience during heightened levels of stress.	*Headspace* provides 10 minutes of guided meditation for beginners. After the trial period, it offers 15 and 20 minute sessions for everything from stress relief to increasing creativity.	*Gratitude Journal* allows users to record positive highlights from their day as well as upload photos to help remind them of what they are grateful for. It also sends out daily reminders to the users to feel grateful each day. Android offers a free version of this app called *Attitudes of Gratitude*.	*Balanced* allows users to set and to track different goals that will enable them to better manage the stressors in their life. Users determine how often they should participate in particular activities, as well as choose from 50 prepopulated positive activities to incorporate into their personal self-care plan.	*The Worry Box* is constructed around cognitive behavioral therapy, and teaches users how to manage and alleviate stress by using relaxation techniques. It also allows users to place their worries in a virtual box on the app.	*Personal Zen* is an animated game that has been clinically proven to reduce stress and anxiety among users. The game consists of two animated sprites, one with a happy face and the other with an angry face, who bury themselves in a field. The goal is to find the happy sprite each time the two faces appear on screen.

Apps for Sleeping

Deep Sleep with Andrew Johnson	DigiPill	Relax Melodies	Sleep Well Hypnosis	White Noise	Nature Sounds Relax and Sleep
iPhone and Android	iPhone and Android	iPhone and Android	iPhone and Android	iPhone and Android	Android
$2.99 (both platforms)	Free	Free	Free	iPhone—$.99 Android—$1.99	Free
Based off of Andrew Johnson's CDs and MP3s, this step-by-step app helps users to meditate and unwind in order to help them fall asleep. The simple design and soft blue background gives users the ability to focus and relax.	*DigiPill* provides users with "digital pills" for a variety of situations. Examples are a "sleep deep pill" that helps users get to sleep, and a "sanctuary pill" that allows users to clear their minds and relax. Users may also buy additional pills from a pill store.	*Relax Melodies* provides various melodies, white noise, and other soothing sounds to help users fall asleep. It has a timer and alarm feature, individual volume control of each sound, and allows users to mix and share sounds with others.	Each *Sleep Well Hypnosis* session uses relaxing tones, as well as the soothing voice of a trained hypnotist. Users can repeat sessions, as well as moderate volume control for voice, background, and sleep boosters.	*White Noise* creates a relaxing environment for its users by reducing stress, thereby allowing one to fall asleep and stay asleep. The sound catalog includes crickets, white noise, rain, and pink noise. Users can also upload, create, and share sounds.	*Nature Sounds* provides users with six different sounds, including thunder and song birds. Users can listen for as long, or as little, as they choose, and sounds from the catalog can be used as a ring tone or an alarm tone.

Apps for Mood

T2 Mood Tracker	Optimism	Emotion Sense	Pacifica
iPhone and Android	iPhone	Android	iPhone and Android
Free	Free	Free	Free
Developed by the National Center for Telehealth & Technology (T2), *Mood Tracker* allows users to track their mood using one of six different scales (depression, stress, PTSD, brain injury, anxiety, or general well being). Users can also custom build their own scales for tracking moods, as well as record daily events, medications they are currently taking, and mental health treatments they are participating in.	*Optimism* allows users to selfreport "Core Data" such as rating your mood, the amount of sleep you get on a nightly basis, and your eating habits. For this information, *Optimism* then collates this data to help users track how they are doing in three categories: "Stay Well Strategies" (i.e. exercising), "Triggers" (i.e. poor diet), and "Symptoms" (i.e. anxiety).	Developed at the University of Cambridge's Computer Lab, *Emotion Sense* collects data two ways: passively and selfreporting. Examples of passive data are the amount of text messages you receive in one day, or the number of times you get up to move around. Users may self report data on their current moods and thoughts. The app then compiles a report to show the user how his or her mood is affected by day-to-day activities.	Based on cognitive behavioral therapy, *Pacifica* was designed to provide users with the tools needed to improve one's mood by providing relaxation techniques and allowing users to self-report their moods throughout the day. The app allows users to enter information into a "Thought Diary" so they may learn how to identify and amend negative thoughts. In addition, users can complete daily challenges, such as "Go to work," to also assist with improving their mood.

Apps for Fitness

Yoga Studio	Map My Walk	WalkLogger Pedometer	My Fitness Pal
iPhone and Android	iPhone and Android	Android	iPhone and Android
Free	Free	Free	Free
Yoga Studio comes with 65 installed yoga and meditation classes, and allows the user to create and upload their own classes. In addition, there are over 280 yoga poses in the app library, along with a comprehensive list of instructions and advice for each pose.	With over 600 activities, such as walking, running, and cycling, Map My Walk also allows users to track equipment they use or wear for workouts. Designed for all fitness levels, users can import data and link Map My Walk to more than 400 various devices (e.g. Adidas miCoach, Fitbit products).	WalkLogger allows users to count how many steps they take daily, either through routine activity or exercise. Users are able to receive activity logs, which provide them with detailed information on how they did walking or running. In addition, WalkLogger lets users unlock various themes on the app once they have completed a prerequisite amount of steps. It also allows users to upload their progress to various social media sites.	My Fitness Pal lets users track their daily calorie intake, develop diet plans, and create an exercise journal. All information is self-reported, and My Fitness Pal will create various progress reports for the user. This app can be used on a smart phone, tablet, or home computer.

Apps for Inspiration and Motivation

Inspirational and MotivationalQuotes	Sunrise Inspiration	Fabulous – Motivate Me!	Forest: Stay Focused
iPhone	iPhone	Android	Android
Free	Free	Free	Free
Inspirational and Motivational Quotes provides users with daily quotes, allowing them a moment of reflection. Each quote has been carefully selected, and users are given the opportunity within the app to save the quotes they enjoy the most.	Sunrise Inspiration provides users with daily inspirational and motivational quotes that they may save and share with others vis social media. The app also allows users to upload their own favorite quotes. Sunrise Inspiration provides free eCards, inspirational videos, and inspirational books for purchase.	Fabulous – Motivate Me! focuses on users well being by targeting four specific areas: feeling more invigorated; sleeping better; losing weight; and improving focus. The app allows users to create personal goals based on lifestyle and habits, and then maps out a gradual approach the user can follow to help achieve his or her goals.	Unlike most motivational apps, Forest wants users to stay away from their phones and just focus. Users plant a virtual tree, and then set a timer within the app (from 10 minutes to 2 hours). The only way the tree will grow is if the user does not touch his or her phone for the specified time period. If the user does, the virtual tree will not grow.

Professionalizing Crime Victim Services

Objectives

After reading this chapter, you will be able to:

- understand the development of professionalizing the field of crime victim services,
- understand the progress in creating formal crime victim services in the United States,
- describe the variety of primary service provider agencies at the national, state, and local levels,
- understand the role of victim service providers in the recovery of victims
- understand the history of professionalizing the field of victim services,
- identify and recognize the need for training and certification as part of the professionalizing of the field,
- identify and recognize the need for education designed specifically for careers in victim services, and
- recognize the variety of careers and specific job position opportunities in victim services.

Introduction

This chapter discusses the need for the professionalization of crime victim services and provides in-depth look at the development of formal victim services in the United States. As the field has evolved into a comprehensive service delivery model for a wide range of victimization and diverse populations, the knowledge, skills, and expertise required of service providers have also significantly expanded. In a relatively short period of time, the field grew from a grassroots informal delivery model to a sophisticated, comprehensive direct service prototype that defines itself as a separate discipline. However, the framework for defining the field as "a separate discipline" imposes a mandate on individual service providers to gain the appropriate knowledge, skills and expertise to meet the needs of the population it serves. To achieve such success, standardized training, credentialing, and university education is required.

This chapter provides an overview of the expansive efforts that have been made to professionalize the field. This overview includes the efforts that have targeted legislation, funding, training, certification, and formal education. The enormous role that victim service providers have in the recovery of crime victims necessitates the professionalization of victim services to ensure that quality and accessibility of services be available to all crime victims. While a wide range of victim service "job positions/titles" exists, those working in the field understand that a new category of victimization may present itself and require additional resources or services to support a new population. As we have witnessed over the evolution of victimology, many crimes remained unnoticed and well-hidden for centuries. While the significant developments in the growth of victim services may appear to be exhaustive, the reality is that the field as a discipline is still in its youth, with victim services emerging only since the 1970s.

History of Crime Victims Services

"No matter what population we serve or where we provide services, ours is a kinship that arose from the similarity of our work with those victimized by crime" (J. Adkins, 2001)

The evolution of crime victims' support and services has been an exciting, albeit challenging journey. The field has largely been a grassroots effort primarily driven by former victims of crime. The first evidence of victim services appeared as mostly "underground" or informal services. For example, in 1964, California established the first shelter, Haven House, where supporters would "shelter victims" in their homes to protect them from their domestic abusers who often were alcoholics. However, the field of victim services grew from several powerful social and political movements in the 1960s and 1970s. The women's rights movement gave a voice to the once silent victims and brought awareness to the plight of the hidden victims of domestic violence, sexual assault, and child abuse—categories of victimization that had been largely ignored in the past; and the victims rights' movement in the 1970s led to dramatic changes in support of victims leading to the first formal (and mostly unfunded) victim service programs. Early in this decade, the first three victim service programs were established to support sexual assault and domestic violence victims: the Bay Area Women Against Rape (San Francisco, California), the Aid for Victims of Crime (St. Louis, Missouri), and the Rape Crisis Center (Washington, DC). A year later , in 1974, the first formal domestic violence women's shelters opened: the Women's Advocates in St. Paul, Minnesota; Rosie's Place (which began in a private home) and Casa Myrna Vazquez shelter for multiracial victims in Boston, Massachusetts; and, the Union Mission in Atlanta, Georgia. By 1977, 89 women's shelters were available throughout the United States, and in 1983 the number grew to over 700 shelters nationwide (NCADV, 2019).

While the first types of victim services targeted specific victims (e.g., domestic violence, sexual assault, child abuse, homicide survivors, drunk driving), the field expanded as more funding and resources were made available. The early services that were established mostly by volunteers, slowly grew into nonprofit or non-governmental organizations. And the first government-based victim assistance programs were soon established. The first of these were set up by law enforcement agencies in Fort Lauderdale, Florida and Indianapolis, Indiana; soon afterward the first victim/witness programs were established in the Brooklyn, New York and Milwaukee, Wisconsin District Attorneys' Offices. And after the Crime Victims' Legal Advocacy Institute and the National Association of Crime Victim Compensation Boards were established in 1979, government-based victim assistance services rapidly expanded.

President Reagan's 1982 Task Force on Victims of Crime led to the establishment of victim-witness coordinators in every U.S. Attorney's Office, and the passage of the Victims of Crime Act (VOCA) of 1984 affirmed the nation's commitment to supporting crime victims in their recovery. In 1986, VOCA established the Crime Victims Fund to support state compensation programs for victims in communities throughout the United States. And in 1988, an amendment to VOCA was passed that established the U.S. Department of Justice, the Office for Victims of Crime (OVC), which was to be charged by Congress with administering the Crime Victim Fund. Two hundred new victim services programs were funded that first year, and those funds supported the growth of local nonprofit victim assistance programs spread across the country throughout the 1980s. Because the fund is financed with fines and penalties paid by federal convicted offenders, it is a sustainable source of funding that has only grown over the years. These funds have gone from supporting roughly 4,000 programs in the 1980s to more than 30,000 programs by 2017 (Oudekirk et al., 2018). In 2018, the fund balance was over $12 billion, and more than $3.4 billion was awarded to thousands of local victim assistance programs across the country.

After the passage of VOCA, the International Association of Chiefs of Police (IACP) adopted a Crime Victims' Bill of Rights. IACP's new Bill of Rights mandated that the criminal justice system incorporate legal and/or victim services within law enforcement agencies. As state constitutional amendments were passed and VOCA funds made available, victim services became more integrated throughout the criminal justice system at all jurisdictional levels. Today, victim services can be found in law enforcement, states' attorney offices, corrections, courts, and parole and probation agencies. Some criminal justice agencies provide legal advocacy, while others include a variety of support services.

The leading federal agency for victim service providers is the Office for Victims of Crime (OVC). OVC describes the occupation of victim assistance as "a full-fledged advocacy and service field dedicated to meeting the physical, financial, and psychological needs of victims their families" (OVC, 1998). OVC's description of the field is general enough to include all categories and types of service providers, whether specialized or generalists. OVC sets the priorities and standards for best practices in the field. When a newly recognized form of victimization emerges, OVC works toward meeting the challenges and needs of those victims, frequently leading to discretionary funding to establish new resources and aid to assist those victims across the country, and. updating the professional standards, research, and education to support new categories of crime victims.

With the passing of both VOCA and VAWA federal legislation, the development of victim assistance programs began to rapidly expand across the United States. A wide range of federal agencies, national coalitions, networks, and organizations dedicated to supporting and advocating for crime victims were established. Some agencies are embedded into federal government agencies, but most are non-government organizations (NGOs). Periodically, new national agencies are developed to address new types of crime victimization issues or to expand services in typically underserved parts of the community. A list of some of the active national agencies are provided in Table 10.1. Some agencies, as suggested by their title, are very general in their mission, while others specialize in a specific typology of crime victimization (i.e. domestic violence, elder abuse, homicide, child abuse, etc.) or specific population (i.e. children, adults, elderly, LGBTQ, immigrants, cyber-victims, etc.). National organizations have supported and advocated for advancing the professionalism of victim services and supporting global communities and partners in their efforts to provide quality services to victims. Many of those organizations provide the blueprints for best practices, resources, advocacy, data and research, clearinghouses, education, conferences and networking, credentialing and certification, and standards for professionalizing the field. Although they routinely provide leadership, guidance and support to local victim service agencies and providers; none have the authority over practice.

It's important to note that while this book does not focus on international victim services, the field of victim services has grown globally beyond the United States. Some countries have grown faster than others in establishing model programs, while many countries are far behind in addressing crime victims. In communities where services may not be readily available, international resources such as the United Nations, U.S. State Department, and many international agencies and organizations direct their attention and resources to parts of the world where victim services are non-existent. And an interest to expand scholarship to include a more international focus has also grown exponentially. For example, the World Society of Victimology has hosted a symposia for researchers and practitioners every three years in all major regions of the world.

Table 10.1 National Crime Victim Related Agencies

National Agencies	
Office for Victims of Crime, U.S., DOJ	National Organization for Victim Assistance
National Center for Victims of Crime	National Crime Victim Law Institute
Violence Against Women Office	Court Appointed Special Advocates (CASA)
Vera Institute of Justice Center on Victimization and Safety	National Crime Victims Research and Treatment Center
National Advocate Credentialing Program	National Association on Crime Victim Compensation Boards
National Coalition Against Domestic Violence	National Sexual Assault
National Center on Elder Abuse	National Coalition of Anti-Violence Programs
National Association of VOCA Assistance Administrators	National Children's Alliance
National Center for Prosecution of Child Abuse	Rape, Abuse and Incest National Network
National Center for missing & Exploited Kids	Grief Recovery Institute
Prevent Child Abuse America	National Victim Assistance Academy
National Center on Domestic Sexual Violence	National Center for Injury Prevention & Control
National Sexual Violence Resource Center	National Indigenous Women's Resource Center
National Coalition to Abolish Slavery and Trafficking	Mothers Against Drunk Driving
Parents of Murdered Children	National Teen Dating Abuse
National Crime Victim Bar Association	American Psychological Association
Substance Abuse and Mental Health Administration, DHHS	National Suicide Prevention
National Alliance on Mental Illness	National Center for Child Traumatic Stress
International Society for Prevention of Child Abuse and Neglect	Polaris (Protect labor trafficking victims)
Office on Trafficking in Persons, DHHS	National Center on Elder Abuse

Source: D. Stanley (2020)

Challenges for the Field of Victim Services

Time has revealed that the problem of crime victimization is constantly evolving, and thankfully, the trauma and impact of victimization is better recognized today. Subsequently, services have become more diverse, resulting in more multi-faceted and complex recovery models. Service agencies may find their mission changing in response to the current needs of victims. Many agencies have shifted to serving a variety of victims, not one specific population or category of victimization. Moreover, as funds from VOCA and VAWA increased, more victim service agencies were established, and the number of victim service providers grew. The growth of the field throughout the 1980s and 1990s was rapid; some agencies were successful, while others faded away. As the variety of services continue to increase, so too has the diversity of resources, with a range of basic support to more advanced services. The diversity of services may range from legal advocacy, shelter, to trauma recovery and mental health services.

One of the main challenges confronting the field today is the continuously changing categories of victimization; crime patterns change over time, impacting the type of victims' services required. The recovery model for crime victims varies with the type of victimization, i.e. level of trauma and impact of the victimization, and the diverse populations. An area of significant need are victims with disabilities. Access to disabled victims can be challenging if appropriate technology is not integrated into the service delivery model; often services are not tailored around the needs of the disabled. For example, many services are available via hotlines or the internet, which prevent those with hearing, speech, or vision difficulties from reaching out for assistance. Developing comprehensive service delivery models is essential to serving victims.

In the early development of the field, victim support and services were managed by volunteers who were often former victims or concerned citizens with enormous compassion for those who fell victim to crime. In the 21st Century, the role of a service provider has become more than a person supporting those in need; providers have become key agents in the lives of victims navigating the criminal justice system and restoring victims' lives. Therefore, the knowledge, skills, and responsibilities of victim service providers have grown significantly over time. Agencies are hiring more experienced and educated individuals to serve victims. Current demands on the field necessitate standards and professionalism of victim service providers.

Victim Service Providers: What it Takes to Work in the Field

Victims have their own unique victimization experience that manifests differently, and therefore their needs differ significantly; no one service model fits all victims. For example, how crime victims react to trauma and to what extent it influences their ability to recover are different for every victim, regardless of the type of victimization experience. Therefore, victim service providers are what one might refer

> "Victim service providers are change agents; they understand the impact of criminal victimization and how best to effectively intervene with those who have had the unfortunate experience of being victimized by crime. They know how to prevent 're-victimization'" (Atkins, 2001).

to as "generalists," with a little bit of knowledge about a lot of topics. Yet, to do their job successfully, they need a comprehensive set of knowledge and skills to help victims recognize their strengths, and to direct them toward solutions for recovery and secure the safety they deserve. As noted in Table 10.2, there are at least 50 areas of skills and expertise required of victim assistance providers. The complexity of victim assistance makes it difficult to establish standards of professionalism for the field, hence its slow emergence as a recognized profession. In the past thirty to forty years, however, the field has experienced a rapid growth of services and reached the point at which professional standards and training are viewed as essential. Today, there are greater expectations for more comprehensive and coordinated responses to adequately serve and protect victims.

Table 10.2. Victim Assistance Skills

Safety Planning	Crisis Counseling and Intervention	Conflict Management	Intervention on behalf of victims
Case Management	Crime Scene Cleanup	Navigating Social Services	Professional Development
Advocacy for victims' rights	Family Services	Immigrant Services	Vicarious Traumatization
Client Assessment	Community Organizing	Cross-cultural Services	Nonprofit management
Counseling	Change Management	Grant Writing	Property Repair
Navigating the Criminal Justice System	Community Crisis Response	Research	Navigating Public Housing
Information and Referral Agent	Civil Litigation	Program Administration	Public Speaking
Trauma intervention and recovery	Coalition Building	Program Development	Resource Development
Historian	Death Notification	Program Evaluation	Identifying specific needs of victims assistance
Public relations and media outreach	Public policy and implementation	Victim restitution	Victim compensation
Strategic Planning	Stress Management	Substance Abuse and addiction assessment and interventions	Support Group Facilitation

Training	Translation and Interpretive services	Technical Assistance	Information Technology
Victim activism	Victim/Offender programming	Violence Prevention	Volunteer Management
Mentoring interns and new staff	Grant Management	Legislative Protocols	Navigating Mental Health Services
Medical Services	Monetary Support Services	Material Assistance (food, clothing, etc.)	Forensic Examiners

Source: D. Stanley (2020)

Victim service providers include both part-time volunteers and full-time paid employees, and their backgrounds and levels of expertise can widely vary. Some have only had minimum training while others hold advanced degrees; some have survived the trauma of crime victimization and others have no history of victimization; some are trained as generalists, while others are highly educated specialists providing a specific service for a designated category of victims such as interpersonal violence, elderly, cybercrime, human trafficking, immigrant victims, disabled, and drunk driving victims; some provide legal expertise, or highly sophisticated modalities of clinical services, while others provide support and information. Thus, the more complex the services they are expected to provide, the more education, training, mentoring, and "on the job skill building" is required.

Professionalizing Victim Services

Professionalizing the field of victim services will lead to greater success in serving victims. Trained victim service providers increase victims' access to services, improve the compliance of victims' rights, and give a voice to victims. Working in victim services is a multifaceted undertaking that requires a breadth of skills and knowledge in a variety of areas. Those providing services to victims should recognize the impact and effect they have on people's lives; they often serve as first responders to crime victims, provide support, establish safety, and lend a listening ear. In addition to the skills and knowledge related to the profession, they need the compassion and patience to work with individuals experiencing trauma and loss. It takes a good deal of passion, resiliency, and confidence to ensure that crime victims receive the quality of support and services they need and deserve.

While victim services as a profession has developed rapidly in size, greater progress is needed for the field to attain appropriate recognition and respect for the roles and responsibilities of the profession. The field has only minimally accomplished many of the professional characteristics required to establish itself as a profession.

A characteristic of victim services that affects the professional subculture is the grassroots nature of the field. Providers lack a common identifying job title and clear standards for entering the field. As an emerging profession, standards and competencies are needed to move the field to a higher level of professionalism (Turman and Adkins, 2001).

In 2000, the National Victim Assistance Standards Consortium (NVASC) brought together diverse leaders who represent national, state, and local victim organizations to examine and define common standards for all victim service providers (Dehart, 2014). In an NVASC blueprint (est. 2003) core individual and program standards were identified for promoting competency, ethical integrity, and quality and consistency of service. The outcome of the NVASC efforts were written guidelines, published and titled "Model Standards for Serving Victims & Survivors of Crime." The goal of the standards was to gain respect and greater professional recognition for service providers. The guidelines identified three sets of standards: 1) *competency standards* to address attitudes, knowledge, and skills, 2) *ethical standards* that define behavioral expectations based on core values for the field, and 3) *program standards* that address appropriate documentation and administration of victim services. The blueprint of *Model Standards* is one of the first resources toward professionalizing the field; the guidelines set standards for victim service providers, programs, and communities. The standards were designed to promote competency, integrity, and ethical behavior of providers, and quality and consistent practices within service programs.

Credentialing

Another way to help professionalize the field of victim services is through credentialing. One of the most reputale credentialing organizations for victim services is the National Organization for Victim Assistance (NOVA). NOVA is a nonprofit organization that was established in 1976 by a group of victim service providers, criminal justice professionals, researchers, former victims, and others invested in the recovery of victims. NOVA is committed to recognizing victims' rights in four areas: national and local legislative advocacy, direct victim assistance, member support, and professional development. Today, it is the longest standing national victim assistance organization of its type in the United States. NOVA is recognized for its leadership in victim advocacy, education, and credentialing.

In 1976, the first NOVA conference for victim service providers was held in Fresno, California. The annual NOVA conferences became the first formal opportunity for victim service providers to network and share their expertise and experiences, discuss their concerns, and share their practices. NOVA conferences are noted for being the first to train and provide publications for victim service professionals. NOVA established the first draft on standards for victim assistance programs; the earliest version published in 1980 focused on victim service agencies. *The Victim Service System: A Guide to Action* (NOVA, 1983) presents the necessary service elements to be included in a victim service program or collaboratively across several local programs to appropriately support crime victims.

In 2003, NOVA established the first national credentialing program – "*The National Advocate Credentialing Program*" (NACP). Oversight of the NACP is provided by a Review Committee comprised of subject matter experts (SMEs) in victim advocacy and victim services. The Committee determines the credentialing process and revisions and standards for the program. This enabled the field to establish uniform standards to hold programs and agencies accountable for quality victim services, and to establish competency and ethical standards for service providers to achieve status as professionals. According to NOVA, elements of professionalism in victim services include:

- Theoretical or intellectual base of knowledge and skills;
- Relevance of field to social values;
- Training and education opportunities
- Motivation for becoming a member of the profession;
- Autonomy in setting standards and holding individuals accountable for "unprofessional" behavior;
- Sense of commitment pervasive throughout the field;
- Sense of community; and
- Codes of Ethics

According to the NACP, by 2017, more than 6,000 advocates had applied for NACP credentialing.

Following the publication of NOVA's guide to action, OVC recommended a a code of ethics for victim service providers be developed to increase accountability. Hence, NOVA partnered with Mothers Against Drunk Driving (MADD) to develop a code of ethics for victim service providers. An example of the Code of Ethics are shown in Figure 10.1 as it relates to victim service providers' relationships with clients. Additional codes of ethics are also included as they relate to professional relationships with colleagues.

Code of Professional Ethics for Victim Service Providers

In relationships with every client, the Victim Assistance Provider shall:

1. Recognize the interests of the client as a primary responsibility.
2. Respect and protect the client's civil and legal rights.
3. Respect the client's rights to privacy and confidentiality, subject only to laws or regulations requiring disclosure of information to appropriate other sources.
4. Respond compassionately to each client with personalized services.
5. Accept the client's statement of events as it is told, withholding opinion or judgment, whether or not a suspected offender has been identified, arrested, convicted, or acquitted.
6. Provide services to every client without attributing blame, no matter what the client's conduct was at the time of the victimization or at another stage of the client's life.
7. Foster maximum self-determination on the part of the client.
8. Serve as a victim advocate when requested and, in that capacity, act on behalf of the client's stated needs without regard to personal convictions and within the rules of the advocate's host agency.
9. Should one client's needs conflict with another's, act with regard to one client only after promptly referring the other to another qualified Victim Assistance Provider.
10. Observe the ethical imperative to have no sexual relations with clients, current or past, in recognition that to do so risks exploitation of the knowledge and trust derived from the professional relationship.
11. Take client referrals to other resources or services only in the client's best interest, avoiding any conflict of interest in the process.
12. Provide opportunities for colleague Victim Assistance Providers to seek appropriate services when traumatized by a criminal event or a client.

Source: National Organization for Victim Assistance (1997)

FIGURE 10.1

Interest in credentialing the field of victim assistance began with the development of NOVAs program in the 1980s. By the early 1990s, several states had credentialing programs, often offered through a higher education partner. he first of this kind was created in 1985 by California State University, Fresno, who offered a Victim Services Certificate Program for academic credit. The program continues today, and other academic institutions have followed suit. A more recent example is the Roper Victim Assistance Academy of Maryland (RVAAM), which is housed at the University of Baltimore. In 2007, RVAAM (refer to Spotlight on Model SVAA) developed and implemented a three-tier certification program that is approved through the State VOCA Administration Office, Governor's Office of Crime Prevention, Youth and Victim Services and Maryland's State Victim Services Board.

In the 21st Century, professionalizing the field of victim services has continued to gain momentum, and become a priority for the field. For example, most local victim service programs now require a minimum number of foundational training hours for all new-hires, and continuous annual in-service training to stay informed of changes in laws, policies, practices, and issues. While service providers are not expected to be experts in all areas of service, it is imperative to have the foundational knowledge of the discipline, as well as the basic requirements of their position as specified by their organization of employment. Foundational skills require interpersonal skills, ethical behavior, professional decorum, preservation of the victim's confidentiality, and basic case management skills that include retaining accurate recordkeeping. Skilled providers recognize the urgency of victims' needs, and they can look at the issues from the victim's perspective, building on the strengths of the victims. Skilled providers support the development of quality programs and services to victims, ensuring competency, integrity and protection from further harm. Victim service providers often interact with highly skilled and experienced allied professionals; this allied support is often a necessity to refer clients to services not available within their agency. These collaborative relationships are critical to the safety and recovery of victims. Therefore, providers must continue their training, education, and skill development to expand their understanding of the needs of victims and the available services outside their own agencies, and learn how to interact more effectively with highly skilled experts outside the domain of victim services in order to better serve victims.

Training

Another important element to professionalizing the field is training. Training programs are designed to provide knowledge and professional skills relevant to serve and support victims. Prior to the formation of formal training programs, training would typically require on-the-job skill building and mentoring upon being hired. This type of training was typically not standardized and ad hoc. Discovering that on-the-job training was insufficient, agencies found that more foundational training with specific competencies designed around victim service modalities and victims' needs is required. Thus, agencies developed training programs based on the specific needs of their organization and the victim populations they served; however, this became an arduous task with all the changing laws and practices within the field,. Consequently, these ad hoc trainings often lacked the standards needed to keep up with the field and were inconsistent across agencies.

Therefore, national organizations began to sponsor and support conferences, networking opportunities, training, and certification programs. Much of the initial training was offered at state and national level conferences, workshops, and professional meetings, shifting away from the on-the-job agency level training. This practice continues today with most of the national organizations, such as NOVA and NCVC, offering a variety of programs at conferences or by using distance learning technology for web access training.

© fizkes/Shutterstock.com

The mission of the national victim assistance academy (nvaa) is to provide an intensive learning experience to develop and promote professional skills and knowledge for victim service providers.
The nvaa training helps to protect and support crime victims.

Ovc, 2019

However, the Office for Victims of Crime (OVC) recognized there was still a need for a comprehensive standardized training curriculum, so they established and funded the National Victim Assistance Academy (NVAA) in 1995.

The NVAA was established to encourage professionalization of the field through an academically-based curriculum developed in partnership with universities that would assist victim service providers in becoming more skilled and knowledgeable in their profession. The goal of the NVAA was to provide comprehensive, academically based, foundational education and skills-based training for victim assistance providers, victim advocates, criminal justice personnel, and allied professionals who routinely deal with crime victims. The NVAA foundational curriculum was offered as a residential, 45-hour course delivered to victim service providers and allied professionals over five and a half days. The residential format of the NVAA fostered an environment that allowed participants to engage in collaboration and networking (OVC, 1999). For the first several years, the NVAA was held in Washington, DC. However, in 1997 and 1998, the NVAA shifted to a regional model and hosted its training at four university campus sites across the country - California State University, Fresno (CSU), South Carolina University (SCU), University of New Haven, and Washburn University along with the nonprofit organization Victims' Assistance Legal Organization, Inc. Between 1995–2002, more than 2,000 participants were certified through the NVAA.

While the NVAA provided invaluable information and resources for victim service providers and allied professionals, its curriculum adopted a more general focus of national laws, policies, and practices that related to victim services, hence it lacked the specific information participants needed to learn to assist them in their own states. Therefore, in 1998, Michigan State University submitted a request to OVC to fund a State Victim Assistance Academy. Using the NVAA as its blueprint, the faculty developed a state specific curriculum that included victims' rights, laws, policies, criminal justice system and best practices in victim services within Michigan. OVC agreed to adopt and fund the pilot test. OVC funding was supplemented with university and State VOCA funding, and the first state victim assistance academy was brought to life. The Michigan program was so well received and the outcomes so positive that a separate grant program was established with the goal, over time, of funding all 50 states and U.S. territories in developing a SVAA (OVC, 2019). The grant program was designed to give grantees the tools, knowledge, and training to both develop an SVAA and sustain it after OVC funding ends.

As states began to develop their SVAAs, NVAA continued to offer its annual training, and eventually began to collaborate with them. In 1999, the NVAA continued to run simultaneously with the SVAA via distance learning technology for a portion of the 45 hours at CSU, Fresno, Washburn University, SCU, Sam Houston University, and American University. By 2002, the NVAA model had shifted fully to an online service delivery platform and the curriculum was split into two areas. The first is the foundational academy, and the second area was an online leadership academy that would be implemented by NOVA's National Advocacy Leadership Center (NALC), an online training and professional center. With the increase in the number of SVAAs, in 2011, NOVA phased out its foundational academy and turned that portion of the training over to the SVAAs.

Once the first SVAA was successful, OVC encouraged the SVAA model to continue as a course of study in victim services at a partnering academic institution. OVC and its co-sponsors saw the university partnerships as a huge step forward in professionalizing the field. The expectation was that the SVAA would either be reflected through the integration of victim issues into the university curricula or would become a separate course or degree program in victimology or victim studies. While OVC provides seed money to states to develop SVAAs, the intent is for the SVAA to become institutionalized in the state and continue to offer training after OVC funding for the program ended.

Since its inception, OVC has provided startup funding to 47 states, Puerto Rico, and Washington, D.C. However, the grant program ended in 2016, and the State Victim Assistance Academy Resources were transferred to the National Crime Victim Assistance agency. Today, states are encouraged to use VOCA funding to establish or restart their SVAA. Currently, twelve states are relying on VOCA funds; and, fifteen states are relying on multiple sources of funding. Only four states have secured sustainable funding. The SVAAs of sixteen states and Puerto Rico are inactive. Of the sixteen inactive states, eight are in the process of re-establishing or developing a state academy.

Spotlight on Model SVAA

- The Roper Victim Assistance Academy of Maryland (RVAAM) (circa 2003) is one of four SVAAs initially funded by OVC, to secure sustainable state funding. RVAAM represents a highly successful and sustainable model for both training and credentialing victim assistance providers. The Academy offers a rare opportunity to live, work, study, and interact with victim service providers from all areas of advocacy from across the state.

- To prepare students for the harsh realities related to the challenges of serving victims, RVAAM provides intensive, standardized training during its annual Academy, as well as post-academy professional development.

- The training provides a fundamental overview victimization, theory, best practices. policies, and victim services for residents in Maryland. Sessions are led by recognized leaders and practitioners in the field of victimology, criminal justice, and victim rights, and focuses on skill building and best practices. For more information about the Academy, go to: http://rvaam.us.

- RVAAM's leadership has strategically instituted progressive plans to equip victim service professionals and victim advocates with a unique blend of information and connections to a diverse range of resources.

- There are six noteworthy features that sets RVAAM apart –

1) Its diverse population of participants. Its 800 plus alumni have come from every county in Maryland, as well as Virginia, Pennsylvania, West Virginia, Washington, DC, Tennessee, and Texas; and three countries China, India, and Italy.

2) The Academy's forward-thinking approach to subject-matter content keeps it relevant to the emerging needs of the field. For example, some of the recent topics covered at the Academy include human trafficking, cyber-victimization, forensic interviewing, trauma-informed services, etc.

---

3) RVAAM has attained a level of sustainability that is unprecedented in the field, securing a line-item in the state's annual budget (est. 2005)

4) RVAAM developed the Maryland Victim Assistance Certification Program (MVSCP) (2010) to help further professionalize the field of victim services. The program offers three levels of certification that reflect a candidate's varying years of experience in the field and level of professional training

5) First SVAA with an active alumni association, the Victim Services Professional Network (VSPN). Like other similarly situated organizations, VSPN provides alumni with a multitude of professional and social opportunities to network with colleagues and to take an active role in supporting the Academy.

6) RVAAM established an advanced training program, Victim Services Training Enhancement Program (V-STEP) (2017). V-STEP is a regional training program, through the coordination of regional advisory boards, specific regionally based training needs are identified, and the training is provided in that designated community. The traveling training program has served more than 6,900 service providers throughout Maryland. More recently, the V-STEP has added virtual training, offering numerous webinar topics that run throughout the year.

RVAAM was recognized in 2013 by the Office of Victims of Crime as the "gold standard" for other state victim assistance academies to emulate.

As RVAAM welcomes its 20th and 21st classes in 2021, there is no doubt it has proven itself to be an invaluable training experience for hundreds of victim service professionals, and as such, has helped to improve the quality of victim services in the state of Maryland.

Source: www.rvaam.us

Today, there are several publicly funded training programs for victim service providers, as well as nonprofit and privately-operated training programs beyond the foundational SVAAs. There are programs that target special populations (e.g., underserved victims, international victimization, immigrant victims, elderly, children, teens, adults, LGBTQ population), while others focus on specific skills, such as those discussed earlier in this chapter. The programs that have established standards and comprehensive academic curriculum in line with OVC's model standards have grown throughout the 2000s. While there are a variety of examples, two are presented below to demonstrate the diversity of options for victim service professionals. The first is presented in detail under Spotlight on Training #1: Illuminations Program, and a second is highlighted in Spotlight on Training #2: Breaking Silence – Interpreting for Victims. Each program is unique and offers several levels of training, and both are nationally recognized as model training programs.

Training is one of the primary conduits to successfully professionalize the field of victim services. As the field continues to evolve and modification of knowledge and skills are needed, it is imperative that we continue to develop training to address current needs in the field. Well into the 21st Century, ongoing development of comprehensive training will be required; universities need to respond by supporting the growth of professional development opportunities, expanding higher education, certification, and credentialing.

SPOTLIGHT ON TRAINING 1: Illuminations Program, Inc.

The Illuminations Program is a best practice training program that presents a series of artwork and journal entries created by two brothers who were sexually abused by the same offender during their childhood.

It is the desire of both boys that by sharing their story it may help broaden others cognitive and empathic understanding of the experience and behavior of victims, the impact victimization and trauma have on families, and the mindset and behavior of offenders. The art portfolio provides the opportunity for participants to explore each piece of artwork, and its corresponding written material, in a manner that will enhance their engagement and increase the potential for gaining new or expanded knowledge of victimization. To accomplish this, the training portfolio is comprised of three seminal pieces of artwork, each of which is accompanied by written material (e.g., journal entries, letters, and poems) that reinforces and expands upon the narratives encapsulated within the artwork.

- The first piece of artwork in the Illuminations portfolio addresses the question *"what was this experience like for you?"* It provides the viewer an opportunity to explore how this type of trauma may affect an individual's attitudes, beliefs, and behaviors about self and others; and, explore shared narratives with individuals who have experienced other types of trauma.

SPOTLIGHT ON TRAINING 1: Illuminations Program, Inc. (Continued)

- The second piece of the portfolio addresses the question "what are your thoughts and feelings about your perpetrator?" It provides the viewer the opportunity to explore the often-complex relationship between a victim and offender within the context of intimate relationships, and how those dynamics may affect a victim's attitudes, beliefs, and behaviors when processing their abuse.
- The third piece of the portfolio addresses the question "what did this do to your family?" It allows participants the opportunity to explore the concept of secondary victimization, the varied responses to trauma within the family, and how those responses can exacerbate or mitigate the negative effects of trauma for the victim.

By presenting their story in such an interactive manner, the audience may engage in a dynamic discussion about the experience and impact of victimization and trauma, and then explore how they may adapt their own communication skills when interacting with victims and witnesses that will increase a victim's willingness to engage and help reduce the likelihood for re-traumatization.

What do Participants Gain?

- A deeper understanding and awareness of the impact of victimization and trauma on the individual, and its potential consequences.]
- Enhanced communication skills to facilitate interviews with victims and witnesses.
- Strategies to help reduce the risk of revictimization/ re-traumatization of victims and witnesses during the criminal justice process and in recovery.

The Illuminations Program has trained thousands of professionals in victim services, criminal justice system, counseling, social work, schools, faith-based communities, and other allied professional services.

Illuminations Program, Inc.
School of Criminal Justice
University of Baltimore
illuminations@ubalt.edu

SPOTLIGHT ON TRAINING 2:
Breaking Silence: Interpreting for Victim Services

The Breaking Silence program prepares interpreters to work in a specialized field: victim-centered, trauma-informed interpreting, such as interpreting for victims of violent crime, domestic violence, sexual assault and child abuse. The training addresses how to interpret for any victim of violent crime. Breaking Silence has a particular focus on interpreting for victims of domestic violence, sexual assault and child abuse. The key service areas that are addressed include medical, mental health, legal, court and social services interpreting (whether for government and nonprofit agencies or large health care institutions) as well as interpreting for law enforcement, emergency services and disaster response.

Deaf or hard-of-hearing, and English deficient individuals are growing each year. The curriculum is designed to assist interpreters to appropriately support crime victims and survivors by removing the language, cultural, and social barriers. In the past, those barriers may have prevented victims from receiving appropriate services and consequently led to revictimization or re-traumatization, rather than assisting them successfully through their recovery. The Breaking Silence curriculum trains interpreters to better serve the needs of this growing population (Bancroft, et. al, 2016).

The program is intended for interpreters who have had basic training in community, general and/or legal interpreting, whether for spoken or sign language interpreting. The training is designed for both spoken and sign language interpreters. The program consist of 8 intensive modules that cover the following topic areas: 1) an overview of victim services, 2) vicarious trauma and self-care, 3) interpreting skills and modes 4) note taking for consecutive interpreting, 5) sexual assault and domestic violence, 6) techniques to promote survivor autonomy, 7) cultural mediation, and 8) terminology in victim services. the program includes a training manual and a companion workbook of exercises and roles plays.

Interpreters in Victim Services are often needed for domestic violence, sexual assault, and child abuse cases; however, they are also needed for Survivors of torture and war trauma,

Education

In place of a credentialing body, accredited academic programs or certifications within universities provide the knowledge and skills deemed necessary to be employed in the profession. The first form of crime victim-related education was developed at the university level in the 1960s in the form of subtopics or single courses within other disciplines such as criminology, sociology, psychology, social work, and human services. As separate victimology or crime victimization courses were developed, they were integrated into criminal justice and/or criminology education programs. Most criminal justice undergraduate degree programs offer a victimology course; however, few are required as part of the core major, and are more often treated as electives. The primary focus of most of these courses are based on the study of crime victims.

The first victimization research to impact the advancement of victimology curriculum was published in 1968 by Stephen Schafer in his book *The Victim and His Criminal*. As the national crime victimization survey data became more standardized (1970s), the data began to describe a more vivid image of crime victims, the scope of the curriculum grew, and eventually disputed much of the historical research. Research findings from the seventies and eighties formed the basis for a renewed respect as a field. As the field of victimology progressed, academic courses expanded their scope by highlighting the various categories of crime victims, victimization trends, and the basic characteristics of victimization.

It is important to point out that there is a distinction between courses in victimology that focus on crime victimization and the study of crime victims versus victim service-related courses that focus on the needs and recovery of crime victims. While victimology grew out of the early research of crime victimization, it was much later in the evolution of education programs that we began to see courses in victim services and recovery. As the victims' rights movement continued to increase the public's awareness of the plight of crime victims and their need for services and support and lobby for the integration of crime victims within the criminal justice system, more academic programs began to expand their course curriculum to include victim service-related courses.

The evolution of higher education was further advanced by the faculty in the Department of Criminal Justice at California State University (CSU), Fresno (Refer to Table 3 for a list of higher education victim related programs). CSU, Fresno's program is considered a best practice for victim-related education and as a model for other universities to follow. As noted in an early section of this chapter, CSU, Fresno established the first victim services certificate program in 1985, and the first undergraduate victimology concentration in 1992. By 1996, Fresno was the only university in the nation to offer multiple programs: an undergraduate victimology concentration, a specialization in victimology in a graduate degree program, and a certificate program offered as a month-long summer institute on victim services training. Although the summer institute was open to participants from across the United States, Fresno's four-course certificate program became the model for other universities to develop their own programs.

Fresno's summer institute was the impetus for developing a national consortium to provide a standardized curriculum and annual training; the founding participating institutions included California State University, Fresno, University of South Carolina, University of New Haven in Connecticut, and Washburn University in Kansas. The consortium of victim-related experts from the four universities became the foundation for building what became known as the first National Victim Assistance Academy (established in 1995). As noted under the "training section" above, the National Victim Assistance Academy (NVAA) was founded by the Office for Victims of Crime in collaboration with field experts in academe and the field of victim services. The NVAA was the first linkage between academia and the field of victim services.

Universities soon began to follow CSU, Fresno's lead. In 1996, the second university undergraduate concentration and certificate in victim services was established at the University of New Haven in Connecticut. In that same year Kansas City Community College developed one of the first Associate two-year degree programs in Victim/Survivor Services. Four universities added additional degrees in 1998; Washburn joined forces with the development of an undergraduate concentration and degree program in Victim/Survivor Services (1998), and a Masters of Public Administration in Domestic Violence was established at the University of Colorado (Denver and Colorado Springs). A graduate concentration was created at the University of New Haven, and two Victim Services undergraduate degrees were developed at Sam Houston State University. In the 2000s, the University of Baltimore's School of Criminal Justice established sustainability of the Roper Victim Assistance Academy (est. 2003), and later began developing a victim-related curriculum. Today, the University of Baltimore has a victim studies minor, a victimology specialization at the graduate level, and a Trauma Informed Certificate. In 2009, the first doctorate with a specialization in victimology was established at CSU, Fresno as a joint degree with CSU, Davis. As indicated in Table 10.3, university-based victim related programs continue to exist in limited number.

Table 10.3. List of Universities with Victim Related Programs

Higher Education Institute	Certificates	Baccalaureate		Master's	Doctorate	Training
		Degrees	Minors			
California State University Fresno Doctorate is Joint with CSU, Davis	Victim Services (1985)		Victimology Option (1992)		Criminology-Victimology specialization (2009)	Summer Institute Victim Services (1989)
OVC – 1st National Victim Assistance Training Academy						NVAA (1995)
University of New Haven (UNH)	Victim Services Administration (1996)		Victim Services Admin (1996)	Victimology and Victim Services Management concentration (1998)		
Washburn University	Victim/Survivor Services (1998) Trauma and Recovery Services (2018)	Victim Survivor Services (1998)	Victim-Survivor(1998)	Victim-Survivor Services (1998)		
Sam Houston University		Victim Studies B. A. and B.S. (1998)		Victim Services Management (2013)		

University of Colorado-Denver & Colorado Springs				Public Admin in Domestic Violence (1998)	
Michigan State University 1st State Victim Assistance Academy					1st SVAA (1998-present)
University of Baltimore	Trauma Informed Certificate (2014)		Victim Studies (2010)	Specialization in Victimology (2007)	SVAA (2004-present)

Source: D. Stanley (2020)

Today, courses are more advanced, and the research is more readily available with richer data and resources to examine and explore some of the more difficult questions around the plight of crime victims. The curriculum now spans across half a century's worth of research and provides broader scope of the extent and impact of crime victimization, responses to victimization, and the restorative needs of victims. As such, the field of victimology is now considered a separate discipline with its own data, research, theories, and practices. It is able to examine more closely the characteristics of crime victimization, the relationship between victims and offenders, circumstances and mitigating factors, and place and time of victimization, and a greater emphasis is placed on the restoration and recovery of victims and society in general. Equally encouraging, more students today are preparing for careers in victim services, advocacy, legal rights, and reparation. Thus, more colleges and universities are expanding their curriculum to include victim-focused courses, minors or concentrations, certificate programs, and degree programs.

However, the education requirements for employment in the field of victim services varies from state to state or even from district to district. Generally, aspiring victim service professionals should hold a minimum of a bachelor's degree in victimology or criminal justice or a four-year criminology degree. Some agencies require additional training in counseling or psychology. For some agencies, a master's degree is often preferred. At the minimum, providers need to be knowledgeable of the criminal justice system and the legal process specific to their jurisdiction where they are working.

Careers in Victim Services

Victim Service Providers serve in various disciplines, such as child advocacy, domestic violence, sexual assault, law enforcement, prosecutor's programs, community and institutional corrections, juvenile justice system, and emergency assistance. They may specialize in legal advocacy or victim advocacy, direct services working with victims or indirect services working in research, community engagement, advocacy, or community awareness campaigns and outreach. As illustrated in Table 10.4, there are a wide range of career positions in the field of victims services. All of these positions may be found in both public and private victim service agencies. Some agencies may have one victim service provider (for example, in criminal justice agencies there may be one victim service position for an entire organization), whereas in nonprofit victim services agencies, there may be a team of professionals working together at various levels. Regardless of the size of agency or unit, victim services providers are most effective when they collaborate and network with other providers within their community.

Victim service providers are volunteers, interns, survivors, caseworkers, outreach workers, counselors, legal advocates, administrative staff, and social workers. Today, providers continue to have varied educational and training backgrounds; some have extensive formal education, while others have  little or none. Many nonprofit agencies that work with victims of crime provide extensive support, thereby requiring their providers to possess strong interpersonal communication skills that will enable them to interact with people of all levels of education and background. Every victim service agency requires that providers are empathetic, understanding, and patient.

Table 10.4. Career Positions in Victim Services

Anti-Human Trafficking Outreach Specialist	Counselor Advocate
Child Trauma Responder	Criminal Court Victim Advocate
Child Victim Advocate	Victim Services Specialist I or II or III
Crisis Management	Mediation
Crisis Response Victim Advocate	Director, Domestic Violence Shelter
Data Analyst	Victim Assistance Program Manager
Domestic Violence Victim Advocate	Family Advocate
Elder Victim Support Specialist	Intake Counselor
Homicide Survivor Advocate	Victim Notification Specialist
Legal Support Coordinator	Elder Abuse Coordinator
Legal Victim Advocate	Service Coordinator
Sexual Assault Response Coordinator	Victimology Researcher
Victim Advocate	Trauma Specialist
Victim Advocate Coordinator	Trauma Victim Advocate
Victim Services Director	Case Management Specialist
Victim/Witness Coordinator or Assistance Specialist	Victims Services and Relocation Coordinator

Source: D. Stanley (2020)

Job Growth

Career opportunities for victim service professionals are increasing as more victim organizations recognize the importance of having a trained professional on staff to work with victims of crime. These victim services positions are available in a variety of fields, including criminal justice, social services, medical services, schools, and community outreach programs. Victim advocates are an integral part of the social services landscape. They have been common in larger cities and suburban areas for some time, but now even smaller communities are seeing the benefits of supporting programs for victims of crime and abuse. These professionals are often employed by nonprofit organizations, state or federal legal offices, and shelters and community centers. While victim services are still in its relative infancy as a profession, opportunities may become more available as offices expand and evolve their roles. Looking into the future, for the would-be victim service professional, this field will continue to provide a wide range of employment opportunities.

Conclusion

The field of victim services has gained a great deal of recognition and is gradually gaining respect from allied professionals. The NVAC standards have been adopted by both the federal Office for Victims of Crime (OVC) and the National Organization for Victim Assistance (NOVA) credentialing programs for both individuals and programs. The nine elements of victim service standards have become the standard for most victim service organizations throughout the country. As one of the recommendations made in OVC's New Directions from the Field (1998), and Vision 21: Transforming Victim Services (2013), certification or credentialing of victim service providers has received a great deal of attention. Today, every state and many organizations have training programs that include some form of certification. The field of has gained academic recognition by universities at all levels of education.

The goal for the 21st Century is to fully move victim assistance into a professional field. All service providers would be required to complete foundational training through an SVAA, and providers working in the more advanced areas of the field should be required to hold a Bachelors degree at a minimum, with the goal of attaining a graduate degree before moving into a leadership role.

Discussion Questions

1. Describe the historical benchmarks in the development of victim services.
2. What role do victim service providers play in the recovery of victims?
3. Describe how are service providers saving lives. What is their most critical skill?
4. Explain the importance of professionalizing a field and maintaining certification and training.

References

Academy Forum. (VSPN (2013), January). *Victim Services Professional Network – A year in review.* Roper Victim Assistance Academy of Maryland, University of Baltimore.

Academy Forum. (VSPN (2018), May). *Roper Victim Assistance Academy: A week of learning and building connections.* Roper Victim Assistance Academy of Maryland, University of Baltimore.

Atkins, J. (2001, Summer/Fall). *National Center for Victims of Crime (NCVC), Networks Newsletter*. Retrieved from: www.victimsofcime.org/docs/Networks/networks_sumfall_2001.pdf

Bancroft, M., Allen, K., Green, C., & Feuerle, L. (2015) *Breaking silence: Interpreting for victim services*. Washington, DC: Ayuda.

Davis, R.C. (1987, MayJune). *Crime victims: Learning how to help them*. [NationalInstitute of Justice, Report No. 203]. Washington, DC: National Institute of Justice.

Dehart, D. (2014). A university partnership for victim service professional development: Model standards for serving victims and survivors of crime. *Journal of Criminal Justice Education, 25*(4), 421-434.

Dussich, J. P.J. (2006). *Victimology – Past, present and future. United Nations*. [NCJ # 219635]. http://www.ncjrs.gov/App/publications/abstract.aspx?ID=241427

National Coalition Against Domestic Violence. (2019) *History of battered women's movement*. Retrieved from: https://ncadv.org/

National Organization for Victim Assistance. (1983). *A victim service system: A guide to action*. Retrieved from https://search-ebscohost-com.proxy-ub.researchport.umd.

Office for Victims of Crime. (1998). *New directions from the field: Victims' rights and services for the 21st century*. Washington, DC: U.S. Department of Justice, Office of Justice Programs.

Office for Victims of Crime. (1999, December). *Report to Congress*. [NCJ 178933]. Washington, DC: U.S. Department of Justice, Office of Justice Programs.

Office for Victims of Crime. (2013). *Vision 21: Transforming victim services*. [NCJ 239957]. Washington, DC: U.S. Department of Justice, Office of Justice Programs.

Oudekirk, B., Langton, L., Warnken, H., Greathouse, S., Taylor, B., Welch, V. & Howley, S., (2018, February). *Building a national data collection on victim service providers: A pilot test*. [Document 211524]. Washington, DC: U.S. Department of Justice, Bureau of Justice Assistance.

Young, M. (2005, August). *Present and future development in victim services. Developments in victim services*. The International Organization for Victim Assistance Conference. Oregon: Newberg. Unpublished paper.

INDEX

#BlackLivesMatter movement, 171

Blanchard, Lisa, 209

blood alcohol concentration (BAC), 101

Bloom, Sandra, 200

Booth v. Maryland (1987), 126

Boston Children's Friend Society, 85

Boynton-Jarrett, Renee, 219

Brace, Charles, 85

Breaking Silence program, 276–277

bullying, prevalence of, 39, 62

Buncombe County ACE & Resiliency Collaborative, 219

Bureau of Justice Statistics (BJS), 28

    National Crime Victimization Surveys (NCVS), 18

Burke, Tarana, 98

burnout, 237, 246

    occupational stress associated with, 237

    on-the-job, 14

C

California Endowment, 218

California's Victim's Bill of Rights Act (2008), 144

careers, in victim services, 281–282

Casa de Esperanza, 214

Census Bureau for the Department of Justice (U.S.), 28

Center for Court Innovation, 208

Centers for Disease Control and Prevention, 36

Challenge of Crime in Free Society, The (1967), 91

charging, guidelines for, 146

chastisement, right of, 84

child abuse and neglect, 84, 168

    anti-institutional child neglect responses, 85

    child fatality as the result of, 60

    definitions of, 41

    Fletcher v. People (1869), 89

    Hewlett v. Georgia (1891), 89

    Kempe's research on, 95

    minor child protection from parental violence and wrongdoing, 89

    need to intervene in cases of, 85

    official reports of, 42

    patterns of, 41

    as punishable offense, 93

    sexual abuse, 42

    social work movement against, 87

    trauma and effects of, 92

    victim–offender relationship, 69

Child Abuse Prevention and Treatment Act (CAPTA), 41, 93

Child and Family Traumatic Stress Intervention, 204

Child Development-Community Policing (CDCP) program, 201, 204

child fatality, as the result of abuse, 60

childhood trauma, 68, 186, 189, 204

    history of, 186

childhood victimization, trauma associated with, 68

child maltreatment

    among African Americans, 60

    among Native Americans, 60

    due to intimate partner violence, 58

Crime Victims Fund, 9, 120, 151
    management of, 121
Crime Victim Specialist (CVS), 143
Crime Victims' Rights Act (CVRA, 2004), 100, 114, 122–123, 148
Crime Victims' Rights Movement, The (1970s–1980s), 91–96
    legal remedies and rights, 93–94
    socio-political context of, 91–93
    victim services, 94–96
crime volume, 20
criminal justice system, 4, 9, 29, 91–92, 95, 115, 138, 173, 191
    initiating of case, 138–144
    prosecution, rules of, 145–150
    on protections, redress, and services, 150–156
    responses to victims of crime, 114
    "retributive" approach of, 163
    rights afforded to victims in, 8
criminal victimization, 98
Crisis Response Line, 206
culpability of the victim, 4
cyberbullying, 62, 178

D

'dark figure of crime' researchers, 32
dating violence, 67, 100
    physical, 40
    sexual, 40
Davis v. Monroe County Board of Education (1998), 123
DC SAFE, 206–207

DeAndrea, A. J., 233
Dear Colleague Letter (DCL), 174
death notifications, 197
    best practices for, 197–198
decision making
    evidence-based, 72
    to resist the risk of re-traumatizing, 191
DeGeneres, Ellen, 171
demographic characteristics, predicting victimization
    age, 58–59
    citizenship status, 65–66
    gender, 57–58
    individuals with a disability, 64–65
    marital status, 61
    race/ethnicity, 60
    religious affiliation, 61–62
    sexual orientation, 62–63
    socioeconomic status, 60–61
digital activism, 171
directories for services, 177
direct service prototype, 258
distance learning technology, 271
divorce
    as legal remedy, 88
    women's right to, 86
DNA databases, 178
domestic violence, 8, 36, 58, 67, 84, 99–100, 121, 125, 146, 214
    hidden victims of, 259
    services for domestic violence victims, 86
    temperance movement (1830s–1920s), 86
    trauma and effects of, 92

Domestic Violence Housing Continuum, 207

Domestic Violence Units, 205–206

DOVES Program, 217

E

early crime victim typologies, 53–57

e-counseling, 177

education, crime victim-related, 277–280

    list of universities with victim related programs, 279–280

Elevate Montana initiative, 220

Ellen, Mary, 90

emergency protection order, 143

emotional distress, 141, 155, 234

emotional stress, 233

empathy, 234

empowering victims of crime, 168–170

End the Backlog project, 142

evidence-based decision making (EBDM), 72

evidence-based practices, in victim services, 72

evidence, collection of, 141

F

false imprisonment, 154

family group conferences, 166–167

Family Justice Center Alliance, 201–202

family violence, 87

Family Violence Prevention and Services Act (1984), 93

Family Wellness Warrior Initiative, 214–215

Federal Bureau of Investigation (FBI), 18

    supplemental homicide report, 24

    Uniform Crime Reports (UCR), 18, 19–26

Federal Trade Commission, 43

felony, 22

Felson, Marcus, 70

female victimization, forms of, 8

Fenway Institute, 216

financial assistance, provided to crime victims, 151

Fletcher v. People (1869), 89

Foderao, Joseph, 200

follow-up protocol, 143

forensic examination, of sexual assault victims, 143

forensic experiential trauma interview (FETI), 195–196

    versus traditional interviewing, 196

FORGE, 215

Futures Without Violence, 202

G

Garrison, Todd, 220

Gather v. Tennessee, 128

gay rights movement, 171

GEMS, 213

gender-based violence, 214

gender identity, 62

gender, risk of victimization, 57–58

Gerry, Elbridge T., 89

global financial crisis (2008), 43

global positioning system (GPS) tracking, 177–178

government-based victim assistance programs, 260

grassroots informal delivery model, 258

grassroots movements, 171

Grateful Garment Project, 209

Great Depression, 89

gun violence, 58–59, 67

    as leading cause of death among children, 59

H

Hagerman, Amber, 173

Handle with Care Act (2018), 205

"Handle with Care" initiative, 204–205

Hatch, Orrin, 121

hate crimes

    against African Americans, 60

    because of religious affiliation, 62

    committed by or directed against juveniles, 24

    incidents of, 24

    against LGBTQ community, 62, 172

    Matthew Shepard and James Byrd, Jr. Hate Crimes Prevention Act (2009), 24

    for religious bias, 25

    for sexual orientation, 26

    victims of, 24

Haven House (shelter home), 259

Head Start program, 204

"Healthy KC" initiative, 220

HEARTS Initiative for ACE Response, 218

Hewlett v. Georgia (1891), 89

homicide, 38, 56, 61

    victims of, 57

Homicide Outreach Project Empowering Survivors (HOPES), 211

HOPE Court, 212

House of Ruth, 206

Hullinger, Charlotte, 95

Hullinger, Robert, 95

Human Rights Campaign (HRC), 172

I

identity theft, 154

    Identity Theft and Deterrence Act (1998), 100

    prevalence of, 43

Illinois ACEs Response Collaborative, 220

Illuminations Program, 274–275

Indian Child Welfare Act (1978), 93

individuals with a disability, risk of victimization in, 64–65

initial report, filing of, 139–140

initiating of case, 138–144

    arrest, 144

    initial report, 139–140

    investigations, 141–142

    presentation of options, 143–144

Integrated Domestic Violence courts (IDV), 208

interactive voice response (IVR) technology, 176

International Association of Chiefs of Police (IACP), 260

    Crime Victims' Bill of Rights, 260

International Symposia on Victimology, 4

interpersonal crime victimization, 12

interpersonal violence, 6, 8, 86

    male victims of, 99

intimate partner violence (IPV), 33, 57, 61, 143, 168

    age group with highest incidence of, 58

arrests in cases of, 144

female victims of, 35, 58

male victims of, 35

in racial and ethnic group, 60

repeat victimization, 68

investigation, of crime victimization, 141

It Gets Better project (2010), 172

J

Jeanne Clery Disclosure of Campus Security Policy and Crime Statistics Act (1990), 96, 102

job growth, for victim service professionals, 282

job satisfaction, 243

Justice for All Act (2004), 97

juvenile justice system, 117

K

Kelly, Florence, 88

Kempe, Henry, 92

Key Federal Victims' Rights Legislation, 119–124

Crime Victims' Rights Act (CVRA, 2004), 122–123

Title IX, 123–124

Victims of Crime Act (VOCA, 1984), 120–121

Violence Against Women Act (VAWA, 1994), 121–122

KidGuard app, 178

Kids' Court program, 203

Klaas Kids Foundation, 130

L

Lamb, Cindi, 95

landmark cases, on crime victims' rights, 124–125

larceny-theft, 22

Larkin, Heather, 218

law enforcement agencies, 20

Law Enforcement Assistance Administration (LEAA) fund, 9

law enforcement officers, 139

Ledray, Linda, 208

legal relevance, theory of, 128

Lethality Assessment Program (LAP), 143

LGBTQ community, 98, 100

hate crimes against, 62, 172

issue of suicide in, 172

It Gets Better project, 172

media and, 171

Network/La Red, 216

Northwest Network of Bi, Trans, Lesbian and Gay Survivors of Abuse, 216

prevalence of intimate partner violence in, 63

Stonewall Inn, 171

Stonewall Riots, 171

targeted for bias crimes, 62

as victim of

hate crime, 62

intolerance and hate, 172

violent victimization, 62

Lightner, Candace, 95

litigation

    against the perpetrator of crime, 154–155

    third party lawsuits, 155

Lloyd, Rachel, 213

M

Mandatory Victims Restitution Act (1996), 154

marginalized groups

    LGBTQ community (*See* LGBTQ community)

    media and, 171–173

marital status, risk of victimization due to, 61

Marsy's card, 144

Marsy's law, 144

Maryland Victim Assistance Certification Program (MVSCP), 273

mass shooting, in San Bernadino (2015), 233

Matthew Shepard and James Byrd, Jr. Hate Crimes Prevention Act (2009), 24

Maz, Veronica, 206

media and crime victims, working with, 170–175

    crimes against children, 173–175

    marginalized groups, 171–173

mediation programs, 155–156

    Umbreit's review of research on, 156

    victim-offender, 163, 168

Megan's Law, 129, 173

Mendelsohn, Benjamin, 4–6, 53–54

    as father of victimology, 55

    victim typology, 55

mental health services, 263

#MeToo movement, 98–99, 171

Miller, Terry, 172

Mobilizing Action for Resilient Communities (MARC), 218

Model Victim Assistance Program Brief (1986–1988), 96

Mothers Against Drunk Driving (MADD), 9, 95, 168, 267

N

Najavits, Lisa, 200

National Center for Injury and Prevention and Control (CDC), 207

National Center for Victims of Crime (NCVC), 154

National Child Abuse and Neglect Data System (NCANDS), 41–42

National Child Traumatic Stress Initiative, 204

National Crime Victim Center (NCVC), 130

National Crime Victimization Survey, 114, 139

national crime victim related agencies, 262

National Crime Victim Survey (NCVS), 28–33, 57, 64–65, 91

    database, 6, 12

    difference with Uniform Crime Reports (UCR), 32

    principle goals of, 6

National District Attorney's Association (NDAA), 146

National Domestic Violence Hotline, The, 103

National Incident Based Reporting System, 26–28

National Intimate Partner and Sexual Violence Survey (NIPSV), 33–36

    on intimate partner violence, 35

    on sexual violence, 35

R

race/ethnicity, risk of victimization due to
    intimate partner violence, 60
    sexual violence, 60

rape, 46
    definition of, 22–23
    female victims of, 58
    lifetime prevalence of, 63
    rape shield law, 93

Rape, Abuse & Incest National Network (RAINN), 209

Rape Crisis Center (Washington, DC), 259

rape kits, 142

Reagan, Ronald, 9, 114
    Presidential Commission on Drunk Driving (1982), 95
    Task Force on Victims of Crime, 91, 115, 260

RECOVER program, 211

Redemption Project, The, 165

refugee crisis, 171

religious affiliation, risk of victimization due to, 61–62

repeat victimization (multiple victimization), 67–69
    of children and adolescents, 68
    in intimate partner violence (IPV), 68
    violent victimization, 67–68

Resilience Network of the Gorge, 219

restitution, 151, 154

restorative justice, 163–168
    family group conferences, 166–167
    peacemaking circles, 167
    principles of, 164–165
    victim impact panels, 168
    victim impact statements, 167–168
    victim-offender conferences (VOC), 165–166

Restorative Retelling and Criminal Death Support Group, 210–211

retraumatization, issue of, 190

Revolutionary Era, 104

rights *versus* laws, 82

risk assessment screening, 143

risk of victimization, 53

Roberta's House program, 211

Robert Wood Johnson Foundation, 218

Rodino, Peter W., Jr., 120

Roper Victim Assistance Academy of Maryland (RVAAM), 269, 272–273

Ryan, Ruth Ann, 200

S

Saenger, Robin, 217, 222

Safe Horizon, 202

SAFE Space Program, 207

safety, issue of, 192

Sanctuary Model, 200

San Diego Trauma Informed Guide Team (SG-TIGT), 221

Savage, Dan, 172

Schafer, Stephen, 55
    victim typology, 56

school violence, prevalence of, 39

secondary trauma, 14, 234

secondary traumatic stress (STS), 233–238, 235–236

Vital Village Community Engagement Network, 219

Vital Voices Democracy Initiative. *See* Vital Voices Global Partnership

Vital Voices Global Partnership, 173

von Hentig, Hans, 4–5, 53

    victim typology, 54

W

Wald, Lillian, 88

Walker, Lenore, 92

War on Crime, 93, 98

War on Drugs, 93

Weinstein, Harvey, 98

welfare of children and child life, 88

welfare of children, public's concern about, 8

Wellbriety Movement, 215

wellness

    emotional aspect of, 243

    intellectual aspect of, 243

    occupational aspect of, 243

    physical aspect of, 243

    six domains of, 243

    social aspect of, 243

    spiritual aspect of, 243

Wetterling Act (1994), 132

White Bison, Inc., 215

white-collar crime, 33

    credit card fraud, 43

    defined, 43

    forms of, 43

    household victimization by, 44

    identity theft, 43

    National Public Survey on White Collar Crime (NPSWCC), 42–44

    scope of, 43

    victimization of, 43–44

wife abuse, as a public harm, 86

wife beating, 88

Wilson, Mary Ellen, 89

witnesses, rule on, 148

Wolfgang, Marvin, 56

    victim typology, 56

Womankind, Inc., 207

Women's Christian Temperance Union (WCTU), 90

women's movement, 7

women's rights movement, 259

Women's Rights Movement (1860s–1960s), 86–91

    legal remedies and rights, 88–89

    socio-political context of, 87

    victim services, 89–91

women's right to divorce, 86

women's suffrage, 87

World Society of Victimology (WSV), 4, 261

Y

Yale Childhood Violent Trauma Center, 203–204

Youth Risk Behavior Surveillance System (YRBSS), 38–40

    development of, 38

    on prevalence of health-risk behavior among youth, 38